SHIFTING GEARS IN CHINA

INADVERTENT TRAVELS, 1980-2020

Richard Kirkby

Shifting Gears in China

By Richard Kirkby

ISBN-13: 978-988-8843-05-3

© 2023 Richard Kirkby

BIOGRAPHY & AUTOBIOGRAPHY

EB184

All rights reserved. No part of this book may be reproduced in material form, by any means, whether graphic, electronic, mechanical or other, including photocopying or information storage, in whole or in part. May not be used to prepare other publications without written permission from the publisher except in the case of brief quotations embodied in critical articles or reviews. Richard Kirkby asserts his moral right to be identified as the author of this book. For information contact info@earnshawbooks.com

Published in Hong Kong by Earnshaw Books Ltd.

*To Louise, Jonathan, William, Sophie
& the kindness of people in China*

Foreword

THE TRIALS OF writing are almost at an end, the body of the book long since with my intrepid publisher. Now for the final push, the last stone in the archway — a foreword, a summary.

With the book's twelve chapters despatched for a proofreader's scrutiny, *en route* for the Aegean I had the mis/fortune to pick up a volume from our library of 19th and 20th century China tales, mostly missionary. An astonishing number of China sojourners, both short- and longer-term, literate and semi-literate, seem to have felt that there was a book crying out to be written. I'm hopeful, though not confident, that my own current effort isn't one more which should have been consigned to the slush pile.

The volume I'd chosen quite at random both delighted and humbled me. The American Graham Peck *Through China's Wall*, was a *real* adventurer and a great writer.[1] It was the mid-1930s, and he ventured into the far interior with the slightest of resources, and the slimmest pretensions of knowing China. Unlike some of our celebrated travel writers of today, who lift their copious historical fillers from Baedeker, and retail long conversations on Yangtze river boats which would have challenged the best of linguists, Peck is unpretentious, elegant, ingenuous. Yet occasionally he too does his back-stage research: Peck's delving into the origins of the oddly named 'Washing

---

1   London: William Collins, 1945.

the Elephant' monastery high up on Emeishan, where we both stayed 80+ years apart, is a case in point. I wish that I'd worked out that odd name for myself.

At the end of the long project, there's often the writers' lachrymose. I think that you can sense what's troubling me isn't just author fatigue, but rather author *envy*. In truth, I would far rather be Peck, penning the introduction to *his* 1930's masterpiece. But needs must, and off I go.

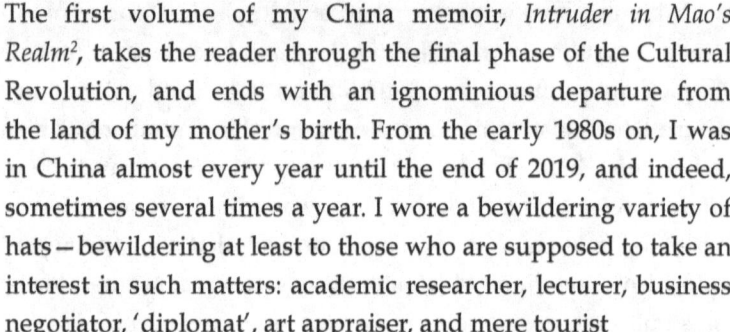

The first volume of my China memoir, *Intruder in Mao's Realm*[2], takes the reader through the final phase of the Cultural Revolution, and ends with an ignominious departure from the land of my mother's birth. From the early 1980s on, I was in China almost every year until the end of 2019, and indeed, sometimes several times a year. I wore a bewildering variety of hats — bewildering at least to those who are supposed to take an interest in such matters: academic researcher, lecturer, business negotiator, 'diplomat', art appraiser, and mere tourist

Back in the 1970s, when few foreigners were permitted to stay in China, I'd been determined to witness life from the 'rice-roots'. Several years of surreptitious observation in town and country allowed the accumulation of insights, and then some pioneering analysis of China's post-1949 urbanisation strategy. *Pioneering* only because none of my fellow China buffs had bothered to make the effort to breach what we once called the 'Bamboo Curtain'. Their China research was usually insulated in Taiwan, or rarefied in Hong Kong. There, many a scholar tried to work out what was going on in China by interviewing eager, well-paid refugees at the premises of the mysterious Universities

---

2   Hong Kong, Earnshaw Books Ltd, 2016.

Service Centre, where I too once had a desk. A tangible result of my hanging around the country in the 1970s, a 1985 book about urbanisation during Mao's times, was now to my surprise (and dismay, given the disappearance of the years) republished by Taylor & Francis as a 'classic'. This was without my knowledge and permission, and when I enquired, the answer was 'Sorry – we thought you were dead'. Not quite.....

On my final trip to China at the end of 2019, just before the menacing global madness hit us all, I was to meet several of the then-young and now mostly retired Chinese urbanists whom I managed in the mid-1980s to inveigle into the University of Sheffield. In those heady days of China's new relations with the world, I was pushing on an open door: the British Council coughed up munificently to cover three years of short courses for 'young Chinese planners'. Actually, such a category of persons didn't then exist, but it suited everyone to go along with the pretence. China's urban planning in its infancy was solely the business of bureaucrats and engineers. Most of the three dozen participants were to rise to the commanding heights of China's urban and regional planning scene as it took shape; in my first Sheffield group was an individual who even ascended to ministerial rank. The abortive trip to Lhasa, Chapter 4, arose because of the network amongst China's new planning bureaucracy which I'd long been nurturing.

My longest time in China post-1980 and lasting months, was to direct a team of Liverpool and Shanghai University researchers in a ground-breaking fieldwork-based project. This centred on township citizens' perceptions of environmental degradation in the new age, one in which world industries were being parachuted onto China's virgin soil. We ran three research stations, from Jiangsu in the prosperous East, to the inland province of Anhui, and in the very far West in a county 'famous for being poor' of Gansu province. The project was properly published. Here, however, in order to give a sense of the unexpected flowering of eccentricity in a minority of China's educated, who back in the 1970s were to a man and woman cowering in the corner as the Ninth Category of Class Enemy, I write only of the extraordinary professor who was my research partner.

Two chapters relate the experience of 'twinning' between a British and a Chinese city, the arrangement supposedly for mutual economic gain. The forlorn outcome, and one which I tried my hardest in Sheffield's case to thwart, is today emblematic of the death-knoll of Britain as workshop of the world (the same fate, of course, awaited every Western industrial heartland, Germany excepted).

As we're all too aware, the West, for want of a better shorthand, has in industrial terms now been supplanted by low-cost production elsewhere, principally in China. From the mid-1980s on, the commanding heights of global capital set about offshoring most of the significant non-military productive activities of the Western heartlands. These latter are, of course, now so bereft that it will be impossible under existing polities to sustain livelihoods in North America and Europe in the manner to which they have long been accustomed. You can't live, as the saying goes, by taking in each other's washing.

My misbegotten 1980s role as director of a North of England China business centre produces another chapter on the quest for China riches. It tells of an unlikely hunt alongside a bevy of Yorkshire scrap merchants for a fabled slate mountain in the depths of Shaanxi.

Two chapters follow a quite different tack, and arise through my association with what is politely called 'China's material culture'. In the new Millennium, largely departing my three-decades-long field of specialisation in modern Chinese studies, I crossed over into the highly-charged world of Chinese antiques. On this explosive terrain, I appraise collections and advise auction houses on that enduring, and sometimes truly $64,000 question, 'genuine or fake?' Somehow or other, I should declare, I've managed to miss making my own fortune from China's diasporic cultural legacy.

Three journeys to Tibetan lands feature amongst the book's twelve chapters. In contrast to the tales of 1930s travellers such as Peter Fleming — and of course our Peck — my retellings seem pedestrian. Yet at the time, with years of being restricted to brief trips within heartland (Han) China, *for me* their actuality was hardly hum-drum. No, they were truly eye-popping adventures. First came my serendipitous arrival as a pilgrim at the monastery of Kumbum, in hitherto-closed Qinghai province, to be greeted by a mystified Panchen Lama. Then I was in Lhasa on the fool's mission I mentioned above. And in 1999, my wife Louise and I journeyed perilously from my grandparents' city of Chengdu to the Khampa region of eastern Tibet, there only to be rebuffed by a nervous abbot.

The number of chapters was initially a baker's dozen. For reasons diplomatic I retracted two of them, judging that they wouldn't go down well in certain quarters. My moral fibre restored itself, and I reinstated just one of the two chapters, to achieve, finally, the hallowed total of twelve. The rescued chapter tells of a delegation reluctantly but graciously hosted by the most senior figures I'd ever stumbled across in all my time in China. This was 1984, and for four years Western Europe and even North America had been shaken by the rise of massive, millions-strong anti-nuclear weapons protests. Broadly, the Chinese Communist Party, steeped in atavistic anti-Sovietism, had long decided that Western peace activists were, either knowingly or naïvely, no more than Moscow dupes. But in Beijing's corridors of power there was curiosity about the mass protests. An unexpected summons to make tracks for Beijing thus was issued to the most vociferous of the European peace organisations, the Campaign for Nuclear Disarmament. I was the adviser to the CND delegation; we decided when in China to focus upon a terrible consequence of even limited nuclear conflagration. Carl Sagan and others had termed this the 'nuclear winter'.

I end this introduction on a sombre note. Back in July 2022, when I began cogitating about how to go about it, news came of the death of a person unsurpassed in the British peace movement. Bruce Kent, ex-Catholic prelate, was the man to whom the London Chinese embassy had turned in 1984 when they contemplated issuing an invitation to a Western peace group. Right up to his death at ninety-three, Bruce Kent was shouting out the dangers of nuclear conflict, which he rightly saw as even greater now, in the 2020s, than in CND's heyday during the Reagan/Thatcher era.

The extraordinary blossoming of protest 40 years ago arose because on both sides of the Iron Curtain, the two Superpowers had deployed new classes of land-based cruise missiles. The unstoppable force of the anti-nuclear movement in the West was eventually to push Ronald Reagan to the negotiating table with the Soviet Union's Gorbachev. In 1987 the two signed the Intermediate-Range Nuclear Forces Treaty, known as the INF Treaty. This banned further deployments, and with verification inspections, in the next years each side eliminated over one thousand cruise missiles. There were additionally the immensely vital agreements, the bilateral US-Soviet Union treaties of SALT 1 & 2; the later Strategic Arms Reduction Treaty (START) remains at least on paper between the United States and post-Soviet Russia.

The rest is not, unfortunately, history. What Eisenhower

in 1961 dubbed 'the military-industrial complex' today has an immensely strengthened grip. The most dangerous moment for our world came when the Donald Trump presidency, under the thumb of the most rabid of U.S. warmongers, decided in 2018 to withdraw from the long-standing INF Treaty. Russia, with no counterpart now in the INF, later also withdrew. The Treaty was dead, with nothing to replace it. Unfathomably, Trump blamed China's missile developments as his excuse for abandoning INF.

Though representing signal belligerence against Russia, the elite faction behind Trump had decided that of their 'adversaries', China had to be the first to be brought down. Once that process was underway, the metaphorical and perhaps real guns could be turned on Russia. The faction running the U.S. Democrats took a different view: first get Russia, then China. But it wasn't as though China had been entirely neglected by the Obama/Clinton team, which had already pushed their 'Pivot to Asia' strategy, explicitly aimed at 'containing' China. As journalist John Pilger has vividly described in his 2016 film *The Coming War on China*, the 'Pivot' consolidated dozens of potentially nuclear-armed U.S. bases in a wide arc around China.

Now, in 2022, the position of the eminences behind the Biden regime is this: to up the *ante* against both Russia and China simultaneously. The right-wing think-tanks which inform the U.S. administration, the Pentagon and the multitude of 'intelligence' services send an unambiguous message: the end-game is dismemberment of both continental giants. The advance of NATO to Russia's borders since 1991, and the resulting proxy war in Eastern Europe of 2022 represent a major push with regard to Russia. As for China, authoritative voices in Washington call for a ten-year programme to diminish the People's Republic. To show they meant business, their RIMPAC exercises in the Pacific and Indian Oceans of mid-2022 deployed an unprecedented number of warships as well as 170 aircraft. In the midst of this, Speaker of the House Nancy Pelosi arrived in Taiwan with insouciant innocence, to promise more advanced U.S. military hardware. Such never-ending deliveries certainly breach the spirit, if not the letter, of the internationally endorsed Taiwan Relations Act and the One China policy.

Back in 1945, Albert Einstein and a group from the University of Chicago came to the realisation that the United States' use of the ultimate weapon of mass destruction on Japan presaged a potential end to life on earth as we know it. The Bulletin of the Atomic Scientists set up their virtual Doomsday Clock, and ever since, each year in January they've had to advance the hands towards midnight—towards Armageddon. In January 2022, even prior to the Ukraine War and the ramping up of the West's anti-China policies, the Bulletin and its 11 Nobel laureate sponsors declared that it was now a mere 100 seconds to midnight, to Doomsday. Will the world take notice?

Let's return to where we set out—Graham Peck. August 1937: his last pages see him back in Beijing with the intention of an easy life, catching up with his sketches, sipping beer in the roof garden of the Hôtel de Pékin with its jazz band, and meeting old friends. He ensconces himself in a comfortable courtyard house with a couple of youthful servants seeing to his every need. And then the city falls to the Japanese. He understands—as I essentially do too about further possible wanderings—that his coursing through the byways of China was essentially frivolous. Now things seemed very different to Peck:

> The beginning of fighting meant that the individual life, pleasant and unconstrained, had become painfully inappropriate, really impossible.

RICHARD KIRKBY

Relinquishing his levity of mind, Peck throws himself into the dangerous business of rescuing wounded Chinese soldiers from their hiding places way beyond the city walls. The stench of putrefaction never then leaves his remaining pages. With the self-destruction of incipient civil society now proceeding in China, and the ever-louder drumbeats of war from a belligerent West, it is one which today pervades my own nostrils.

It should, therefore, be obvious why this, my second volume of China memoir, could never have dispensed with the Chapter 5, *The Mission*. Yes — most of the book maintains a light, often tongue-in-cheek tone. But besides the issues brought to mind by Chapter 5, that is the ever-heightening danger of nuclear war, Chapter Three's complexion is also deadly serious. I was a hands-on witness to the onset of a process which, within a couple of decades, was to scythe through the West's centuries-nurtured capacity to produce actual things. Enthusiasts may well speak of the comparative advantage of dispersing production, of cross-continental supply chains. The displacement of the West's manufacturing capacity has, however, irrevocably diminished the livelihoods of hundreds of millions in Europe and North America.

An even more sombre note — it's the Autumn of 2022 and I'm finally completing this memoir at the very moment that the unprecedented crises of war, of energy and food supply begin to press hard on a global citizenry already much wearied by the horrendous response of governments worldwide on a seemingly relentless 'health emergency'.

Contents

Foreword   vii

Chapter I: Kumbum (1983)   1

Chapter II: Lord Mayors, Leaders and Limos (1983-4)   30

Chapter III: The Captains of Industry Hit China (1985)   48

Chapter IV: Lhasa (1984)   87

Chapter V: The Mission (1984)   107

Chapter VI: Turtle Soup (1989)   141

Chapter VII: Intelligentsia (1996)   162

Chapter VIII: The Heist (1996)   187

Chapter IX: Kangding (1999)   200

Chapter X: The Treasures of Dr Luo (2007)   235

Chapter XI: Chasing the Chicken Cup (2017)   264

Chapter XII: Emeishan (2019)   293

About the Author   319

I
KUMBUM (1983)

MY CHARGES had been suitably banqueted, gorged on sea slugs, limo-ed from meeting to meeting, and they no longer needed me. It was now late May, and I'd been playing nursemaid to a group of eager Sheffield city councillors who'd just tied the knot with their new twin city of Anshan up in China's Northeast. Somewhere I'd picked up a copy of the *China Daily*: 'Xinjiang Province welcomes Foreign Friends' signalled a brief inside column.

Back in the 1970s, when travelling was at all possible for the tiny number of 'foreign experts' in the country, it was all political tourism to a handful of cities, revolutionary shrines and 'scenic spots' in the East of the country. Occasionally, if we behaved ourselves, travel might extend to interior provinces such as Shaanxi where the Communist forces had foregathered after the Long March; 'Red tourism' was just the thing to improve foreign minds. Such was the tightness of the circuit that, when 'going out' was permitted in the summer break, you were certain to bump into others on well-shepherded release from their posts. You might be aware of the foreigners in ones and twos in half a dozen of the provincial capitals, and now if you were in luck you could put faces to names and even spend a few hours in company, in whatever guarded hotel on the circuit you had arrived at. Our over-solicitous minders, brought up on spy paranoia, did all in their power to keep us vacationing foreign devils from exchanging gossip. But they were at a loss when a chance encounter led to a pleasant evening in a hotel room, lubricated by a bottle of hooch amongst the plastic combs, Maxam toothpaste, and Double Happiness cigarettes from the little sales booth in the lobby.

'*Go West*' was the unforgettable Marx Brothers' call, and since first arriving in China I'd been desperate to heed it. During the Cultural Revolution, though, absolutely no chance. But like the famed 1930s adventurer Peter Fleming, I'd long dreamt of the Silk Road and the fabled city of Kashgar which lay at its farthest hem. Now, in the early 1980s, Xinjiang wasn't merely opening to routine foreign tour groups. The powers-that-be were offering to issue the treasured travel permit to individual travellers, though certainly not for Kashgar. To be finally free of the hugely costly sheepdogs of the China International Travel Service was a going to be glorious.

That *China Daily* article apart, in this new age there were no grand announcements: it was normally through the bush telegraph that you discovered that such and such a place was now *kaifang*, 'open'. All you then had to do was get your local public security office to stamp your little green booklet with the newly opened destinations. I was to discover that so lax had matters become that if you managed to infiltrate yourself into some obscure interior 'closed' place, the authorities were anxious just to get you off their patch. Rather than cause themselves (and you) difficulties, they would usually despatch you to some distant destination. For the local cops it was a case of pass-the-human-parcel, the higher-ups none the wiser that you'd strayed where you shouldn't. It was pot luck, but you might be sent off to just the exotic, far distant places which you had in mind. This was, as I shall relate, how I managed to launch myself the hundreds of kilometres from Xinjiang, through Gansu Province, and up into the Qinghai plateau, a region which I knew as China's *gulag*.

RICHARD KIRKBY

~~~

Xinjiang, the 'New Dominion' — a vast area of China's Northwest and the native home to a Turkic-speaking ethnic minority, the Uyghur. Only with the advent of the People's Republic have the territories of the Uyghur and the other Xinjiang ethnic groups, all Muslim, been brought firmly within the control of a Chinese state. In the third decade of the 21st century no-one with an interest in the region will be unaware of the repressive hand said by China's increasingly hostile Western adversaries to weigh upon the non-Han population of Xinjiang, particular the Uyghur youth. Rarely acknowledged by China's critics, however, is the deep geopolitical dimension to a neurotic state stance towards minority rights in Xinjiang.

Urumqi, Xinjiang's capital, was some three thousand kilometers distant from my mission in Liaoning. This detour to China's periphery hadn't originally been on my schedule, and if I were to get back home to submit my Liaoning mission reports on time, a leisurely train journey was out of the question. Traversing China's great expanse in a deafening but solid old Ilyushin, four hours out of Beijing we were at last landing; I rode almost alone in a rickety blue and white CAAC airline bus to the city centre. A kindly local led me to the steps of the only hotel newly catering to foreigners, a Western-style building which might have dated from the Soviet dominance of the region in the 1930s. Long corridors, spacious suites, dribbling plumbing, and of course, no public spaces, let alone a bar where people might mingle with tongues loosened. Too tired to venture out into Urumqi's dark streets, I dined miserably at the hotel on chewy *shashlik* served with yoghurt and tired salad.

In the morning I wandered through an immense indoor bazaar, its corrugated roof adorned with a huge red metal star. Stalls were sparsely loaded and the shopping desultory. The only bustling section turned out to be where white-capped Muslims were butchering sheep. Further down on the waste land behind the market, a cacophony of squeals arose where Hans were slaughtering pigs. Urumqi no doubt had its attractions but I had no intention of searching for them in this forlorn outpost of empire, where Han migration was clearly just starting to outnumber the natives.

Emerging into the brightness at the far end of the bazaar, I approached a Uyghur woman, her hair and forehead concealed in a purple chiffon scarf, and asked directions to the bus station. She couldn't or wouldn't reply in the language of the Han, but pointed me towards a nearby compound. As I stepped through its arched metal gate, again with rusty red star, a grime-laden bus lurched into the pot-holed enclosure, cases, bags, sacks and a goat roped to its roof. The passengers emerged looking deadbeat, and I was surprised that amongst them were the first and only foreigners I was to meet in Urumqi. Two camera-laden young men, their heads tied in dusty red-spotted bandannas. No doubt about it—their sparse beards and expensive cameras yelled 'Japanese'.

'Where have you come from on this bus?' I tried in English. They answered with one word: 'Kashi', the Chinese name for Kashgar hundreds of kilometers to the southwest. Kashgar, where in the late 19th century cultures mingled, and where the British kept an eye on their rivals in the Great Game, conjuring up many a story of Russian encroachment. 'We want Pakistan,' one of them explained, with a grin. I knew that west of Urumqi was still strictly off-limits, and there was no way that any foreigner could slip over the distant Pakistan border onto the amazing Karakoram Highway.

'Police!' the talkative one said, crossing his arms over his body in the way indicating capture. It seemed they'd got all the way to

Kashgar in various buses and trucks, and stepped out of the final vehicle straight into the cold embrace of the authorities. After a few hours, the two were simply put on the next Urumqi-bound bus. Their journey had come down to fifteen long days staring out of vehicle windows. Officially stamped travel permits could be useful things. So the only option would be to head not west on the Silk Road, but eastwards. A blue-painted signboard offered a surprisingly long list of Xinjiang destinations and it appeared that in the early afternoon a bus was scheduled for the desert oasis of Turfan, a few hours' journey to the east. I peered through the cut-out hole in a glass window and the face behind it never batted an eyelid when I asked for a single to the place the Han call 'Tulufan'. Never before being able to do so before in all my years in the country, I was still bashful about conducting such simple transactions in Deng Xiaoping's new China.

I consulted my trusty 1950s Nagel guide, and its descriptions of the ancient Silk Road. With its famous mosque and strange grape-drying towers of mud bricks Turfan was an alluring prospect. I was excited by its distinctive geography: at more than 150 meters below sea level, the Turfan Basin is the second lowest region on the earth's surface. Fortunately, it wasn't yet the height of summer. Flaming Mountain close by to the town had the reputation of being China's hottest place, with August temperatures sometimes over 50 Centigrade.

It seemed that the Japanese duo were heading towards Turfan too. They retrieved enough of their school English to explain an interesting rumour that had come their way: an unusual public security man with a restless official seal could be found in the town. 'Qinghai,' whispered one of the Japanese. That remote province was hundreds of miles to the southeast of the Silk Road oases where we'd be heading. If true, in Turfan gold would be struck. In recent decades few foreigners had entered Qinghai.

SHIFTING GEARS IN CHINA

That afternoon I squashed onto the back seat of a homemade bus which was to rock alarmingly on its truck chassis. We were soon bumping over the sharp black stones of the desert, at one point half-braining me as I hit the ceiling. In recovery position, head between hands, on the dusty floor I spotted a tiny red padlock, which to this day I keep on my desk as a memento of the Xinjiang desert. It was a balmy evening when we arrived in Turfan's wide main street flanked by low buildings, many of them of a mellow mud-brick. I soon located my accommodation, lately the local hostelry for visiting cadres and a pleasing, well-ventilated single-storey building of many chambers connected by covered walkways. Led along by a young white-jacketed Uyghur girl, we arrived at a sign announcing that the area ahead was for the 'foreign friends' anticipated in this corner of the desert wilderness. That reminded me of my earlier encounter – I seemed to be the sole occupant and there was no sign the Japanese. But I was soon unburdening myself in a clean cell with cool stone floor and window onto a little melon garden. And next door was a primitive shower room with a goodly supply of sun-warmed water from the tank on the roof.

The next day, with a fine breakfast of eggs, unleavened bread and strong sweet tea, I headed out to see the town. It was market day, or perhaps every day was market day in an oasis. The main street was thick with the local transport—miniature, sloping flat-topped carts on outsized tyres drawn by straining mules. This, and the pedestrians wandering the main street were so unfamiliar and so unlike anything I'd ever experienced in China that I felt I'd stepped through the looking-glass. If there were Han Chinese in Turfan, they certainly weren't in evidence, for the sights around me put me in mind of a visit I'd made to a small town in Tunisia. I followed the road up to the market place, an undulating field already full of buyers and sellers, mainly of livestock and farm things—spades, mattocks, plastic jerry cans. This was an exclusively Uyghur market, the males in square embroidered caps and baggy trousers, the women unveiled but wearing headscarves, long skirts and the thick brown nylon stockings which seemed to be all the rage in Xinjiang. An ancient, white-bearded and turbaned elder rode up to me on a diminutive donkey, his feet akimbo, and addressed me with some remark which amused the crowd. Hens in large split bamboo cages squawked and pecked. A gnarled farmer was striking the hand of a happy customer who'd just agreed to buy his horse. All was as un-Chinese as you could get.

As I gazed around open-eyed, I found myself being sidled up to by a stout bearded fellow in a kaftan. Smiling conspiratorially, he addressed me in Chinese: 'Lai, lai, genzhe wo'. 'Come, come, follow me,' he repeated. In the centre of the field lay a line of low stalls with enclosed huts behind. The man was now grabbing my arm quite tightly, half-dragging me along, heedless of my efforts to resist. We passed through the nearest stall towards its rear enclosure, the stranger unnervingly digging his nails into my palm while pushing his face close to mine and fixing on me guilefully. We pushed through a cloth partition into a windowless smoke-filled chamber half taken up by a long wooden table, dimly lit by a dangling bulb. As if making a speech, at the far end of the table stood a man, perhaps forty, good-looking in a collarless tunic shirt, riding breeches tucked into high leather boots. A peaked woollen cap completed the impression that he's stepped straight out of Tolstoy. This was a European, no doubt about it. Another man, similarly dressed and un-Chinese, gross and with a drinker's visage, was seated to his right, a pile of cigarette stubs mounting in front of him on the bare table top. My unwanted guide said a few words, poured me a beaker of liquid from a plastic carafe and hovering with clasped hands, pushed me into a chair at the end of the table. The two strange characters stared at me drunkenly, the one on his feet spitting some words, certainly not Chinese, at which he and his companion laughed raucously. He raised his hands high as though expecting some response.

It was a weird situation, and all I could manage was a Chinese mumble—a *nimen hao* and something about being in Turfan to *kanykan*, to look around. The standing man raised his glass in my direction, draining it. It seemed I should do likewise. Some kind of smoky-tasting homemade spirit which bit into my throat, causing me to gag. He addressed me again, and I repeated my meagre explanation, but now his expression turned dark. He banged his glass on the table, punctuating a stream of angry words in which 'Russkiy' was emphatically repeated. Was his anger because I'd addressed him in Chinese and not in what was evidently his own tongue?

Peter Fleming's account of his epic journey from Beijing to Kashgar in the 1930s (*News from* Tartary) suddenly came to mind. He'd written much about the Russians then in Xinjiang, but throughout my time in China I'd never heard that ethnic Russians had survived in this far-flung Chinese region. 'Chinese Russians,' I now thought, 'and they've taken me for one of their tribe.' With no contact for decades between Xinjiang and the world at large, the idea of foreign travellers in this distant part of the Chinese universe would never have crossed my drinking companions' inebriated brains. The uncomfortable moment passed, the two men talking animatedly together while sinking more of their brew. Then the mood changed again, the seated man scowling at me and the belligerent one swaying menacingly in my direction. It was time beat a retreat, though my kaftan-clad guide didn't seem to think so as he tried to block my exit. But I slipped through the curtain and was soon out into the bright sunshine and amongst the Uyghur crowds.

During my years in 1970s China, the mindless barrage of anti-Soviet (and anti-Russian) propaganda had been a constant irritation, a reminder of China's unseemly alliances with the perpetrators of death and destruction upon the Indochinese peoples. Who would have thought that all along, ethnic Russians lived under the five star flag of the People's Republic? Later, however, when back in Beijing and in the unlikely setting of a gathering in the home of one of the daughters of Long March veteran Marshal Ye Jianying, I came across another Russian. He was a plump young man in standard Han garb but with distinctly Caucasian features who introduced himself as a *Xinjiang-ren* — a native of Xinjiang.

'I'm on my way to Australia Sydney' he told me in the Chinese way. 'It's a state secret,' he said with a wry smile. He went on to explain that prior to the Cultural Revolution there was a number of scattered Russian communities in Xinjiang, descendants of settlers who'd arrived in the 19th and early 20th centuries. Most had been harassed, jailed or hounded over the border into Soviet territory. The handful who remained, an unlikely Fifth Column now numbering in the hundreds the young man informed me, were being shipped *en masse* to Australia. 'It's a secret deal, and China will get lots of wheat in exchange,' said the young man. I often wondered how it all worked out for him and his fellow Russians, and just what else the Australian government was aiming to get out of this strange arrangement.

———∞∞———

The rumour I'd heard from the two Japanese concerning Turfan and travel passes had substance. Back at the hostelry I tracked down the amenable public security man who seemed inexplicably eager to write 'Xining' and 'Huangzhong *xian*' (county) on a blank page of my travel pass, and then wield his certifying chop, his seal. Getting a potentially troublesome foreigner off his patch or genuine helpfulness, and why so very far distant? Xining I knew was the capital of the province of Qinghai, in days gone by more properly a northern appendage of Tibet, though in People's Republic terms just another Chinese province. The identity of Huangzhong county was only to be revealed once I got to Xining, though I couldn't imagine how, in the vastness of the Qinghai plateau, the man knew that this was where I should be heading. It was only later that I discovered that I was by no means the only traveller passing along the Silk Road in the direction of Gansu province, and thence on to Qinghai.

The accommodating policeman had wanted to know whether, before leaving his turf, I'd be visiting a place he called Gaochang. A must, he assured me, for all Turfan visitors from afar. I'd noticed mention of this place in my guide book—an ancient city which ruled the desert for two millennia, successively home to Manicheans, Nestorian Christians, Mongol Buddhists, and lastly Uyghur Muslims. The following morning, I hailed one of the many local taxis, a flatbed donkey cart commanded by a lad barely in his teens, and we trotted off over dried-up streams until a green and marshy area appeared, a miniature oasis with a few small willow trees. Beyond it rose the turrets and walls of an abandoned city of the Silk Road, a place extending over a great area, the layout of streets, squares, and buildings still entirely legible. Whilst the lad curled up in the shade and slept, I wandered amongst the crumbling city of decayed ochre mud brick which towered still above the desert landscape. To be alone in a place where so many had lived and died was an eerie experience. In a place of almost no rainfall it would surely take another thousand years before the ancient city melted back into the desert.

RICHARD KIRKBY

I wandered, too, that afternoon past Turfan's grape-drying towers, cone-like and as high as minarets. Dusk was coming on, and the great mosque of Turfan I admired only from the outside, for I was eager to get started on the next leg of my journey. Next day, I said goodbye to the town and hitched a long lift on a donkey cart to Turfan's railway station—a bleak installation of grey concrete walls and slab roof standing alone in the midst of the endless desert of black stones. When I stepped up a little uncertainly and requested a one-way ticket to Lanzhou, capital of neighbouring Gansu, the elderly station master took it in his stride. I still hadn't got used to the idea of travellers' *zili gengsheng*, that universal slogan of the Cultural Revolution exhorting 'self-reliance'.

A few young army men were squatting on the cracked concrete of the low platform, smoking and spitting melon seeds. I wasn't sure if I should be pleased or miffed that no-one seemed the slightest interested in a lone foreigner appearing out of nowhere in the middle of nowhere. Long before the rails began to sing, still well over the horizon the eastbound Urumqi to Shanghai express announced itself with lazy smoke plumes. The giant train drew into the station, looming monster-like over us. Running down its length, I found my carriage and to the urgings of a gnarled female coach attendant, I clambered up. Where, I wondered, were the young women with short plaits and huge peaked caps who were the usual custodians of China's long-distance trains?

Until fairly recently, no foreigners had been allowed to travel in anything but 'soft bunk' (*ruanwo*) class, sleeper compartments where they were sealed away from their fellow passengers, especially those of the more humble variety. And it was unusual for single foreigners to travel anywhere. But in this new world where foreigners were no longer obliged to be part of a tour group, officialdom couldn't care less whether one squashed in amongst the cost-conscious 'hard seat' passengers, or paid a small fortune for *ruanwo* car luxury with their four bunks, antimacassars, little table with reading lamp, not forgetting the attentions of the carriage chief and her giant can of boiling water for tea. But this turned out to be my first long distance train with no *ruanwo* cars. In any case, the ticket of choice in this new age of foreigner's freedom was always going to be *yinwo* – 'hard bunk'. The open carriages with their lateral tiers of bunks offered a great way to meet the natives, share their snacks and be quizzed by the ever-curious about oneself, and always – the cost back home of anything and everything. Good language practise. I soon reached my spot with its little oval enamel number marking it, an upper bunk (superior, as one could retire at will from the throng below) but already occupied by a reclining body. I tapped on an olive-green shoulder and a wrinkled face turned to me, muttered, and swung himself slowly down. On the lower facing bunks sat four youngish army men, their jackets unbuttoned to reveal grey undershirts. They were deep into a noisy game demanding a demonstrative slap as each card was offered. From the way in which they now solicitously hovered over the older man who'd been on my bunk, I decided that he was likely a high-up in the People's Liberation Army and the young PLA men were his bodyguards. In my direction, the old fellow consistently showed a grumpy face. But yet again I was largely ignored, as though it was the most normal thing ever for a red-haired stranger to emerge out of the great Xinjiang desert. Back in East China, bored with the incessant public attention, I'd often persuaded enquiring peasants in the street that I was a *xiaoshu minzhu*, a (Chinese) ethnic minority. Perhaps these Han soldiers were so inured to Xinjiang's ethnic diversity that they'd grown to expect heterodox individuals.

RICHARD KIRKBY

Of all the dozens of train trips I'd taken in China, this was the oddest, for the customary order was glaringly absent. Rail journeys in Mao's China had always been a transmission belt for the 'socialist discipline' pressed by the authorities. The railway carriage was a sealed microcosm where this was to be incubated, the twin enforcers being the car attendant and the ubiquitous loudspeakers — which could be switched off in 'soft' class, but never in these carriages.

'Passengers must maintain socialist discipline and refrain from spitting, dropping peel and other litter on the floor,' a strident voice would remind everyone. The car attendant would patrol her narrow patch, her constant skittering by with energetic sweeps of her mop ensuring no infringements of the rules. The tiny towels, essential accoutrement of the Chinese traveller, had to be wrung out and hung on the metal bar in the corridor with perfect symmetry, and any slacker would know her sharp tongue. From time to time she'd put down her mop and appear with an oversize aluminium kettle swathed in a blue-padded cosy; for a couple of cents, passengers' lidded jars of bloated tea leaves would be refilled. As the train drew into a station, the loudspeakers would sound with a sprightly *erhu* folk tune as the woman ensconced in the train's tiny broadcasting cubicle would enlighten her captive audience with a litany of the socialist achievements of the place in question.

On the Urumqi to Shanghai express, however, all this was oddly absent. The floors were strewn with debris — apple peel, cigarette butts, melon seeds — the little towels were disgracefully unruly on their rail, and the attendant had her legs up in her little cabin with a cartoon book on her lap. Thirsty passengers had to help themselves from her spitting geyser if they wanted to top up their tea jars. The train rattled eastwards through the encroaching dusk, a capsule of wanton disorder.

SHIFTING GEARS IN CHINA

All around me I could hear the impenetrable cadences which I knew was Shanghainese only because *nga gok ning* — the Shanghainese for 'foreigner' — regularly sounded as I passed down the crowded corridor to the toilet. Indeed, the train seemed to be a purely Shanghai affair, and on the way to replenish my own mug with hot water, I seated myself on one of the spring-loaded folding seats in the corridor. I knew that before long curiosity should get the better of someone, the ice would be broken by an offer of a cigarette, prelude to the customary interrogation. And so it was: a man with slicked-back hair and polished black shoes was soon unfolding the little window seat facing me. After the usual preliminaries, he became unusually candid:

'We're all from Shanghai, going home on leave,' he offered in passable Mandarin. 'We hate Xinjiang,' he went on. 'We all want to return to Shanghai, but the government won't let us.' The *crie de coeur* of any enforced exile in this nation and especially those ejected from China's greatest metropolis.

In 1950, at the end of their victorious war over the Nationalists, Shanghai regiments of the People's Liberation Army had found themselves in this Northwest province. The soldiers were commanded to stay put, to settle down for good in this far-flung corner of the new People's Republic. Most were assigned to the land near the town of Shihezi, some 150 kilometres northwest of Urumqi, which became the headquarters of the Xinjiang Production and Construction Corps. After 1962, the growing conflict with Moscow meant that the military status of the Corps was never done away with. And in the late 1960s, when Mao ordered millions of young people out of the cities, the Shanghai migration to Xinjiang was bolstered by tens of thousands of the city's youth. For more than one generation of Shanghainese, Xinjiang had become a kind of distant, lacklustre and alien home-from-home.

By now on my third Peony cigarette, the man was eager to let me know how it was that he'd become a Xinjiang exile. 'I was one who answered Chairman Mao's *da haozhao,*' he said, referring to Mao Zedong's 'great call' to the youth of May 1968, after which, nationwide, some 16 million school leavers were excised from the cities.

'Many of my group got back to Shanghai a few years ago, but I'm still trying,' he went on with a mournful smile. I was well aware of the little-advertised return of 'sent-down' youth to the cities, as it was one of the matters I'd researched while in Shandong in the late 1970s, especially after I'd been caught up in a mass protest of Shanghai youth who'd been despatched to remote Yunnan. So a good many of the 16 million had managed to re-acquire their precious urban household registration papers, but then the government put a stop to the great return. Again and again, the man insisted that no Shanghainese could stand living in Xinjiang. Hyperbole perhaps, but then to the Chinese, the long-ingrained view of the lands 'beyond the Great Wall' held them to be places of exile and misery. For the Shanghainese in particular, who to the annoyance of their fellow citizens were generally given to flouting their urban sophistication, the scattered towns in the deserts and mountains of Xinjiang had to be hard to bear. I'd joined a train full of unhappy exiles, returning on brief leave to their beloved city which had, by and large, permanently disbarred them. At least, that was certainly how it was back in 1983.

With my hot water 'white tea', I munched a dry snack and retreated to the top bunk. Beneath me, the card games, the spitting of peanut shells and melon seeds, the peeling of apples (the Chinese never eat apple peel) and the deft shelling of boiled eggs continued apace. And not forgetting the smoking, from which the top bunk offered no retreat. Far from it: I was to spend the next thirty hours fending off the acrid fumes of the five chain-smokers beneath me, and longing for some fresh air. But unlike any other Chinese train I'd been on, the windows were sealed. When it all became unbearable, I reclaimed my corridor seat, and in the hour before dusk darkened to night I stared out at the desert landscape and its fleeting images of human occupation — the occasional farmer driving a mule by the trackside, and once a cart drawn by a shaggy brown Gobi camel.

Unusual for a train journey, I started to wish it was all over. End it did in the late afternoon of the second day at Lanzhou station, where I was to change trains. At least I'd finally managed to get something pleasant from the journey. In those austere days, the dining cars on Chinese trains always seemed to serve an excellent bowl of noodles with shredded pork, and just before we arrived I found a seat in the dining car and lapped up an oversize portion, complete with garnish of coriander. At Lanzhou's barn-like two-storey station I headed straight for the ticket office and got myself onto the next train to Qinghai, once again no questions asked. More novelty, my first ever *yinxi* – 'hard seat', the only class on offer for the half-day journey up to Xining, which stands at over 2,000 metres above sea level on the great Qinghai plateau. The Xining train wasn't due to leave until the early hours of the next morning, and it was going to be a long and uncomfortable wait in Lanzhou station.

A ragged chorus yells were coming from somewhere just outside the building; I went out onto the flight of steps to investigate. Ranked on the concourse were perhaps five hundred young lads, very obviously farm boys. They stood uneasily to attention, eyes front; on the steps nearby me was the PLA's version of a sergeant major, bellowing commands through a megaphone. The sudden appearance of my outlandish self was proving a distraction, and the man cast annoyed looks my way until I retreated. I learned later that it was the annual army recruiting season and this must have been the rostering point for Lanzhou.

Back in the station, I found my way to the upstairs waiting room, the usual dark chamber with damp concrete floor and long lines of benches, each section marked out with a metal sign for a particular destination. I lugged my rucksack towards the end of the Xining benches and seated myself next to the only other people waiting. In downtown Beijing you might stumble across a token Tibetan, brought to the capital for study at the Minorities Institute or to add colour to the government's congresses. Such individuals were always immaculately turned out in colourful tunics, expensive woollen gowns and decorative felt boots. My new neighbours were more authentic. Next to me on the bench was a man of middle age, with round face, pepper-and-salt hair and an even, tanned complexion. His gown, *chuba*, was a typical nomad's of sheepskin with the woolly side concealed. In the way of Tibetan herdsmen, his right arm was out of the chuba. Under it he wore a red tunic and a pair of army trousers which had seen better days. A worn pair of laceless faded plimsolls comprised his footwear. An older woman — was she the man's wife or his mother? — with careworn face grooved with deep smile-lines leaned over and took a good look at me. Her wispy dishevelled hair was long down her back and in the dim light I glimpsed silver in her long braids. The woman's chuba was of some thick material from which the blue dye had long faded. The third Tibetan, a woman perhaps in her thirties, would be good-looking in most cultures. Her costume was altogether finer, a white blouse showing under it. The man dipped into the side of his chuba and extracted what appeared to be a burnt bone, which he then offered in my direction. Smiling my appreciation,

I was glad to be able to point to a plastic bag containing my own snacks—a packet of dry biscuits and a tiny Hami melon.

How, I thought, would these un-scrubbed Tibetans be received in the very Han territory of a modern concrete train station? A blue-uniformed woman with peaked cap headed towards us, vigorously sweeping with broom and hinged dustpan. She wore on her lapel the little red and white symbol of the railways, stylised *ren* and *gong* characters shaped something like a train on a rail. The meaning of the character is 'worker', an appellation conveying all the pride of China's labour aristocracy. In the Party's class formulations, the workers were at the top of the pile. Unspoken but in effect, the bottom tier in this schema was occupied by the benighted people of Tibet, scarcely out of theocratic feudalism. As she neared us, the woman scowled, and her broom turned into a weapon. We hastily raised our legs from the bench as she directed it under and around us. I understood that this act of intimidation was in honour not of myself so much as my companions, and was meant to signal her disdain. The threesome were nonplussed and merely smiled a little dolefully.

I thought it time to introduce myself and did so in Chinese. The man waved his hand languidly which took as a sign that he had no knowledge of the language, so with communications flagging I decided to get some sleep in the hours before the train's departure. I awoke to a hubbub of conversation, of rustling bags, of coughing and spitting. It was now well after midnight and the Xining enclosure was jammed with travellers and their bags and bundles. A couple of hours on, and the same officious female showed up wielding a bullhorn, into which she yelled 'Xining, shang che'—'Xining, board the train'. We lined up and squeezed through a narrow steel barrier into the underpass leading to the platform. Touchingly, the three Tibetans had linked hands in order better to face any unpleasantness. The man's chuba, swollen with his possessions, caught in the barrier, provoking reprimands and knowing scowls from two ticket checkers. But soon we were all climbing into a hard seat carriage, I alongside my new friends. 'Four outlandish creatures together', I thought to myself. The man pointed at his nose, in the way of the locals, and carefully enunciated 'T-u-n-du'. I countered by mouthing 'Li'.

We settled in companionably for the four-hour journey. As day dawned, I stared out at a desiccated landscape of deeply eroded cliffs and gullies. The carriage had developed a moist fug and into it suffused the rancid aroma of Tundu's sheepskin; like the Lanzhou train, none of the windows could be prised open. As we approached our destination, the railway flanked a fast-flowing river, a hundred metres wide. Tundu launched into an animated communication with me, raising and lowering his clasped hands in a devotional manner and mouthing the two words 'Kumbum' and what sounded like 'Banchen'. He then added a third, pointing at his little group in turn: 'Lhasa' he repeated. He then put his folded hands against his head in the attitude of slumber and proceeded to count on his fingers. Watching carefully, I realised that he was telling me that it had already taken his family twenty days since they'd left Lhasa. This then was a real pilgrimage, but as yet I knew not the purpose.

The train was suddenly jerking into Xining station. Stepping out, first impressions were not of a provincial capital but rather a sleepy rural town. Was there a hostelry which allowed foreigners? The question was quickly answered by the Qinghai Hotel, a two-storey building near the station proclaiming itself by rusting characters on its roof. My new friends wandered off to find, I supposed, more modest accommodation. The surprised receptionist, who had in all likelihood never before had a foreigner come knocking, handed me a key and sent me off to an upstairs passage and a dimly-lit chamber. The bed lacked the usual cotton-filled quilt: instead, there was a thick but stained green blanket encased in a sheet with diamond-shaped aperture. On a bedside cabinet was the customary thermos, and next door to the bedroom a bath tub of black composite concrete fed by a red-hot steam pipe. I soaked off the long journey, and then there was just time for a stroll down some of Xining's village-like streets before dusk set in.

It was a clear morning of blue skies, and I wandered out of the hotel door to take soundings on the day. Apparently awaiting me, Tundu and his companions were in a huddle on the pavement. My new friends greeted me with warm smiles, and I realised that I was now an accepted, honorary member of their little pilgrimage group. Knots of Tibetans in diverse dress were coursing along the street—some in smart chubas of ersatz satin, others wrapped in stained sheepskins their upper bodies half exposed, and still more in conventional blue Chinese garb. 'Why all the crowds?' I asked myself. I was still in 'go with the flow' mood and hadn't thought too much what it was all about and where I might be heading next. But that 'Huangzhong county' which Turfan's policeman had happily entered in my travel pass hadn't been quite forgotten.

We were soon in a noodle shop where the threesome seemed happy with idea of some breakfast; we stood around a high ledge slurping our *miantiao*. I guessed that Tundu's whirling gestures, engine noises and his pointing at the crowds meant that we should be off. Trusting to instinct, I followed them and we soon were joining a crowd in a bus station yard, jostling in a good-natured way around a dozen vehicles. Doors were firmly closed, drivers slumped in the seats or taking a last drag on their cigarettes. Red and white windscreen signs on each vehicle displayed the two now-recognisable characters 'Huangzhong', as well as the three characters 'Ta-er-si'. A sprinkling of females in Tibetan garb stood around, but the crowd was mostly bronzed-cheeked men from the high plateau, some rather oddly dressed in standard Chinese blue jackets and peaked caps. I sat down on the fringe of the yard and got out my old guide book. 'Taersi' was, of course, none other than the Chinese name for the great monastery of Kumbum.

Later I turned once more to my Nagel. That intrepid mid-19th century traveller to the remote Western reaches of the Qing empire, Abbé Evariste Huc, had written of his visit to Kumbum. And I was to discover that the Belgian-French explorer and mystic, Alexandra David-Néel had actually spent a couple of years at the monastery imbibing Tibetan scriptures. A decade and more on, in his east-to-west odyssey across the great wastes and deserts of China, Peter Fleming in his *News from Tartary* describes the same journey from Xining to Kumbum. Historically speaking, at least, I was in good company.

Fleming in 1935 was accompanied by a bodyguard thrust upon him by nervous local officials:

> The transport was a Peking cart. The escort was a spindle-shanked and defenceless dotard.....At one o'clock, breasting a low ridge, we saw below us the great monastery of Kumbum. Its coloured roofs, the tiles of one of them plated with pure gold crowded the steep slopes of a narrow, sparsely wooded ravine. Figures in dark red robes, diminished by the distance, threaded the narrow, climbing passages between the buildings. A gong boomed lengthily. [1]

We were soon squeezing onto a bus and heading out of Xining. In

---

1   Fleming, Peter, *News from Tartary: A Journey from Peking to Kashmir*, London: Jonathan Cape, 1936, p78.

less than an hour of dry brown hillocks, we were at the terminus, a dusty area with food stalls to one side and peddlers in a line to the other. I noticed that many of the Tibetans were now removing their Han-style clothing and donning their Tibetan dress. Unlike my companions, they must have been too bashful to assert their identity on their long and arduous journeys, often through Han territory. Around us now were pilgrims in every variety of chuba, and adorned in an array of headgear. You could write a learned paper, I thought to myself, on contemporary Tibetans' choice of headwear. Most of the older men favoured broad-rimmed felt Pampas cowboy-style hats, but there were plenty of battered trilby-like head covers; many younger men had colourful fur-lined silk bonnets, and all of the tall warrior-looking youths, the Khampas, were hatless, their long locks entwined with bright red silk.

More buses were arriving and around us now were hundreds of Tibetans. Tundu beckoned to me and we were swept by the crowd up a dusty road lined with covered stalls selling garments of all kinds, alongside Buddhist votives and trinkets. My friends waited while I successfully bargained for a small green jade carving of water buffalo, ancient and missing a leg—another memento of this strange journey. The stall holders with their white skull caps were all Chinese Muslims, Hui traders from Ningxia and Gansu, fulfilling once again their traditional role as intermediaries between the Han and Tibetan worlds.

Half a century after him, my first glimpse of the golden roofs of the great Kumbum monastery half-concealed at the top of the hill was just as Fleming had described. We arrived at an open space with a series of eight ancient stupa — *chorten*. Several dozen pilgrims were moving around them, the most devout 'measuring their bodies', a painful forward progress requiring a falling almost flat to the ground, a full stretching out, then a rising to the feet. For the most devout, this went on without respite over the days and even weeks of a pilgrimage. Around them, antique matrons pounded the ground with many genuflections. A young man seemingly in a deep in trance was being dragged by his father and brothers from shrine to shrine. Wild-looking holy men from the mountains ripped their sheepskins from their blackened torsos in strange witness. Next to the stupa, a bank of large prayer wheels spun lazily on bearings greased with yak butter.

A half-naked drummer beat eerie time to an ancient Tibetan score, while floating over the scene from some distance came the plaintive sound of a *dungchen*, the long copper horn of Tibetan Buddhism. I skirted the chorten platform in search of the horn-blower, going down into a nearby hollow where Tibetans in every variety of dress — and undress — were taking their ease. There I encountered a handsome young man in the most princely of chubas and headdresses, all satin with fox-fur linings. Alongside him was a beautiful young woman, also lavishly attired. Perhaps I looked at her a moment too long: the young man drew his dagger and waved it at me, and I quickly moved on. An unexpected encounter, and I pondered on it for a long time after. But just like anywhere in the world, the reality is that the Western idealisation of a pacific, meditative culture is belied by a history punctuated by violence (much of it internecine), banditry and oppression.

Beyond the pilgrim crowds loomed those golden roofs of the monastery's many chambers. I was back with my companions, and quite suddenly a strange, constant humming like the sound of a score of bee hives seemed to be emanating from a banner-bedecked temple above us. The people around me shifted restlessly, and when Tundu unmistakably waved a 'hurry', we were funnelled into a rough scramble up a muddy bank, bringing us near the portal of a temple chamber. From there, I could see that it was being defended by half-a-dozen nervous looking blue-uniformed Han security police. Something dramatic was in the air, something was about to burst upon the expectant crowd. I readied my faithful Olympus OM1: a shutter speed priority setting would do well in that intense plateau sunlight.

Suddenly, violently, great red-lacquered double doors were propelled open from within, and a tribe of scarlet-robed novices, hardly teenagers, cascaded merrily down the steep path. The pilgrims, who now flanked it several deep took up a chant, some prostrating themselves. After the novices, next to emerge was a group of tall and fierce-looking figures, each with a stout staff, whom I recognised from tales of old Tibet such as Heinrich Harrer's as the 'bouncer' class of monk. The procession then became one of large banners, proud monk dignitaries under splendid yellow silk parasols, and clusters of ancient religious elders, some half-bent to the ground. The cacophony of wind and brass became louder and out of the portal emerged a full Tibetan orchestra, flutes prominent amongst other unfamiliar instruments, each musician wearing the curious horn-shaped ochre headdress of the Buddhist sect known to us as the 'Yellow Hats'.

For a minute or so no-one else appeared, and I assumed that was it. But the pilgrims around me were now hushed and even more attentive, eyes glued towards the great door. The procession resumed and a fresh group of figures emerged. Striding in the midst of a group of tall monks, in high black leather boots and a smart black silk gown, came a portly figure whom I recognised instantly from his frequent appearance in the pages of those Beijing glossies intended for a foreign audience. It was none other than the Banqen Erdini, the 10th Panchen Lama. As he passed me within touching distance, the Panchen paused for a few seconds, seemingly for my camera shutter to click. He wore a puzzled expression, which quickly transformed into a broad smile: the unlikely presence of a red-haired pilgrim had amused him. He moved on down the path, and he and the rest of the procession snaked back into another of the monastery's buildings, the Great Hall of Meditation.

In the tail of the procession, several dozen of the faithful had been admitted into the Great Hall, and the doors were clanged shut. Hundreds more, myself amongst them, were left to await events. I followed the crowd around the corner of the temple complex, scaled a steep bank, and alongside a chattering group of pilgrims — who seemed unquestioningly to accept a foreign interloper in their midst — squatted down on my haunches. Well aware of the repression of China's minority peoples during the Cultural Revolution, the degree to which Tibetans had managed to preserve their traditions was very much on my mind. My eyes, my camera too, were drawn to a woman, long past middle age and seated right in front of me on the slope. In an extraordinary attention to effect heartening to observe, her wispy long grey tightly plaited tresses were richly adorned with silver, turquoise and coral.

For the next couple of hours the growing tedium was only broken by chuckles from those around me at a regular little sideshow. One after the other, a bevy of monks would appear in the gully under us, bend down, lift their long russet robes and unashamedly proceed to do their business. But like my neighbours, who seemed to know what was to happen, my gaze was mostly fixed on the high red-lacquered set of double doors some 30 metres below us. Here, a company of security officials in their bright blue uniforms were being regimented by a loud officer half-bursting from his tunic, very much in command and clearly Han. Quite suddenly and half-hysterically, the commander started barking orders and shooing knots of pilgrims clear of the entrance. Meanwhile, I spied a black Hongqi limousine coming slowly up the rough lane, to halt just outside the doors. In a trice and despite the driver's remonstrations, a dozen women pilgrims surrounded the vehicle, festooning it with white silk scarves, *khata* and prayer flags, tying them onto the bonnet, the mirrors, door handles and the car's rear bumper. Some bent in prayer, knocking their heads on the car's windows. Now the driver was yelling and trying to fend them off with a colourful feather duster on a long bamboo stick.

Abruptly, the heavy doors of the chamber were thrown open, and the band sounded from within. First to emerge was a knot of officials with the Panchen at its centre, he under a tilting, oversized yellow parasol wielded by two monks. The Panchen Lama seemed relaxed as he exchanged a few words with those awaiting him, and then climbed into the limousine. It turned jerkily and took off at some speed, kicking up the dust. At this, a collective moan spread through the crowd. Meanwhile the rest of the procession emerged, quickly losing cohesion and dissolving. Nothing more to see, and people around me were already scrambling down the bank and moving away.

But it seemed that thousands of pilgrims were staying put. They hadn't travelled for hundreds of miles just for a single day out at Kumbum. As I wandered down towards the stupa platform, I could see people making makeshift camp amongst the hillocks outside the monastery. Perhaps many too were being accommodated in the huge temple halls. Dusk was already drawing on, and it was time for me to make a move. In the first rush to see the procession I'd lost my three friends, and I found my way alone to the bus terminus.

Back at the Qinghai Hotel, a young man intercepted me, wanting to find out why I was in Xining and where I'd been that day. I told him I'd been to Taersi and had seen the Panchen Lama. He was eager to give me the routine verdict on the Tibetan prelate.

'Banqen Erdini is a very rich man,' he said with a grimace. 'And the 5,000 poor Tibetans who went to see him at Taersi have made him even richer.'

He went on to claim that, on average, each pilgrim had handed over 100 *yuan* to the Panchen's entourage. Perhaps this was true—I'd noticed the roll of dirty notes Tundu concealed in his chuba. How much of the cash found its way back to the monastery was anyone's guess. Judging from the piles of bamboo scaffolding I'd seen everywhere, the huge complex of chambers and temples dating from the late 16th century and spread over forty-five hectares were, at least evidently, receiving some remedial attention.

The 10th Panchen Lama's relationship to both to the Nationalist government prior to 1949, and more particularly to the Communist Party in power, was throughout his life a snakes-and-ladders one. Having initially, in the 1950s, decided to cooperate with the new power in the land, and having been granted symbolic high office in Beijing, in the early 1960s he made a tour of Tibet which resulted in his submitting a long and highly critical report. Soon the Panchen was denounced for his 'separatist' views; what followed was long years of imprisonment and house arrest. In 1979, the Chinese state encouraged him to marry, to not just *any* woman but the daughter of one of China's senior Long Marcher generals. I recall John D of Hong Kong's Universities Service Centre telling me a tale, perhaps apocryphal, of how the Panchen had virtually kidnapped this already-married woman whom he had regularly seen walking along a Beijing street as he whizzed by in his official car. His unorthodox betrothal, and to a Han at that, was obviously intended to cement his support for Beijing's post-Mao stance on Tibet. And after Deng Xiaoping firmly grasped power in 1979, the Panchen was again accorded high positions in the Chinese state machinery, though really only on an honorary basis. Despite his harsh words for Beijing following his 1962 tour of Tibet, and given his tortuous history with the Communist Party, the Panchen's stance towards Beijing had coalesced into an uneasy but liveable ambivalence. He might easily be dismissed on the basis of his later life, his supposed amassing of a fortune in the decade following his marriage, his property interests and his penchant for fast cars, but his earlier record stands. To every Tibetan nationalist, his premature death in 1989 is regarded as highly suspect. The Panchen controversy continued after his demise, with competing claims regarding the succession. The outcome has been the promotion of two different Panchen Lamas, one by Beijing and one by the Dalai Lama, each denying the legitimacy of the other's choice.

All Panchen Lamas have cultivated a relationship with Kumbum, the 10th Panchen no exception—his chief assistant Arjia Rinpoche acting as the Party-appointed Abbot. And the Panchen's association with Kumbum was intimate; as far back as 1951 he'd first officiated in religious rites at the monastery. On that extraordinary day in 1983 when I just happened to arrive at Kumbum, the Panchen had not long since been rehabilitated, and this was the first visit he'd been permitted to make to one of the great Tibetan religious communities. I wondered what had detained him for hours within the confines of the monastery, while the faithful awaited him outside. Perhaps as in 1951 he was once more performing the peace rites, the Kalacakra Initiation, set around a large mystically decorated sand mandala. But how many of Kumbum's monks were now still genuine believers, how many simply placemen—and worse—remained a question.

Certainly, the efforts made by thousands to journey for weeks from all over the vastness of Tibet to this one spot signalled foreknowledge of a special day. Lengthy pilgrimage trips are a deep part of the culture, and after the repression of the Cultural Revolution, few Tibetans would pass up the chance to witness the reappearance of the second most revered living figure in the their pantheon. Perhaps too, after years of suppression, the Panchen's well-advertised visit to Kumbum was simply a chance for ordinary Tibetans to find a common focus, and for the first time in years to assemble together in large numbers..

Whatever the reason for that huge congregation, it was my ignorant good fortune, hastened by the willing seal of a policeman hundreds of miles distant, which had made me the sole foreign witness to the Panchen Lama's long awaited and much heralded return to the greatest monastery of the Gelukpa School, aka the Yellow Hats.

II
LORD MAYORS, LEADERS AND LIMOS (1983-4)

When China first loomed in my life back in the early 1970s, Britain was all factory sit-ins, militant miners and a Conservative government—Edward Heath's—brought to its knees. When we returned from China after six years' absence class strife was still very much in the air. Britain's coal miners were now fighting for the very survival of their industry. Soon, massed strikers would be pitted against the forces of the state. Their eventual defeat in 1984 was to set the tone of British politics until the present day.

It was 1980 when we'd re-entered Britain's dispiriting terrain. Massive shifts were underway in the architecture of Western economies and the web of global institutions of the post-Bretton Woods era. Spearheading these shifts, with Margaret Thatcher at the helm, a newly confident global financial elite were consolidating their power. From the heartland of the City of London, its interests were now assured of an expansive reach far greater than ever before. On both sides of the Atlantic the regulatory fetters on financial institutions were in the cross-hairs. In the City of London, they were cast aside in what was benignly named the 'Big Bang'. Meanwhile, Wall Street saw the abolition of the crucial Glass-Steagall legislation which had long kept apart commercial banking and the speculative shenanigans of 'investment banking'. The scene was thus set for an increasingly virulent financialisation of economies, and two decades on, the inevitable descent towards the 2008 global financial crisis with all its dire consequences.

———∽∽———

In the Spring of 1980, our little family was reunited in Durham. The departure from Shandong had been ragged, Jo in ill-health travelling with our new-born, while I arrived three months later, surviving a drama in Jinan and a 'heart attack' in Hong Kong (told in *Intruder in Mao's Realm*). We were given temporary refuge by my China-born mother in picturesque Durham, with its improbably massive Norman cathedral. From our terraced house on the edge of the city, we made timid forays onto streets which seemed almost as alien after years of absence as had Cultural Revolution China when we'd first arrived there. Jobless, and with the economic downturn promising few immediate prospects, we wondered what would happen when our meagre savings had expired. As an aspiring academic, my central purpose in China, since first arriving there in 1973, had been to cut through the obscurity which shrouded the process of migration, capital accumulation and urbanisation during the period of Mao Zedong's ascendancy. Despite securing a book contract, I had yet to write a single page and the publisher's deadline was nigh. In a desperate move, I invested my slight China savings in a state-of-the-art IBM golf ball typewriter, its cost equivalent to a quarter of a modest professional's annual salary. The book was stuck firmly in my craw, and my plan was that this magic machine would somehow unloose all and do the writing for me.

'Whichever of us gets a job first in a half-decent northern metropolis, that's where we'll go,' we'd agreed. It was my partner who had the marketable credentials, and so we ended up in Sheffield. That city had been in the steel-making business since Chaucer's time, its famed cutlery industry nurtured by local iron ore and water power. In the first of many technological paradigm leaps, the mid-18th century Huntsman's crucible process meant that high grade steel could be produced in significant quantities. A century on, Sheffield companies adopted the Bessemer system capable of transforming pig-iron into hitherto unimaginable quantities of steel. In the ensuing decades, Sheffield's primacy in the world of steel was never in question, the demands of empire and warfare a constant spur to innovation.

We arrived in Sheffield at a real turning point in the city's industrial history. At its beating heart was the swathe of industrial territory stretching from the commercial centre several miles eastwards, up to and beyond the Tinsley viaduct carrying the M1 motorway. Crammed within this wide corridor were countless steel-making, forging and engineering enterprises accumulated willy-nilly over the previous century. And now Thatcher's anti-manufacturing policies were to bring this, the Lower Don Valley, to a dreadful pass. Factory closures, already trundling through in the 1970s, greatly accelerated. By 1981, the local unemployment rate had soared to over eleven percent. In the early 1970s, half Sheffield's workforce had been employed in manufacturing; a decade on, and it accounted for only a quarter of those working. In devastating measure, the newly empowered financial architecture was, in effect, conspiring against an industrial heritage forged through generations.

The disaster went far beyond Sheffield. Now feasible on a mass scale with the newly standardised shipping container and the exponential advance of computer logistics, off-shoring to low-cost centres overseas became an irresistible option. Almost overnight, world-wide industrial supply lines stretching to the Far East were a viable proposition. So alien was this entire notion back in the 1980s that I recall my astonishment at learning that Rolls Royce had already shifted their production of basic castings to Shanghai. For those in the know, the 'unpatriotic' behaviour of Britain's iconic company caused raised eyebrows. Of course, today when everything comes from everywhere, no-one would give such a thing a second thought.

But what was all this to me, a humble barefoot academic concerned with the little understood development processes in Mao's China? By investing in one of the first home computers—and casting aside my IBM goofball—I'd actually managed to write the book, which turned out to be something of a success, even landing me an unexpected doctorate. Thus equipped, I was in for one of the best university jobs in my field, but was thwarted by the manoeuvring of unseen hands: because I'd been in China during Mao's day, I just *had* to be a dangerous Maoist and thus unappointable. A bit like my Quaker forebears, who when denied university entrance or civil service jobs turned instead to banking, engineering and chocolate, I found myself forced into other fields in order to make a living. Thwarted in my high ambitions in the academy, ensnarement in the web of transnational interchange blithely termed 'globalisation' was hardly uppermost in my thoughts. But due to the modest socialistic aspirations of an English town hall and the law of unintended consequences, in the spider's web of trade and finance I was now to play a walk-on part. Improbably, Chinese manhole covers and 'hand-made' bricks were soon pouring into Yorkshire by the tonne and at the flick of a few telex keys. The ruination of several companies in Yorkshire and beyond was a foregone conclusion. But more of my role in Sheffield's eccentric foray into China in what follows.

―――∞―――

How was it that two antagonistic forces—Sheffield's leftist Labour civic leaders on the one hand, and the city's Thatcherite, troglodyte captains of industry on the other—were soon happily parading together on the Great Wall of China? Nationally, the break with the *noblesse oblige* 'One-Nation' Conservatives signalled by Thatcher's rise had also caused deep ruptures in the defeated Labour Party. With the backdrop of ferocious riots in London and Liverpool, the rift soon came to a head in the election campaign for its deputy leader. The right-wing of the Labour Party prevailed and the torch was left in the hands of municipal socialism. Here, at the sharp end of politics, the struggle continued apace. True to the contrived 'family grocer' narrative, the Thatcher regime of the early 1980s had made it illegal for town halls to set deficit budgets, and councillors who did so were to be held personally liable, fined and disbarred from office. Not at all typical was the response of Liverpool's administration, the ruling Labour Party in the hands of a small group of determined gut-socialists, adherents of what was known as the Militant Tendency. Large areas of their city were scourged with poverty, and in their thousands Scousers were fleeing the misery. In an act of defiance, Liverpool City Council went to the capital markets and obtained funds which they targeted on the city's atrocious housing conditions. Thousands of families were removed from high-rise council slums, and rehoused in 'homes with gardens'. But in the end, with the open collaboration of the Labour Party hierarchy, the Liverpool councillors were traduced by the Tory government and removed from office. A few years later, I was in Liverpool working at the city's old university. I was left in no doubt by the menials—the locals such as my office cleaner with whom I always passed the time of day—that the radicals' short-lived reign in Liverpool was the best thing that had ever happened to the city.

But back to the Sheffield of the early 1980s. With large scale unemployment facing Steel City for the first time since the Great Depression, the Labour council decided to take action—a rather different action to that of Liverpool, but nonetheless bringing to the city and its region the often insult-laden soubriquet 'Socialist Republic of South Yorkshire'. When the chips were finally down, the City Council led by one David Blunkett notoriously did forget their promise to set an illegal budget. But the highly popular 'Socialist Republic' label was happily played by the leftish coterie ensconced in Sheffield's town hall. Actually, in essence the whole 'socialist' thing was really nothing much beyond a high local subsidy to the publicly-owned South Yorkshire bus service, as well as a little ineffectual dabbling in workers' cooperatives. If truth were known, the Chamber of Commerce (redoubt of the reactionaries) was just as happy as everyone else that people could get to work on the buses for a few pence and on time and in a relaxed state of mind. Good for both productivity and the damping down of wage demands. But subsidies to public transport, cheekily supplied by local government which 'had no business interfering in the economy', were a heresy to be firmly stamped upon. Of the over eighty seats in the Sheffield Council chamber, the Tories had a pathetic handful. So how to make way against the 'Socialist Republic', and specifically against Sheffield's Labour-run council? In London, the Tory House of Commons was planning to simply abolish the Greater London Council, a hotbed of quasi-socialist activity under the leadership of Ken Livingstone. The government eventually got away with this because they could push through an Act of Parliament with the GLC as its sole target, but no way could the tactic be extended to a local authority, a Metropolitan District Council such as Sheffield. Instead, Conservative Central Office assigned to the Sheffield Chamber of Commerce the task of bringing troublesome council leader Blunkett & his comrades to heel. And despite my obvious sympathies with the city council, it was to fall to me to work alongside both antagonists — with China the arena of battle.

———∞———

In the People's Republic of China on the other side of the globe, big changes were underway. The post-Mao leadership of the Communist Party was now firmly in the hands of the 'veteran reformer' (read 'Rightist'), Deng Xiaoping. At a session of the Communist Party's 11th Central Committee in late 1978, a monumental change in strategy had been signalled. China's economy, until then scarcely trading with the outside world, was to open up, the market to play an increasing role at the expense of central planning. But unlike the 'shock capitalism' imposed upon the former Soviet Union a decade later, Western bankers and corporations were ill-equipped to mould Chinese developments into a market-based free-for-all. Far from it: within constraints, naturally, it was the Communist Party which was to dictate a carefully planned, gradual and always highly controlled process of development which used, but never depended upon, foreign interests. And of course, there was to be very little change in the way that power would be dispensed by the Communist Party.

In the early days, the crucial objective of the Chinese authorities was to fuel the new Great Leap Forward by gaining access to Western technology on the cheap. For centuries China had been imagined as the elusive prize of Western imperial dreamers. Now, foreign companies were to be persuaded that the surest way to breach the Bamboo Curtain was to embrace the *joint venture* formula. In this, the Chinese partner would supply the land, the factory building, the infrastructure, and a carefully disciplined if not well-trained labour force, all at a fraction of the cost in the home country. For its part, the foreign joint venture company would install the modern hardware and software demanded by markets which were in the main to be export-oriented, earning for both sides the great incentive of foreign exchange. A capitalist-style top-down hiring-and-firing labour management regime was to be the norm, meaning an end to the 'iron rice bowl' of the Mao-era planned economy. Instead, the rice bowl, at least for the mass of China's workers, would henceforth be one of increasing fragility.

How to get those Western foreign devils wedded to the joint venture (JV) idea in a land the other side of the globe and in a culture, political world and language which for decades had been mystically hidden away? The problem was uppermost in certain Chinese minds. In corners of obscure Beijing courtyards, superannuated Party leaders and 'democratic party personages' beavered away at the magic concept of 'friendship'. Now, this word (*youyi* in Chinese) is almost exclusively employed in the context of China's official relations with 'the foreign'. 'People-to-people' diplomacy, aka winning foreign friends and bending them towards China's world view, was (and remains) the objective.

Most prominent in the friendship game was an outfit with a rambling English title: the Chinese People's Association for Friendship with Foreign Countries. From deep within its corridors came the command to nurture city twinning with Europe and North America. 'Friendship cities', 'sister cities' (*youhao chengshi, jiemei chengshi*) were going to be crucial bridges in the pump-priming of China's new technological revolution, and joint ventures were to be the vehicle.

'Mutual benefit' is the leitmotif of China's diplomacy, and what could be more mutually beneficial (went the line) than citizens of twinned cities joining hands across the oceans to enrich themselves through joint ventures on Chinese soil? With or without a twinning link, plenty of foreign companies took to the JV idea with enthusiasm and went on to make good money.

But as I was about to discover, the JV way of doing things was definitely not one which appealed to most of the British industrial class, who in the main saw themselves as far too red-blooded and superior to consort as actual *partners* to the Chinese. And in addition, our captains of industry had little time for town halls, leftist-run or not, or for civic niceties and all the awkward ceremonial of the 'friendship' dance. It was to be my own experience, as we shall see, that far from mutuality, the benefits they sought were, naturally, one-sided and short-term.

Now to London. It was no surprise that China's London-based diplomats were casting around for likely places for the friendship city hard-sell, and that Sheffield should be high on their list of targets. After all, the technocrats who increasingly dominated the Central Committee had been schooled since mother's milk (and Stalin) in the Great Truth: steel output is the key to all progress. A byway in my twinning tale brings me to events in the early 1980s at China's renowned embassy building in London's Portland Place. These reveal much about the British government's attitude to a China which had finally seen the sense, as it judged, of taking a leap towards a kind of autarkic capitalism.

I was no stranger to the august building in Portland Place just up from the BBC, where the revolutionary Sun Yat-sen himself had once been held prisoner by Qing diplomats. Since our being interviewed there back in 1974 for our Nanjing posting, I'd passed through the embassy's grand doorway several times, most recently to what seemed to be a soft debriefing following a British Academy-funded research trip to China. Then, in my role as a council member of the Society for Anglo-Chinese Understanding (SACU), the official 'friendship with China' organisation, before every October 1st National Day I would receive those red-fringed invitation cards emblazoned with the five-star flag. Throughout 1983-85 the receptions were held in a building up Portland Place from the George III embassy building which had been inherited from the Nationalists (who in turn had inherited it from the ruins of the Qing empire). The embassy lay hidden behind a massive shroud emblazoned with the insignia of the giant Wates Group construction company.

This shielded, it turned out, some shocking skulduggery. The original highly protected, Grade I Listed building dating from the late 18th century and designed by the celebrated Robert and James Adam had been completely flattened, and a 'Georgian' pastiche was rising in its place. The very right-wing and Tory Party-funding private construction outfit, Wates Group, was hard at it, working to a plan devised in-house as it were by the Beijing Architectural Design Institute. Demolition *was* officially sanctioned by the powers-that-be, but only with a stern stipulation that the original interior mouldings, staircases and the like should be carefully integrated into the new building. In the event, nothing of the sort happened. One very lucky architectural salvage man was able to fill truckloads with Adam cornices, fireplace surrounds, cast-iron stair fittings and wooden banisters from the skips parked on Portland Place. Instead, the interior was done out in the manner of the late 1950s Great Hall of the People—a style which the Chinese designers no doubt thought was modern and international and suitably grandiose in their nation's representation. This wholly illicit arrangement was nonetheless happily OK'd by the London authorities both local and ministerial—no doubt in the cause of good relations with the newest and most unlikely convert to what Mao had castigated as the 'capitalist road'. Indeed, as it turned out, considerable Foreign Office pressure was exerted on the Westminster local authority from the early 1970s on, when Beijing first suggested a 'refurbishment'. To smooth the way, Wates had opportunistically hired a local architect to see through their deranged and illegal vandalism. Colin Penn was more than an architect—with close political ties to the embassy he was also the project's chief fixer. Is it a coincidence that all this took place during the Westminster Council regime of the arch-Thatcherite Dame Shirley Porter, later prosecuted and fined tens of £millions for gerrymandering?

I knew Colin Penn through the Society for Anglo-Chinese Understanding. Penn was a taciturn man who didn't take kindly to those who questioned the twists and turns of the official line from Beijing. I can't say that I had more than a few stilted exchanges with him, and I recall receiving a gruff response when I asked him if he was related to the illustrious Quaker William Penn. Far too petty-bourgeois a question for the confirmed Stalinist. Penn and his wife and a small circle of true believers found SACU's *China Now* magazine insufficiently loyal: their answer was the closely typed and densely packed *China Policy Broadsheet*. Back in the 1970s in Nanjing, this publication had come into my hands irregularly. It could always be relied upon to be a dance of fealty to the Cultural Revolution and its pseudo-Marxist philosophical ramblings. Long after it became evident that things had gone mightily awry with any democracy-friendly strains of the Cultural Revolution, the *Broadsheet* remained true to the ultra-Maoist line. Seeing (if not entirely living) the reality of China in the mid-1970s, I'd always relish getting into a lather of indignation when the latest *Broadsheet* arrived.

It was at the National Day reception of 1982 that Ambassador Ke Hua engaged me over the battered prawn canapés.

'You live in Sheffield, and Sheffield is a very famous steel city. You should ask your leaders to become friendship cities with

Anshan, which is also a steel city and much praised by our late leader Chairman Mao.'

The diplomat was referring to Mao's famed 'Anshan Charter' of 1960. His promotion of the Anshan Iron and Steel Company (known always as Angang), already China's largest state enterprise and employing 100,000, was particularly intended to raise the steelwork's internal discipline as a national model, a paragon of the new socialist order. This was just a couple of years after the launch of the Great Leap Forward; steel was seen as a crucial measure of the Leap's success, Mao's target being to double production within a year and overtake the U.K.'s annual output within fifteen years. Steel, steel, steel....

As it happened, Sheffield was no stranger to municipal diplomacy: the ambassador was pressing on a door which had already been opened many times. Long before David Blunkett became its leader, the city had aspired to a role which went beyond its steelworks-ochre skies. Remarkably, just five years after the end of the Second World War, Sheffield had twinned with the coalmining city of Bochum, in Germany's Ruhr. This act of reconciliation was rare but not alone — in the same era my then home of York had linked up with the North German city of Münster, an arrangement in which my own father had been instrumental.

Next in Sheffield's internationalist crusade came a twinning with a city in the Ukraine Republic of the U.S.S.R. Donetsk is, of course, today the heart of the breakaway territory from a Ukraine turned quasi-fascist with lashings of U.S., EU and IMF gold. But in 1956, for Sheffield to get into bed with Soviet Donetsk at the very height of paranoid, anti-leftist McCarthyism was a brave move. Then there was the Sheffield-Esteli twinning during Ronald Reagan's presidency, the Iran-Contra scandal and the U.S. terror onslaught on Central America. Ideologically driven

SHIFTING GEARS IN CHINA

it may have been, but the Esteli twinning was always practical and helpful—Sheffield teachers I knew went off to work camps there, and people-to-people aid projects flourished. Unlike the fated Donetsk twinning, Sheffield's link with the Nicaraguan city, a legacy of the enlightened Blunkett era of the early 1980s, survives to the present day.

Heir to the selective internationalism of a Communist Party which had always been strong in the leading engineering trade union of the locality, the Amalgamated Union of Engineering Workers, anti-apartheid had become a vocal cause of the Sheffield Labour Party. Indeed, none other than the ANC leader-in-exile, Oliver Tambo, was a regular guest of the town hall. Once when I was at a reception for him in the splendour of the Lord Mayor's Parlour, the very Yorkshire elderly lady incumbent welcomed him as 'Mr Sambo'. The slip of the tongue was taken in good part, as was her desire that he 'give all of our greetings to his comrades back in South Africa'. Mr Tambo had long been in exile and South Africa was the last place he'd be returning to. Such minor blips apart, Sheffield City Council and the local labour movement could hardly be faulted when it came to matters of international solidarity.

―――∾∾――

Back in Sheffield, I walked through the Victorian town hall's grand portal famously opened by the Queen herself in 1897, 'remotely', as she sat in her carriage and pulled a lever. I took a sharp right turn in the building's lobby and was in the Council's spacious Publicity Department for a meeting with a jolly young woman who introduced herself as the International Officer. Elizabeth's was an unusual position to find in a town hall, but not in Sheffield with all its worthy international initiatives. I was led to the Department's chief, a Pinocchio-like fellow sitting in front of an oversize desk in a partitioned office. Peter W was a man who lived on his nerves, a slave to the every whim of the irascible council leader. He once confided in me that he'd overcome the worst of his neuroses by becoming a regular at Sheffield United's Bramall Lane where his therapy was to shout and curse with the best of them. The man claimed to have no politics except those of the football terraces and the golf course—meaning to say, of course, that his tribe was the Tories. I did wonder from time to time whether he was the Chamber of Commerce's Trojan Horse within the town hall.

Within days, a letter arrived with the rubber-stamped signature of David Blunkett inviting me to his lair (for those unfamiliar with U.K. politics, Baron Blunkett of Brightside as he's known today is entirely blind). Blunkett needed little persuading that China was a Good Thing. On the spot and against all Council precepts banning subcontracting, aka outsourcing, I was appointed consultant to Sheffield City Council to develop links with China—and to work as many hours as the job demanded.

Prior to moving to China in late 1974, I'd tried to get a job with a state-funded initiative called the Community Development Programme. The progressive CDP had set up a number of units in deprived urban settings around the country. Unhappily for the government, these rapidly became refuges for university graduates of the late 1960s who were committed to leftist social activism. The Coventry CDP was run by one such, John B Lured by Blunkett's 'Socialist Republic', he'd arrived in Sheffield as the director of the Council's new venture, its Department of Employment & Economic Development, DEED. The Tories now had a target firmly in their sights. To the Chamber and its stooges, DEED, located on an upstairs floor of an Edwardian terrace right opposite the town hall, symbolised all that was wayward about the City Council. Indeed, it was downright impertinent for local politicians (and Labour ones at that) to parade on their terrain, the terrain of the city's 'natural wealth creators'. How things have changed: today in the U.K. there's hardly a town council of whatever political hue lacking a department supposedly devoted to the good of the 'local economy'.

'We can pay you a daily rate plus all expenses,' John B casually declared as we walked from Blunkett's town hall office over the road to the premises of DEED in Pinstone Street. Thinking on my feet, I replied 'How about £40 a day?' That would be, he replied, no problem at all. With the average senior civic employee on about £3,000 annually, I could now look forward to notching up a living wage. I'd voluntarily given up a lectureship at my old college, London's Architectural Association, in order to finish that book on China, and so wasn't eligible for state unemployment benefit. But money was becoming a problem, and after a decade of attaching myself to the coattails of China, I told myself that the hard times were at least beginning to deliver. Rather than answering to Peter W and his team of functionaries, I would be put under the wing of the director of DEED. I'd noticed that John B certainly had the ear of Blunkett, essential to getting any China plans moving. From my new platform, I was to march alongside my fellow socialists (for most of the DEED officers were dedicated to the cause) onto the brave new terrain of a China taking its first uncertain steps into the battleground of the global economy.

———∞———

Liaoning is one of the three provinces in the northeast of China once known to us as Manchuria, native territory to the Manzu (i.e. Manchu) tribesmen who conquered China in the mid-17th century to proclaim the Great Qing dynasty. The province, more than the Northeast's Jilin and far distant Heilongjiang, is the location of an extraordinary array of industrial and agricultural resources and hence the Japanese militarists' invasion of the region in 1931, with the de facto concurrence of the League of Nations. Until their defeat in 1945, large numbers of Japanese were settled in Liaoning, and its coal and iron ore resources were heavily exploited for Japan's war drive. It was during the fifteen years of the Japanese occupation that the great steelworks at Anshan were developed along modern lines.

Once the People's Republic was declared in 1949, and the extraordinary First Five Year Plan inaugurated, huge resources were put into Liaoning. Fushun's open-cast coalmine was to become the world's largest; with Soviet aid, the province capital of Shenyang (formerly aka Mukden) became the focus of China's heavy electrical engineering. On one of my many visits to the province, I was shown around a huge plant creating giant turbines for hydroelectric generation. Even the sleepy port city of Lüda — today's Dalian — was industrialised. In my later wanderings in the province, I was once the guest of a massive Dalian plant producing up-to-date electric locomotives; in the city, too, I visited a modern works making high grade special steels for the aerospace industry and, no doubt, the armaments industry too.

By the 1980s in Sheffield's putative twin of Anshan, the monster iron and steelworks, Angang ('An' from Anshan and 'gang' from *gangtie* = steel), was turning out seven million tonnes annually, a figure equivalent to around half the ever-shrinking output of the U.K. as a whole. In contrast to the small-scale Dalian works I'd been to, Angang was in the business of ordinary carbon steel, known sniffily in Sheffield as 'clog iron'. Sheffield itself, of course, had long moved on to the more refined special steels demanded by the high-tech industries. Angang's blast and electric furnaces and rolling mills had been substantially renewed during the short-lived era of Soviet technical cooperation of the mid-1950s. This meant in many cases being brought up to pre-World War Two standards, for the U.S.S.R. had not moved on greatly itself from the innovations brought in from the West by Stalin's Second Five Year Plan. As a Sheffield engineer demonstrates in his account of an odyssey around China's steel producing centres in the late 1970s and early 1980s, by contemporary Western standards China's entire steel industry was beset by obsolescence.[2]

So despite the gulf steel-wise between Sheffield and Anshan, there was still enormous scope for Sheffield companies to get involved with the replacement of Angang's old plant. But everything depended on the say-so of the overlord Ministry of Metallurgical Industries in Beijing— that behemoth dwarfing all other ministries. Though limited in its foreign exchange allocations, the Ministry was looking towards wholesale modernisation of the huge steel sector. A prime candidate in terms of hardware was the introduction of new and more productive ways of dealing with the molten steel as it flows from the blast furnace. Angang and indeed all China's steel works urgently needed the continuous casting technology already pretty well universal in the West.

Angang and hence the whole of China's steel sector promised untold opportunities to the Sheffield steel industry. And once the U.K. city had sealed the link with Anshan, though scarcely understood back home Sheffield could be the beneficiary of a crucial web of personal relations, the key to getting things done in China. That's to say, because of Angang's status politically, senior personnel in the all-commanding Metallurgical Ministry, including successive Ministers and most Vice-Ministers, were

---

2 Ewan Hewitt, *Rolling Around the World*, Bloomington, ID: Xlibris, 2014.

almost exclusively Angang men. I was later to realise that despite China's long isolation, these people knew a great deal about Sheffield and its steel technologies. And they were eager to do everything in their power to bring these modern ways to their beloved Angang: Sheffield was pushing on an open door if it wanted to do business in China.

Whilst in China, civic authorities identified closely with the enterprises of the city (since they 'owned' most of them). In the U.K. things were very different: the town hall was generally regarded by local business as a hindrance to their money-making. Were the rich prizes offered by the Chinese metal bashing fraternity to their Sheffield counterparts to be gratefully seized or carelessly disregarded? Many a managing director was going to be dragged to the sweet waters through Sheffield's twinning with Anshan, but would they drink? Yet unconscious of any of these questions, let alone their answers, John B and I packed our bags, filled them with tribute gifts consisting mainly of Sheffield's famous cutlery and on a cold winter's morning headed off to China and its great Northeast to see how the land lay.

III
THE CAPTAINS OF INDUSTRY HIT CHINA (1985)

BASIC WORK routines were mostly alien to the chieftains of Sheffield industry. In particular, reading any briefing paper beyond a single page of A4 — the idiot's guide — not to mention taking notes in business meetings, was unknown. This was the 1980s, and senior company men in Sheffield's steel and engineering outfits had mostly come up through the ranks. Or they were the unschooled but breezily confident scions of the family firm. University degrees were little heard of, and viewed almost as a badge of shame. Being a semi-educated 'intellectual' (the Chinese term for anyone who'd ascended beyond primary) and the written word my daily meat, the demeanor of our captains of industry towards me was one of disdain. And 'barely concealed', as the cliché goes.

This attitude had to be a little moderated once we were together in China. The company men would beg me for the lowdown on an official briefing from which we'd just emerged. After all, only secretaries (female) take notes at meetings, while their (male) bosses dunk their biscuits and dream of the golf course. The cultural divide between me and my wayward charges put me in mind of David Lodge's magnificent and comedic 1988 novel, in which a feminist academic is unwillingly entwined by her university's 'Industry Year Shadow Scheme' with the pig-headed chief of a Birmingham steel foundry. At least the Brummy dinosaur learnt weird new words ('semiotics', 'objectivity') and even found deep in himself tender feelings for the unlikely female who'd landed on his lap. In the case of myself and the Sheffield captains of industry though, neither respect nor (I'm happy to report) tender feelings ever rose to the surface. Before the captains of Sheffield industry were to be let loose on Chinese soil, it was going to be essential to prepare the ground with lashings of pomp and ceremony. This was going to be more of a necessity to Anshan's civic leaders than to Sheffield's, for in China matters relating to the foreign world had not only to be done, but seen to be done. The telex machines were chattering away, and between the two cities were flying flowery drafts for the protocols which would bind them together in eternal friendship. I was already getting the message that Anshan had a strong sense of itself. I'd once lived a couple of kilometers from a large steelworks; I could just imagine Anshan's night sky lit by the explosive tapping of its blast furnaces and by the yellow-hot molten waste being tipped with a rushed roar from rail wagons onto an ever-extending embankment of furnace slag. For me, a northerner with heavy industry in his bones, this signalled an almost atavistic power in the land. Ahead of us I could already see the speechifying the banqueting and the consummation at a grand signing ceremony of twinning between two proud steel cities.

In 1979, Beijing had put an end to the long drought of published economic and administrative statistics, so before journeying to China's Northeast I was able to divine some basic information about Sheffield's proposed twin. As is still the custom for all Chinese municipalities, the surrounding rural areas were ruled by Party supremos in the city proper. The then two counties under the city administration were described in official publications as abundant in mineral resources, their deposits of iron ore equalling a quarter of China's total, not to mention the *world's* largest cache of magnesite. Hot metal operations can't happen without the insulating refractory materials formed from magnesite. The coal for the steelwork's coking plants which fed Angang's monster blast furnaces was also right there on the doorstep. Liaoning province had, and today still has, copious reserves, with mega-mines at Fushun and Fuxin. No wonder that after the First World War the vast mineral-rich territory of China's Northeast was coveted by a militarizing Japan. There followed, of course, Japan's notorious invasion and its 1931 declaration of the puppet kingdom of Manzuguo, with the shameless acquiescence of a toothless League of Nations.

With years of official dealings in China under my belt, I was well used to platitudes, not to mention the routine obfuscations of officialdom. From the moment John B and I we were received by Madame Liu — as she announced herself — at Beijing airport, I felt that things looked quite promising. Stolid, middle-aged Mme. Liu, Anshan Foreign Affairs Office, had managed to acquire passable English, though like most graduates before the Sino-Soviet rupture she'd been trained as a Russian speaker. Maybe there was indeed something in the air in this no-nonsense city of Anshan, and its heaviest of heavy industry, that bred straight talking: our exchanges as the train coursed northwest through Hebei and Liaoning were untrammeled by political rhetoric. Liu explained her hope that Sheffield could be central to the huge modernisation programme planned for the steelworks. And Anshan was also eager to elevate its diverse non-steel economy. We were reminded that as well as Angang turning out upwards of seven million tonnes of steel annually, making it the largest producer in China, the company and the municipality itself ran numerous small enterprises. In workshops and little factories in the shadow of the blast furnaces and cooling towers laboured tens of thousands, most of them from steelworkers' households. Typical of the paternalism of large Chinese *danwei*, Angang had had set up hundreds of businesses which soaked up labour and often made use of low-quality materials, some of them byproducts of the works. The city's own light industry bureaux also 'owned' and managed dozens of medium-sized enterprises, and these too would be seeking modernisation. Of less relevance to future economic links between the two cities were the labour-intensive workshops in every neighbourhood which turned out all manner of modest items with the minimum of machinery. These outfits, under 'collective ownership', offered conditions far lower than in the state-owned units, let alone in the steelworks where pay was way above the national industrial average. Their existence in every city explains why, during the Mao era, the urban labour participation rate was nudging 70 percent.

Despite the damage caused by the Thatcher tornado, Sheffield still boasted an industrial base which went well beyond steelmaking. So if the city could get its act together, there would be plenty of business opportunities in Anshan which Sheffield's small and medium enterprises could address. We kept quiet about the damage done to the industrial base after the Conservative government's coming to power of 1979. Thatcher, the instigator of our woes, was, paradoxically, almost a folk hero in China's corridors of power. Insofar as they thought at all of the 'Iron Lady', it was as a staunch ally in Beijing's obsessional project to destroy the Soviet Union.

Throughout China, Angang was a byword for industrial prowess. In his *Charter of the Anshan Steel Company* Mao Zedong had, after all, singled out the steelworks for special praise. But now that the Mao system was fast fading, an old accolade from the late Chairman wasn't going to preserve the company from the winds of change. So the securing of a future for the city's workforce was clearly uppermost in the minds of Anshan's municipal leaders, mirroring the situation back in Sheffield. With deepening capitalist globalisation, the two cities were going to be facing situations in which each economy was going to be subjected to pretty much the same broad forces.

In China, the quality of the local Party leadership was always crucial, especially as the *shizhang* ('mayor', but actually the Party boss) of a city such as Anshan traditionally wielded considerable power, and in the Communist Party's system this was still so in the local economic arena. But I was conscious that the provincials of Anshan would have little idea how things worked in the U.K. Our Chinese interlocutors would have difficulty with the idea that an enterprise located within the bounds of Sheffield was not guided, let alone commanded, by the city authorities. Just as Anshan's leaders would be orchestrating their enterprises in the linking up with Sheffield, they would be expecting Sheffield City Council to be selecting joint venture and other business partners, and even endorsing contracts. The reality was that the twinning relationship might lead Sheffield companies to the water, but the task of making them drink promised to be arduous, no matter what the Town Hall wished for.

In all this, Anshan had a natural advantage: the *shizhang* and civic and industrial underlings would speak with one voice, a cardinal rule of diplomacy. The Sheffield team, an uneasy fusion of leftish civic leaders and Tory business types, was inherently conflict-riven, and this could be expected to surface. But for all their supposed Marxism, my long experience in China told me that it wouldn't occur to Anshan's cadres that private interests in capitalist Britain would be viscerally hostile to local government in general and especially to a left-leaning city council. To the average Party member, the 'class struggle' — the *sine qua non* of their own lives for so long under Mao—halted miraculously at China's borders. In the magic universe of 'the other', all was peace and harmony. I'd long since worked out that this ignorance, this delusional worldview, was one fostered by a Party hierarchy keen to avoid real solidarity with their Third World brethren. If everyone was living felicitously out there in the world beyond the Middle Kingdom (except, of course, in the dastardly Soviet Union), then socialist internationalism could be set aside.

To add to the cultural gulf, the fact that Sheffield's political chief was blind must have mystified the Chinese who, much as we'd been until really very recently in Britain, were still in the pre-Enlightenment age with regard to physical disabilities. As David Blunkett often used to comment, or more accurately, to expostulate, in Britain, blind people had at best been encouraged to become piano tuners. In China, the standard pigeonhole for blind males was traditional bathhouse massage. But this stereotype was on the cusp of change: in 1984 none other than Deng Xiaoping's son had set up the first ever organisation in China to promote the interests of the disabled. Deng Pufang had a personal interest: his persecution in the Cultural Revolution had crippled him. Later, in his efforts to form a kind of worldwide federation of prominent disabled people (with himself at its helm, naturally) Deng Pufang became rather keen to co-opt David Blunkett. But that's another story....

Certain also to confuse Anshan was the fact that in the British system a *lord* mayor with all his/her bells and whistles strung around his neck —his solid gold chains and insignia—is merely a Buggins-turn honorary position with almost no actual authority or powers of decision within the city council. Adherent of one political party or the other, the mayor has a casting vote in the council chamber, but that's about it. Obviously, there was no possible parallel in the Chinese system of governance. How was it, Anshan was bound to think, that the *lord* could be taking orders from the *commoner* – the *Mr.* Council Leader? To the Chinese none of it would make the slightest sense.

Our first day in Anshan, and the municipality laid on the grand welcome. This was the occasion to shower John B and myself with all manner of municipal statistics, and Mayor Zhang Jianzhong undertook his task with enthusiasm, his smiling deputies chipping in. The distinction between these civic personnel and our council managers back home was striking. To a man and woman, the ex-steelworks cadres who ran Anshan's affairs were, we gradually learned, highly qualified technical people, and often graduates of China's top engineering schools. Mayor Zhang Jianzhong was amongst them, and to underline the fact he chose to use a given name which said it all: 'Jianzhong' translates as 'Building China'. The mayor might have come up through Angang's ranks, but there was nothing of the shop floor about him. His black-framed professorial spectacles, his well-cut dark-blue Zhongshan suit, his handsome and intelligent visage topped by a thick head of well-groomed hair (black-dyed as is the custom for middle-aged males), all seemed unlikely against the red dust which shrouded the civic HQ. Anshan's municipal leaders seemed to ooze a similar urbane confidence.

I was comparing Anshan's leaders with those of Sheffield, of course, where the lefty middle classes were already prominent in the Labour-run council. Surprisingly, few of the 70-strong Labour councillors had any technical or industrial background. But the greater contrast was with my own father's experience of the town of Scunthorpe. Like Anshan, Scunthorpe had risen out of its steelworks, but unlike the Chinese steel city, its local officials were men (and a sprinkling of women) of very limited education.

RICHARD KIRKBY

When he talked the local lordship into accepting a peppercorn rent from the local authority for his vacant, stately North Lincolnshire home, my father had the toughest of struggles in persuading the borough council from turning the deer park over to stock-car racing, and the house itself into a glorified bingo hall (maybe that would have been more fun...). Scunthorpe's blue-collar-dominated council, mainly ex-steelworkers, grudgingly came to see things my father's way. He set about furnishing the Regency mansion from top to bottom as the 'visitor experience' which Normanby Hall remains all these years later.

Mayor Zhang concluded his welcome speech by laying out the city's winning card: in the corridors of national power, he informed us, Anshan held special sway. The most senior positions in China's powerful mega-Ministry of Metallurgy were always by tradition occupied by former Anshan Iron and Steel Works engineers. This was no ordinary Ministry: when Sheffield's first trade mission actually finally arrived in Beijing, and was received by a vice-minister (an Angang man, naturally), we were regaled with extraordinary statistics: under the Ministry were three million workers, fifteen large scale construction companies each with up to 30,000 technical staff, twenty universities and colleges, and of course every metallic mineral mining and quarrying operation in the land, along with the plants necessary to process their output. Anshan's intimacy with the Ministry, Mayor Zhang smilingly implied, could put Sheffield in pole position. Far beyond Angang, every one of China's steelworks needed modernising, and what the national model of Angang did today, the rest would follow tomorrow. We'd only half-digested the mayor's presentation when we were shown into the adjacent dining chamber. Following our lunch, John B and I were led to the city's outlying beauty spot, the verdant slopes of Qianshan Park, where we endeavoured to work off the thirteen courses of our welcome banquet. 'After eating, walk a hundred steps and then you'll live till ninety-nine' goes the old Chinese saying.

Later we reconvened for a protocol meeting with the bookish and reticent foreign affairs chief Wang Pengjiu, a man who seemed to have a soft spot for me after I rather cleverly (!) quizzed him on why his given name referred to that gigantic mythical bird, the roc. Wang made clear that in Anshan's eyes, signing of the civic twinning had to come first, and nothing serious on the trade front was possible prior to the ceremony. This should take place in Anshan, he insisted. With the Chinese love for well choreographed theatrics, I knew at least that a good show was promised.

'After the ceremony you will please invite Mayor Zhang and his delegation to Sheffield in order to strengthen the friendship between our two cities,' Wang explained in the direct Chinese way. 'Some of our six vice-mayors in charge of industry will also come to Sheffield with Mayor Zhang,' he went on. It was the deputies who oversaw the city's light industry departments, and they were just as eager as was Angang to get hold of modern technology for their backward factories. It was all quite logical: with the Anshan return visit, it would be clearer which of Sheffield's industries might find Chinese matches, and on that basis, Sheffield, we were informed, would be welcome to dispatch a trade mission and sign contracts. I was already imagining how our civic and business worthies would react to all the razzmatazz which official China throws at honoured guests from afar. Chinese fanfare—lavish banqueting, motorcades of black limos, luxury guesthouses—would be designed to stun parochial Sheffield into a mood of 'yes, yes, yes'. But what Anshan didn't yet realise was that 'yeses' on the part of the city council would be worthless if the Chamber of Commerce's cynical members remained unimpressed. 'Mutual benefit' was a phrase to be drummed into us. Beijing had been busy printing a sheaf of new joint venture laws, though how they would translate in practice in this novel era of engagement with the West was anyone's guess. In Anshan's case, while some direct sales of equipment to the steelworks could happen if the Ministry decreed it, we were left in no doubt that the joint ventures route would be the main one for doing business. The Chinese side would provide the land, factory buildings and all infrastructure, and its well-disciplined labour force which, being paid over the odds, would be very willing. Under the circumstances, the JV model seemed to us to be eminently sensible. But John B and I were as yet unschooled in the prejudices of British industrialists in general and Sheffield in particular.

With the civic formalities done, we two envoys of the West's most illustrious steel city were whisked off to the real power centre in Anshan—the headquarters of the steelworks. Off the tongue of the chief engineer rolled the usual impressive array of dimensions and output figures. The great works, Engineer Long Chunman informed us, had no fewer than ten giant blast furnaces; steel-making was supplemented by three melting shops equipped with large electric arc furnaces. Sixty operating divisions acted as accounting units in this new age of 'planned capitalism'. Unmentioned, naturally, was that major parts of the plant had been laid down in the bad old days by the Japanese, and it was technicians sent by the Soviet Union who had rebuilt the works in the 1950s. We set off with the chief and a group of his hard-hatted senior managers on the site tour, the finale of which was the tapping of one of the ten blast furnaces. Streams of white-hot metal poured forth, workers prodding dangerously close in asbestos suits, sprays and sparks flying high. We were then walked along the grey powder-laden catwalk above a monstrous rolling mill while below us red-glowing billets clattered back and forth at high speed. The cacophony of squealing rollers and the thump of great shears and the clouds of hissing steam created a vision of hell which was not unfamiliar. As a teenager I'd worked in my holidays at the Appleby Frodingham plant in Scunthorpe, one of the few sites of the former great British steel industry to limp into the second decade of the 21st century. The blast furnaces and rolling mills at Ap-Frod were something to behold, but Angang's were on an altogether different scale. Wishing to underline their power in the land, Angang's Party managers laid on an evening banquet befitting their gargantuan enterprise, one which annually turned out not far short of all Britain's then-fourteen steelworks combined.

Back in Sheffield, it fell to me, the anointed local China expert, to prepare the Council's senior members, the Lord Mayor and his elegant consort for the journey of their lifetimes. Travel to China was still in the early 1980s an unusual thing and confined mostly to those Westerners with deep pockets. We met around a huge table in the town hall's board room. In those days, long before PowerPoint, my presentation was all through scrappy overhead projector slides, still in my cupboard all these years later. They painted in lurid colours everything the ingénue would need to know about Liaoning Province (area and population as big as England) and Anshan's civic and company personalities. I was also careful to provide my audience with the basics of modern China's history, politics, economics. Apart from the occasional interjection ('will we have to eat dog?'), my students were wide-eyed and attentive. At least I was lucky with the Lord Mayor, who when not bedecked with his splendid heavy gold chains and insignia of office (the mayoral regalia had its own special guard in the Town Hall), the diminutive, sharp-faced bow-tied Peter J was a doctor, a GP, as was his glamorous Lady Mayoress.

In a rare display of diplomacy, the council's Labour group had decided to let the toothless opposition tag along on the China beano. The leaders of the tiny Conservative group, as well the equally tiny Liberal group, were to be tolerated with the unspoken proviso that they should keep their mouths shut. An all-expenses-paid trip to an exotic realm on the other side of the globe was enough in itself.

Another yellowing and just-legible letter has survived in my garage filing cabinet, a victim of the flooding brought by the horrendous Storm Desmond which hit our county of Cumbria in 2015, just before Christmas.

> 26 September 1983
> Mr Wang Pengjiu, Director
> Anshan Foreign Affairs Office
> Anshan Municipal People's Government
>
> Dear Mr Wang Pengjiu:
> I am writing to you on the instructions and advice of the Second Secretary of the Embassy of the People's Republic of China in London, Madame Wang Zhangli. Firstly, I should say we in Sheffield are extremely grateful for your timely assistance in making the practical arrangements for our forthcoming journey to China and your City of Anshan. As Adviser on Chinese Affairs to the Sheffield delegation, I have had the opportunity to discuss the visit with all the

members, and I can tell you that everyone is excited and pleased at the prospect of Anshan and Sheffield becoming sister cities.....

My missive was also blatantly self-serving: it went on to request some personal favours. By stealth, Beijing was little by little opening up large tracts of the country to individual foreign travellers. Rumours had reached me that parts of Xinjiang and Qinghai province were now opening up to foreigners. Travel passes and airline tickets weren't going to be easy to acquire – and a city foreign affairs chief would have no trouble sorting things out for me. That he agreed to help I've already demonstrated in this book.

It was 5th October 1983, a decade almost to the day since I'd first stepped onto China's shores. The preparations for Sheffield's civic delegation were finally in place, and we were off on our twenty-two hour flight via Hong Kong. The etiquette of greeting and seeing off (*jie* and *song*) by everyone from humble family member to honoured guest had somehow survived the Cultural Revolution. At Beijing airport, we were met by a welcoming party led by one of Anshan's Deputy Mayors. From the programme which he laid before us, Sheffield was to be given the full Beijing treatment before going on to Liaoning province: the Great Wall, Forbidden City, the Beijing Duck restaurant where the management had already got the throughput of coach loads of Western tourists down to a fine art. The Sheffield party was also allowed a little free time to wander, a privilege unheard of only a few years earlier in the paranoid China of the Cultural Revolution.

'How does it feel to be here in this strange environment?' I asked David Blunkett as we picked our way arm-in-arm along uneven pavements in Beijing's Dongdan. In the absence of his famous guide dog, I was taking him to visit an indoor fruit and vegetable market, and then to the famous 'theatre shop' where Beijing opera costumes outlawed by the Cultural Revolution were sold for a pittance to foreigners.

I was surprised by Blunkett's ebullient reply: 'Sounds, smells, everything — it's no different from being sighted. I'm finding everything as interesting as anyone would.'

When the Sheffield group's day tour to the Ming Tombs and Great Wall arrived, at the Badaling visitors' area Blunkett scrambled with the best of them up the steep chariot-wide crest of the Wall to the first guard tower. On the principle of 'keeping your enemy close', Sheffield's Leader had chosen to invite along the Chief Executive of the Chamber of Commerce, one John H, a large, taciturn and perhaps shy man, his task to take the measure of what most of his fellow members probably thought was a hare-brained town hall scheme. I noticed Blunkett and John H, however, in a companionable huddle as they scrambled up the Wall to the first guard tower. Later, on the coach back to Beijing, they sat together and continued in hushed tones.

The following day it was 'soft bed' compartments to Liaoning province, the team occupying two carriages. Anshan's railway station was bedecked with flowers, and a full brass ensemble sounded us in. Curtseying youngsters presented the Lord Mayor, Lady Mayoress and David Blunkett with huge bouquets (I recall Blunkett's unease and his 'What do I do with this?' It was the 1980s, and macho Sheffield men were not meant to wield bouquets). Mayor Zhang led the party to a line of limousines and we were whisked off to the best hotel the city could offer, uniformed flunkies everywhere. Four days of stunning banquets, tours to the local mountains and temples at Qianshan, visits to schools and kindergartens were undertaken, with some tentative business discussions with the top brass of Angang when they took over the party for the day. Later, a Deputy Mayor hosted a lengthy round-table on Anshan's industrial shopping list.

The climax came with the signing ceremony for the twinning protocol. We filed into a large civic auditorium where the stage was decorated with extravagant floral displays, a large red banner strung overhead. With a Union Jack to one side and the five-star PRC flag to the other, a signing table stood in the centre of the stage. Before the event, the Anshan foreign affairs people had led me into the chamber to check that all was prepared satisfactorily. I saw that the banner's black letters had rendered Sheffield wrongly — an inverted 'S'. Without letting on to his chief, I whispered in the ear of one of the juniors whom I knew had been responsible. When the delegation entered, packed with several hundred of Anshan's great-and-good, the banner was in perfect shape. Afterwards, the young man quietly thanked me, terror still in his eyes; his job would have been on the line if the error hadn't been corrected. The punitive habits of the Cultural Revolution might have waned, but age-old customs would never: where foreigners are concerned, nothing must be amiss, not the tiniest crack in the façade.

It turned out that a Sheffield myth had been born on China's Great Wall: the class war had been indefinitely postponed! A study of relations between UK town halls and the business community in the post-Thatcher era gives the flavour of the 'class collaboration' which social democracy betokens:

> The high-profile local conflicts between chambers and local government of the 1980s ... were in many ways an 'unnatural' period. The long-term history had been for strong local collaborations between municipalities and

chambers jointly to promote their area. Even during this period, cordial joint meetings between the various local government associations ... were maintained. Indeed, the evolution of Sheffield illustrates how chambers began to play an important role in assisting adjustments in 'new left' areas. Richard Field quotes the local legend that the director of the Sheffield Chamber (John Hambidge) and leader of a council delegation (Clive Betts), whilst on a promotional visit to China, in 1983, began to explore a new common way forward. A convention was agreed in 1986, under Field, that criticisms between the chamber and council would no longer be voiced in public...' Bennett goes on to describe how by 1986, the council had agreed never again to fly the Red Flag from the Town Hall tower and no longer host the annual Marx Memorial Lecture in the City Hall.[3]

Back in Sheffield, council leader David Blunkett enthusiastically embraced his role as the first ever British city boss to boast a foreign economic policy. Despite the cash-strapped times, John B's newly founded domain, the Department of Employment and Economic Development, was landed with an extravagant China budget and told to get on with it. Meanwhile, it fell to the Chamber of Commerce's chief executive to relay the town hall's foreign doings to the membership. 'Communist China' was always going to be a hard sell to the town hall's nemesis. A slim incentive — government trade promotion grants — was a something of a lure. And a group of city council and Chamber leaders were soon on the London train, heading for the House

---

3 Bennett, R., *The History of Chambers of Commerce in Britain*, Oxford, OUP 2011, pp492-3.

of Commons to do some lobbying. We were received somewhat
disdainfully by Alan Clark, briefly Thatcher's erratic Minister
of Trade and Industry. Undoubtedly the true toff, Clark was
taken aback by the amalgam of Red Sheffield and the be-suited
Yorkshire gentlemen of the Chamber, Conservative to a man.
Whatever, that *tête-a-tête* on the Great Wall had apparently
done the trick, and Clark promised a full Department of Trade
& Industry grant to each Sheffield business joining an Anshan
trade mission. He also spoke of government soft credits to secure
any Chinese big deals which might be in the offing. Down at
the Chamber's HQ was a less dismissive reception than had
previously awaited me. Just over the horizon, Mayor Zhang
and his party would be arriving, and the serious business could
commence.

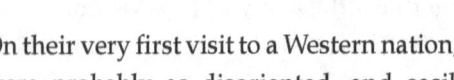

On their very first visit to a Western nation, the Anshan entourage
were probably as disoriented, and easily dazzled too, as the
Sheffield worthies had been when in China. In anthropological
spirit, I was always curious about the way in which people
brought up in the enclosed world of Mao's China and with no
exposure to any society but their own, perceived the strange
environment of a foreign, a Western land. Were children being
sent out to hawk matchsticks on the streets, a tale they grew up
with and which I refused to retail to my students back in Cultural
Revolution days? Or was it that the masses, as deceptively
demonstrated to Deng Xiaoping on his famous U.S. tour of 1979,
were basking in the sunshine of a 'typical' worker's home with
three cars on the drive? Sheffield is a city of hills, and as our
coach passed high over a valley given over to council-owned
allotments, each with its little wooden potting shed, I overheard
one of the Anshan visitors whisper: 'look — those are the squatter

settlements that we've read about.'

Official China, when it wants to impress, pulls out all the stops. The razzmatazz of Sheffield's official welcome was never going to be the equal of lavish Anshan's, but still, with its Lord Mayor's Parlour glistening with the treasures from centuries of gold- and silver-smithing, the city could put on a good show. The late Victorian Town Hall, impressive though it might be, was outshone by the reception at Sheffield's true home of The Great & the Good—the 1830s Cutlers Hall with its even more elaborate gold and silver trophies on display. What Mayor Zhang understood from his encounter with a Sheffield worthy calling himself 'Master Cutler' is anyone's guess.

Perhaps more puzzling for the going-abroad-virgins than Lord Mayors and Master Cutlers was the food on offer by their British hosts. Today, in the third decade of the 21st century, the cuisine of many nations (and none!) can be met on any metropolitan street in China. Not so in 1984, when only a few PRC citizens, and mostly the country's diplomats, had been subjected to 'foreign food', as it was known (in the *yin-yang* binary there was 'food', and 'foreign food'). The idea of slabs of animal flesh alongside a heap of vegetables was alien, if not repulsive. The mode of transferring it from plate to mouth with two metal weapons was outlandish. On the quiet, I gave chief interpreter Liu a little lesson to pass on to her charges—how to wield the humble knife and fork. My tutorial was sadly lacking when it came to the crowning glory of the Lord Mayor's dinner. With a table as long as a cricket pitch, Sheffield's banqueting silverware was out of the closet and each place-setting was a confusing profusion of cutlery.

At another Sheffield Lord Mayoral dinner, staged in an intimate town hall dining room and with a rather more rustic incumbent that the urbane GP Peter J, I'd witnessed the perfect misunderstanding between West and East, as well as a typical case of face-saving by a harassed interpreter. The guest of honour at the Lord Mayor's luncheon was a minister of the Chinese government, no less. With his female interpreter beside him, and me opposite to help out, the prawn cocktails had gone down a treat and now came the *pièce de résistance*. Two waitresses in black uniforms with little frilly coronets emerged from the kitchen carrying a giant silver salver laden with a side of beef and a hillock of Yorkshire puddings. The Lord Mayor turned to the minister, thumped his barrel belly, and came out with 'This'll put the 'airs on your chest!'

The interpreter looked stunned for a moment, then uttered in Chinese, 'Our host says that the food will put the wind in your stomach'. At which each of the Chinese guests affected a smile of the type which said to me 'Whatever will these barbarians be telling us next?' For a young graduate of the foreign languages college, being the linguistic conduit for high officials is a thankless and sometimes risky job. Not losing face and cutting corners are essential.

While on the theme, a tale abounds about the late Zhou Enlai, Premier of China and charmer of foreign dignitaries. When asked 'Mr. Premier, what is your assessment today of the French revolution?' Zhou Enlai is supposed to have responded with the words, 'It's too early to say'. Ever since, this mythical utterance has been offered by Western diplomats as a token of timeless Oriental sagacity. I'm quite certain in my own mind that it was just another case of 'roast beef' face-saving by a wrong-footed interpreter.

The high point of the Anshan mayoral visit was going to be a mini-Sheffield industrial exhibition. We'd prepared a capacious factory shed which had belonged to a bankrupted engineering company, and the Chamber of Commerce was prodded into getting its members mobilised. An eclectic mix of private-sector companies from the city and beyond was eventually inveigled in. I was worried that one of the local big boys, Davy McKee, manufacturer of steelworks equipment, had declined to make an appearance. It was all a little threadbare, with sparse representation from the heavy engineering sector. Improbably, Bassetts, the famed liquorice sweet makers, had occupied a stand. A bemused Anshan delegation had earlier been sent on a tour of the Bassetts confectionary factory, and had only come to life when they were told that the stick liquorice was an import from China. Such humble raw materials were still the mainstay of China's exports: unbelievably today, as recently as 1970 China's greatest export to the U.K. market by value was pig bristles for paint brushes.

I thought it might be another case of the Qianlong emperor and the Macartney expedition's experience. Back in the 1790s, George III had dispatched Lord Macartney and his team of 400 Englishmen to China, to try to persuade the emperor to open up his country to the wonders of Britain's industrial revolution. Too much silver was draining away in payment for Chinese teas, porcelains and silks. The highpoint again was going to be a mini-industrial exhibition, showcasing the most intriguing of British manufactures. After much diplomatic travail, the Qianlong emperor walked straight past the exhibits, and dismissed it all with a caustic comment.

Unlike the emperor, the Anshan mayor and his group lingered politely at each of the stands, asking pertinent questions and generally behaving themselves. Bemusement was hardly concealed when they stopped at a display by a city council-inspired workers' cooperative which dealt with the technology of traffic lights. Much later, it occurred to me that one Sheffield-

Anshan cooperation project which might actually have been a true winner was precisely traffic lights. With China soon hell-bent on clogging its cities with private cars and no automated traffic systems anywhere, a joint venture would have had guaranteed success. But the delegation smiled indulgently and moved on. Then the unanticipated happened: The mayor's whole demeanor lit up when he arrived in front of a neatly mustachioed, elderly fellow in a Colonel Sanders suit and sharp shoes waiting hopefully by a mock bathroom in acrylic avocado, complete with enclosed plastic shower unit and bath tub. What seemed to fascinate the visitors more than anything was the square acrylic shower base. China may now be the land of the plastic widget; four decades ago, though, the only plastic accoutrement in most households was a toothbrush handle, though most were still of bone or wood.

'We must develop our light industry,' announced Mayor Zhang. 'Our city is famous for steel; perhaps we should also try to be famous for making bathrooms!' And from that moment on, the Anshan visitors appeared fixated on acrylic bathroom-ware.

The personable Kiwi Graeme D, Professor of Metallurgy at Sheffield University, was a man whom I was to meet under a different sky. He would later become vice-chancellor of Liverpool University, and just maybe he had a hand in my own 1990 appointment to the teaching staff. On morning, I made my way to his professorial office off Sheffield's West Street to consult about steel and Anshan. The upshot was that in September, along with a couple of Chamber nominees, Graeme D was Anshan-bound on a technical snooping mission, the idea being to fine-tune the planned Sheffield trade mission. My later report to the council perhaps gilded the lily: '...they brought back valuable information on Anshan's and Liaoning's import requirements,' I wrote. No doubt the professor did a competent job; one of the Chamber's men along with him, however, was the very caricature of the plain-speaking professional Yorkshireman. His well flaunted forte was flogging Sheffield steel around the Middle East, Israel in particular.

'It's easy,' he bragged. 'They've got more money than sense over there, even in Israel, and no steelworks to speak of anywhere.' He took the view that if the Chinese wanted anything from Sheffield, they were going to get the best and had to pay the price. He was definitely a 'Sheffield chooses the customers' man. Mayoral visits, twinning agreements, industrial shows, pathfinder missions — time for the meat in all this.

It was now Spring 1985 and brash Yorkshire entrepreneurship was about to be put to the test on the final great frontier for Western entrepreneurship. The Sheffield Trade & Civic Mission, a sprinkling of council officers and thirteen rather disparate company representatives, was set to wing its way towards the Middle Kingdom. It was a mixed bunch of local companies, but then the town hall was in no position to press preferences. Strong and well received hints, however, had been passed the Chamber's way regarding the importance of acrylic bathroom-ware. At the other end of the scale was Sheffield's flagship steelworks engineering outfit, though Davy McKee were ready to remind us that they had their own lines of communication with China, and hardly needed the town hall's assistance. Their participation was something of a relief: I was aware that for a couple of years Davy had been ploughing his own furrow, in mega-steel city Anshan, and also at the Maanshan works in Anhui province and the giant Soviet-built Wuhan works up the Yangtze River in Hubei. As a token to Sheffield City Council, and watching their backs with their well-organised workforce,

Davy's salesman was accompanied by a union representative of the Amalgamated Union of Engineering Workers. The AUEW had long been the power behind Sheffield's Labour Party — already fading perhaps, but still needing to be acknowledged on a council venture which could threaten jobs back home. AUEW official John S was a very quiet member of the delegation who would be paternalistically tolerated, though largely ignored, by the captains of industry.

With some effort, I'd put together a bilingual delegation brochure, and figuring in it was a company from outside Sheffield but closely linked to steel-making in the city. The Distington Engineering Company Ltd of Workington on the far Cumbrian coast arose out of a Victorian iron smelting enterprise. By the late 1960s, under a re-nationalised steel industry, Distington had become the state-run British Steel Corporation's plant-building and contracting arm. As such, its sphere of operations was complementary to Davy's, though I could never quite work out what was going on between these two companies. I'd picked up enough about developments in steel-making to know that Distington/Davy could well unlock many Chinese doors. The vital and relatively new technology for the steel industry, continuous casting, had been a key interest to Distington since the late 1970s, I recall, on the strength of a U.S. licence of the Morgan Steel Co. And continuous casting was the route to modernisation of hot metal forming in steelworks worldwide. I knew that China's metallurgists had had a go at devising their own version of the new technology, but it had been found wanting. Throughout the huge China metals sector — and beyond just ferrous metals — China was ripe for high performance imports. And two companies in the Sheffield delegation held the key to one of the most crucial innovations.

Signed up too were representatives of two high-tech special

ferrous and non-ferrous forging and heavy production machinery concerns. I was fascinated by Hille Engineering, which in its earlier incarnation, like Distington, was linked in various ways to Davy McKee. It was up at Davy's impressive operation at Prince of Wales Road that I'd witnessed the demonstration of an extraordinary creation of an obviously brilliant engineering team. Filling a medium-sized workshop stood a Heath Robinson machine full of tubes and struts and looking somewhat like a moonshot vehicle. As we watched, molten metal was poured in at one end and at the other, out came a fully formed integral forging of a carriage spring. The machine simply did away with those unwieldy separate leaves which are seen in any vehicle's suspension. A world beater for the heavy vehicle manufacturing industry, or so it should have been, before the City of London's financial wolves got hold of it.

Amongst the several other steel-related companies represented was Sheffield's venerable Paragon Razor Company. Sharp-blade technology might be of general interest to China, but in a land of the sparsely hirsute male, certainly not in the form of Paragon's traditional products. On the matter of sharp blades, I have to mention that in the entire land of China at the time there wasn't such a thing as a serrated kitchen knife. Each time a Chinese guest arrived in Sheffield, and on our trips to China, the locally-produced 'Kitchen Devil' product featured amongst the civic gifts. In the space of a very few years, however, China had perfected serrated knife technology and now like most everything else dominates the global market.

On the delegation list too, the name Clugston also showed — familiar because massive Clugston dumper trucks used to block my way, *en route* from Scunthorpe to my parents' home in the little tied village of Normanby. I remember how my father, always one for turning muck into brass as the Yorkshire saying goes, admiringly explained to me how this outfit had developed a highly profitable business. Piled up into mini-mountains for over a century, the millions of tonnes of slag from the blast furnaces of John Lysaght's Normanby Park Steel Works were being excavated and put to use. It all had started with the huge programme of military aerodrome construction in the flatlands of Lincolnshire during the 1939-45 War. Thereafter, Clugston's sights were set on Britain's new motorways: beginning in 1959 with the M1, the network would demand vast quantities of roadstone, much of it Clugston's slag-based product. Dross into gold. With Angang and China's other monster works producing vast mountains of slag each year, largely unprocessed and unused, Clugston could be onto a winner. If, that is, they played their cards right, which my natural scepticism already suggested might be a big 'if'.

The odd one out in the group, for reasons more than one — a female and someone with no apparent real business to push in China — was the elderly, shrivelled, chain-smoking Marjorie F, a Sheffield GP. Ostensibly, according to her self-described entry in the delegation brochure, she was in the unlikely business of selling the Chinese 'business diagnostics'. To my mind, management consultancy services of the Sheffield variety seemed a very long shot for a newly opening China. In the event, Marjorie soon decided this was indeed so, and happily smoked her way through the trip of a lifetime, pleasantly subsidised by the British taxpayer. Very much not least in the Chamber line-up was a sharp pencil-mustachioed, bluff character in a sharp Colonel Sanders suit, Arthur B of the large plumbing hardware shop in downtown's Division Street. The acrylic bathroom-ware man, Mayor Zhang's favourite Sheffield company boss who it was hoped would soon be a key figure in the diversification of Steel City Anshan's economy. Looking back, this wasn't a foolish or vain hope. With China embarking on a massive housing boom for tens of millions of its citizens, perhaps, indeed, Anshan could have shifted from being China's steel city *par excellence* to the nation's capital of acrylic shower and bath units. Stranger things happened in China's economic boom years. There are today specialised cities which turn out the entire world's buttons, others where all manner of electric light fittings are produced, and cities from which the majority of the world's cheap fashion shoes spew out onto the market. But alas, as we shall see, an acrylic future for Anshan was never to be.

For its part, the council's Labour Group chose a senior councillor to head up the civic side of the mission. In line with that famous pact on the Great Wall, the Chamber folk were made to understand that the lefty, long-haired and bearded council figurehead to the mission and his gauche female sidekick were along just for form's sake. With the two councillors came a token bag carrier and note-taker, actually a genuine metallurgist-turned-local-government-officer called Jean. And myself, the un-esteemed China consultant. With the business side of the mission fronted by our professional Yorkshireman, who with his one pathfinder trip was now an expert on all things Chinese, I was far from certain we were in good hands. But we were off.

———~~~———

The Sheffield envoys had the inauspicious start which I'd feared. Arriving in Beijing and met with joyous solicitude by the Anshan foreign affairs people, our first stop was the massively powerful Ministry of Metallurgy. Here we were ushered into a boardroom rather more comfortably furnished than I'd ever seen in China. Seated in pride of place was an urbane cadre in his sixties – Lin Hua, vice-minister. He was, of course, a former Angang man. A lengthy discourse ranged over the entire modernisation plans for China's mammoth but ageing iron and steel sector, and in particular, on some juicy prospects for 'foreign friends', should they care to trouble themselves.

'We plan an up-to-date, brand new steelworks at Ningbo in Zhejiang province,' Lin Hua proclaimed, 'and we would like to offer the lead role to Davy McKee of Sheffield.'

Lugubrious leader of the trade side of the delegation, Albert W coughed mildly into his moustache and when the time came responded to the minister with reasonable aplomb. Others around the huge table registered a certain apprehension. The superior attitude of the Davy man had earlier surfaced back at Heathrow Airport, where the humbler delegates had weighed in their baggage collectively so as to avoid any excess charges. The Davy representative had stood apart and paid through the nose for his overweight suitcase, or at least his expense account had paid.

Affluent China is today, like the salary-men of Japan, golf crazy, but back then, Beijing had just inaugurated its very first course somewhere up near the Ming Tombs. The tall, ill-tempered and stand-offish Davy McKee man had thought it beneath his dignity to join with the lesser mortals and follow Anshan's carefully tuned itinerary. He was simply not in the room. Rather than the boring Ministry meeting, he'd gone off to play golf. Of course, all foreigners look alike, and only at the vice-minister's lunch did it become apparent to him that Sheffield's quorum was wanting. The guest of honour seat to his side lay glaringly vacant. I said nothing to the prodigal when he reappeared that evening at the hotel. But I did later hear old Albert W upbraiding him, and his immortal Sheffield response: 'Forget it! At Davy McKee *we* choose the customers.'

Once in Anshan, the mission received a royal welcome, kicked off by a grand reception. I see that my report afterwards to the council enumerated over thirty leading Party figures of the city and its region. As well as Anshan's mayor, his deputies, his department heads, Angang was heavily represented, from the company chairman down. Over the next days, the Sheffield team was separately entertained by Anshan's shortlist of potential joint venture partners. Except for a couple of lucrative triumphs, though really of the 'own-goal' variety, progress was muted. The first of these involved a business from Sheffield's hinterland town of Chesterfield which produced ingenious equipment for raising and lowering the cradles and slings on the sides of high buildings. At the time, there wasn't a single building of more than five storeys (housing blocks from the 1970s) in the entire province of Liaoning, its land area equivalent to that of England. Along with his acrylic ambitions, perhaps Mayor Zhang was thinking ahead, aiming high, and could see into the dimness of the near future, when almost every modest metropolis in China would become skyscraper city. At the Sheffield exhibition, the Chinese mayor had engaged this inventor and owner, Gilbert S, in prolonged conversation, the upshot being that a joint venture in Anshan was firmly promised.

But plans can change. As our limo swept us through the city towards the next meeting, my fellow passenger suddenly asked our guide to halt in a busy street of typical, small collectively-owned workshops. Gilbert S had spotted a roadside shed where an old Beijing jeep had its engine strung from a heavy steel beam by a chain-block hoist. Visibly excited, Gilbert S demanded to know if such contraptions were made in Anshan. If so, he went on to ask, if so what would be the FOB price to an English port? That evening the answer came back: 'One of our small factories supervised by Angang, and using its steel, produces the equipment. You are welcome to receive it in your country.'

I don't remember the precise price, but I do recall Gilbert

S whooping it up when he heard the news. He could import a high-quality product almost indistinguishable from the home-grown example for a mere fraction of the cost. After that, his joint venture talks were no more than pretence. In truth, he had no intention of getting involved with anything so trying as managing a business in an alien land. Gilbert S had an interesting business card which proclaimed him president of the U.K. Lifting Equipment Engineers Association. As time went by and his orders for Anshan hoists piled up, the demise of British chain-block manufacturing was assured, the U.K.'s steel industry sustained another small kick in the teeth, and the nation's balance of trade slipped a few more digits into the red.

———∞∞———

'When you sit down to negotiate a deal with the Chinese, think of something small you can buy from them. This will help them out with foreign exchange and even support their contribution to a joint venture, if that's what you're about. It's important too because you'll be giving face.'

This had been a signal part of my briefing back in Sheffield. I was aiming it expressly at the spry Colonel Sanders of acrylic bathroom-ware fame

Advice in general was generally wasted on my captains of industry, though not in a way on this occasion. We'd been ushered into the standard meeting room, a long chamber dominated by a low table along the length of which was a line of heavy blue covered armchairs. The flaking, distempered wall behind us was decorated with the usual portrait of the late Chairman. In front of each of the dozen people who had seated themselves around us was a glass bowl of brightly wrapped bonbons, a circular red can of the highest class cigarettes, *Zhonghua* brand, and a large glass ashtray with a box of those colourful and collectible Chinese matchboxes.

Wang Bin, head of the Anshan Second Light Industry Bureau opened the proceedings.

'Our Mayor Mr. Zhang is very happy that you are participating in the Sheffield delegation and we hope that you have brought with you the blueprints for our joint venture bathroom-ware factory,' chief interpreter Liu rendered. Arthur B shifted in his anti-macassared armchair, but seemed equal to the challenge.

'Yes, the plans are in my hotel room and I'll give you them soon, after we've agreed a few things,' he responded.

'What will be the value of the English side's investment in our factory?' a vice-mayor enquired. I caught my man's eye at this point and tapped my cheek. 'Face, face', I willed. Arthur B was never one to be flustered. Rising from his deep seat, he pointed out of the window and said: 'Ow about some of them manhole covers?' I rose to his side, wondering what on earth had entered his thoughts. Right outside the window, in the narrow lane, was indeed a standard circular cast iron manhole cover.

'Mr B seems interested in manhole covers,' I said, rather unhelpfully in English. Mme. Liu was entirely at sea. 'Man hole' — what is that?' she asked quietly. I beckoned her over to the window.

'I want loads of them, as many as you can send,' he declared. That evening after yet another banquet, the interpreter turned up at my room with a thin bit of paper strewn with Chinese characters. 'As Mr B..... will be our good foreign friend in running our joint venture, we have decided to give him the best price for his *paishuidao* covers,' she smiled. 'Drain covers,' I said, helpfully supplying a literal translation.

As for Arthur's famous joint venture with Anshan, the caravan had moved on, and no further opportunity arose in the itinerary to raise the matter. We were soon being whisked off to the province's capital of Shenyang and bathroom-ware plastics no longer intruded in our meetings with officials. The 'key to the friendship between our two cities', as Mayor Zhang had extravagantly dubbed it, was irretrievably lost.

Once back in Sheffield, I got a call from Arthur B to meet him at his large shop premises in the middle of the city. Anshan was offering him unlimited quantities of manhole covers, plus their heavy frames which are sunk into the road surface. All for a song. Arthur had been quoted by the tonne, rather than the piece. He'd calculated that if he could get the Anshan foundry to cast at the same weight as the standard which he already supplied to local councils, he'd be paying just US$7.50 for each set landed at the port of Felixstowe. This was less than one-fifth the price demanded by his U.K. supplier just down the M1 motorway from Sheffield—the monopolisers of the trade in 'donkey iron' was a long-established company called Stanton and Staveley.

Our Arthur wasn't a Yorkshireman for nothing. Birmingham rather than Sheffield is the home of precision metal-casting and there, Arthur B commissioned a company to make the mould for his Anshan manhole covers. A trial casting made from this mould weighed in at 16.5kg. It was then despatched to Anshan, where their best foundry could only manage 17kg.

'This won't do, won't do!' muttered Arthur B. Buying by the weight, he'd be losing a margin. Anshan was ordered to try again—same result. China, of course, is the ancient home of metal bashing: since the Shang dynasty which began almost 4,000 years ago China has been precision casting metals. It so happened that in the provincial capital just up the road, back in the 1950s, the First Five Year Plan had established the nation's premier casting research centre. The mould was sent off to Shenyang, and after a few adjustments the magic 16.5kg showed on the scales.

The canny businessman wasn't finished there. He had to

weigh the test-casting himself, just to make sure he wasn't to be undersold. I was due back in Anshan to review progress in the various, embarrassing non-ventures started by Sheffield, and there I picked up a heavy wooden crate with one manhole cover plus base-frame. The only time I've ever been questioned at Heathrow airport, or any airport for that matter:

'What have you got in that crate?' 'A manhole cover from China'. 'Pull the other one', the customs man chortled. He prised off the spar on one side of the packing case and peered in. Astonished, he waved me through.

Arthur B invested in a chattering telex machine. All he had to do for 5,000 manhole covers to land at Felixstowe was to send the order and pay by 90 days. He became very rich indeed on Chinese manhole covers, and remembering how it had all begun, he once called me and offered me a 'bung'. Politely declined, of course. It was bad enough that Anshan never got their acrylic bathroom-ware plant; the other side of the equation, Stanton and Staveley, lingered on to be taken over by a French company and then was closed down in the early years of the new millennium.

An acerbic paragraph concluded my own report to Sheffield City Council on this first and as far as I know last foray into the China market:

> The eight companies which had no previous China experience did not avail themselves of the many briefing documents offered them by the (Sheffield) Department of Employment & Economic Development. All of them could have done more to inform themselves of essential country background information

SHIFTING GEARS IN CHINA

Of the companies on the Sheffield mission in May 1985, other than the two which involved themselves in shipping into the U.K. quantities of cheap Chinese manufactures, I'm not aware that any one of them managed to do any business with China. At the time of the Sheffield Mission, May 1985, three letters of intent were signed — joint ventures for Arthur B's acrylic bathroomware plant and the lifting gear factor promised by Gilbert S, as well as a straight sale by a representative from the forging company Doncasters Sheffield of a used 1,000 tonne press. None came to fruition.

In the years to follow, the wider political-economic environment on both sides — the U.K. and China — saw the growing hegemony of global forces. But back in the mid-1980s neither Anshan nor Sheffield could imagine how far this would all go. The dominant ideology of market hegemony meant that coal mining, shipbuilding and engineering regions of the United Kingdom were to be leached to the bone. Northeast China, very much including the Anshan region, was to become, just a decade on from the twinning venture, China's very own rustbelt. But not for ever, as has been the case of many chronically sick regions of North America, and indeed Britain. Interestingly, Sheffield's economy, with its special steels and diverse engineering was in the end able to sustain itself, albeit in a scaled-down form and much due to the buoyant automotive, aerospace and armaments sectors. But as elsewhere, an insecure job market and indeed structural under-unemployment was going to be an enduring feature, right from the early 1980s 'shock therapy' down to the present day.

In a final throw of the dice, a last attempt to salvage something from all the efforts put into building a business relationship with Anshan, in 1988 I worked on a potentially massive deal which the Chinese city had put Sheffield's way. On Anshan's outskirts an offshoot of Angang was creating, alongside a Western partner, what promised to be Asia's largest scale steel forging enterprise. There had been problems and the partner had departed, leaving the project high and dry. With David F, a Sheffield-based forging specialist—and friend too—I made a site visit and we came away with a realistic plan on how to advance the project. The plant already in place had been mostly imported from Japan, and Siemens had installed a huge quantity of control equipment. All that was needed was a new expert partner, a relatively minor hard currency injection, and a goodly proportion of the enterprise would be handed to the new foreign partner. We did our best trying to persuade Sheffield interests—Davy McKee and Sheffield Forgemasters to be precise. No joy, so we headed south and tried the second largest U.K. company in the field, Wolverhampton-based. In retrospect, that forlorn effort put me once again in mind of the closed attitudes of Midlands metal bashers portrayed so amusingly in David Lodge's novel *Nice Work*. The man who cast scorn on our proposal, and generally on doing anything in China, was a dead ringer, Brummy accent and all, for Lodge's Vic Wilcox of Pringle's Castings.

The upshot some decades later is, of course, that the Midlands forging operation has gone to the wall, while the Chinese enterprise in question, Anshan Xiangyu Co. Ltd, has prospered. In due course, Anshan had secured a rather more enlightened foreign partner than could be found in Sheffield, or for that matter anywhere else in the British Isles. Incidentally, the entire British steel industry, which years after became largely owned by the Indian conglomerate Tata, staggered from one collapse to the next. Perhaps the final irony: in March 2020, a Chinese steel combine, the Jingye Group, acquired the whole of British Steel for a knock-down price. 'Three thousand jobs saved!' the BBC triumphantly announced.

The Sheffield-Anshan link stuttered on until 1989, when the Chinese authorities put down with ferocity the great popular uprising against inflation and despotic mismanagement. Thereafter, without particular pressure from the Foreign Office, all the many 1980s twinning links established between U.K. and Chinese cities went into desuetude. With the (vain) hope of enhancing their economic bases, the other South Yorkshire towns of Barnsley, Rotherham and Doncaster had all acquired twins in Liaoning province. If anything was actually achieved on the business front apart from more outsourcing of industry and heightened imports, I should be surprised. And as the reluctant director of a Northern England business centre concerned with the China trade, I would certainly have known if there'd been positive outcomes to report.

———∞———

A cursory internet survey of the larger companies on the May 1985 mission makes dismal reading, for mostly it's a series of postmortems. The clever engineering company which had dreamed up the integral carriage spring casting machine demonstrated rather more honour in their own efforts to break into the China market. Their good work also came to nothing, but rather than naked greed, it was the perfidy of the British financial sector which did for them. The highly innovative outfit had already taken a firm order from China's First Auto Works in Jilin province's Changchun. This huge plant had dominated China's heavy vehicle market since the days of Sino-Soviet friendship. The main output was a 2.5 tonne truck, which, though incorporating Soviet engineering, was a dead ringer for the U.S. International Harvester K-7 model supplied by Washington in the Second World War to the Soviet Union and to China. China's *Jiefang* ('Liberation') CA-10 truck was still much in evidence when I first arrived in the country in the early 1970s (as were the many captured Willys jeeps), though it was being phased out in favour of a more modern-looking model. That the Sheffield outfit had already cracked the prime producer of Chinese heavy good vehicles was certainly a feather in their cap, and over £1million in their bank. Their young overseas sales chief who had always impressed me with his quiet intelligence, had joined the delegation principally to push forward a further sale of their contraption to an eager buyer, another of China's growing number of auto manufacturers. He was hoping for Anshan's considerable influence, which was indeed forthcoming and an order was landed. But after a few months we learned that the second sale had fallen through. The Chinese company had asked for extra time to make payment, and guess what? Despite a world-beating product and a promising China order book, the Midland Bank refused to extend credit. In a typical manifestation of the indifference of the finance sector to domestic manufacturing, the bankers simply pulled the plug. The bare bones of Hille Engineering, the people who'd produced the casting contraption, were eventually incorporated into a German advanced engineering company of the type that hardly exists any more in the denuded British Isles.

Davy McKee, a crucial company in the U.K.'s heavy engineering, lingered on in life-support into the first decade of this century. If its mismanagement of China opportunities in the 1980s is anything to go by, I'm surprised it made it past the millennium.

Distington Engineering, with its origins dating back over 150 years, stumbled into the 21st century by being passed from owner to owner and eventually to a vulture fund, which in 2017 disposed of it to an outfit called TSP.

Clugston, which started its life so humbly by picking up the muck from steelmaking, seemed to have left actual productive activity behind when it morphed into one of those conglomerates favoured by our neoliberal establishment, offering every kind of professional service including (unspecified) healthcare. As world leaders in the recycling of steelworks slag, with a Chinese partnership and the steel industry so gigantic, Clugston might have secured contracts with no end. The last I heard of the company was that in December 2019 it was in administration and under the tender care of KPMG, the bankruptcy leeches.

While drafting this chapter, I came across a government review written some three decades after cities in the U.K. and China started to get into bed with each other. The document's subtitle, 'Barriers to developing international relationships', is worth citing as it just about sums up the imbroglio which I'd witnessed when Sheffield politicians, with all the best intentions, attempted not only to intervene in an impervious private sector, but also to enter a major foreign policy arena without adequate resources — of all kinds:

> Given limited resource (sic), many UK cities and regions lack a good understanding of the political system and governance structures in China. They anticipate that this is the same for their Chinese counterparts. For UK cities, a lack of understanding of equivalencies means that the profile of potential visitors is not well understood and they are not always equipped to respond appropriately to requests. There are frequent misconceptions by Chinese counterparts that there are large, dedicated international departments and teams

within city councils. Instead it is the case that most have only a small amount, if any, of resource dedicated to the international strategy and international relations. In cities and regions that do have an international team, these are often limited to one to three employees who work on international connections across the world, often being combined with other work of the City Council. While exceptions to this exist such as in Essex, and others are able to utilise the expertise and coordinating function of external organisations, these options do not appear to be widespread.[4]

Though Sheffield council's commitment of resources went far beyond that of any other city with a Chinese twin, its dependence on the uncontrollable actions of the private sector was the Achilles' heel. Despite the strong production culture of the city, 'buying cheap and selling dear' turned out to be the preferred game of Sheffield businesses in China. And this pattern was by no means confined to our disparate bunch of Sheffield industrialists, but pretty much reflected the stance of British industry as a whole. The German case, by contrast, tended towards investment in productive capacity in China; rather than merely replacing a company's domestic production, this complemented and strengthened it. And the constitution of Germany's banking ensured the necessary provision of capital, all leading to the country's primacy today in the manufacture and export of engineering products.

Offshoring, destruction of British industry, the hegemonic role of finance—an enduring malaise which continues four decades on. For me, it was all prefigured by that tale of simple, donkey-

---

4   Government Office for Science Foresight, *UK-China city region partnerships and network development,* August 2016, p8.

iron manhole covers. Certainly, the Sheffield experience with Anshan was against the backcloth of an increasingly inimical global market environment; poor management of mainly medium-sized enterprises cannot be held solely responsible for the industrial malaise which we find today. But almost forty years ago, the record of some of the nation's captains of industry tells me that as far as China was concerned, much can be laid at their door. Unlike their peers in many other of the Western industrial nations, it seems that the U.K's industrial chieftains mostly shunned the opportunities offered by the joint venture model. An instinctual, patronising view of foreigners sometimes verging on racism might also be mentioned. Minimal involvement with the locals, however, was demanded when the form of business was simply purchasing cheaply-produced Chinese manufactures. As we have seen, in Sheffield's case, the two prime candidates on the joint venture front fell, opportunistically, straight into this profitable game.

But perhaps I'm too hard on the U.K. company management which I saw at work in China. At their scale of operation, it was always going to be difficult to buck the markets, increasingly subservient as they became to overpowering financialisation. In the U.K. in particular, the City of London with its worldwide web of secretive tax havens was even in the mid-1980s becoming the main game in town, and other than a few select sectors such as armaments, it has condemned much of Britain's once renowned heavy engineering sector to a careless withering away. As witness to a strange microcosm of the beginnings of this process, I often think mournfully of that brilliant Heath Robinson contraption for carriage springs, killed off in its prime.

IV
LHASA (1984)

IT WAS MID-1975 that the turgid Xinhua daily press bulletin informed me in Nanjing, and the world in general, that the renowned writer Han Suyin had flown into the Tibetan capital. It was reported that in the small turbo-prop which soared up from the sultry Sichuan plain to cruise just above the six thousand metre-high peaks of eastern Tibet, cylinders of oxygen were on hand in case the acclaimed traveller began to expire. For Han Suyin was definitely a *renshi*, a 'personage', a term reserved for all eminent pro-Beijing non-Communist individuals.

The last great gasp of the Cultural Revolution's paranoia and witch-hunting was well under way, and the few restless foreigners employed by the Chinese were hardly allowed down the road, never mind to the interior provinces — and absolutely not to the closed region of Tibet. The famed novelist, celebrated 'friend of China', recorded her journey by penning a panegyric to Chinese rule. Her book, produced by a state publisher, bore the unlikely title *Lhasa, the Open City: a Journey to Tibet*. Lhasa was so open that Dr Han was only the second foreigner to be allowed by the post-1949 Chinese rulers into the Himalayan redoubt in thirteen years. The first, I believe, was another personage, or perhaps a half-comrade: the polemicist Anna Louise Strong. As for Han Suyin of *A Many-Splendoured Thing* fame, she'd long since 'made the turn to Mao', garnering an unflattering nickname amongst those foreign residents who derided those they called 'sunshiners'. Dr Han was cruelly known by them as '*Da Gongbao* in a skirt'. *Da Gongbao* was the Communist Party's slightly more intellectual daily broadsheet, so you can easily catch the idea.

Of course, Lhasa and Tibet as a whole had almost always been closed to outsiders. After 1949 it was the Chinese who were the gatekeepers. But for centuries, it was Tibet's own theocratic, feudal rulers who barred the gates. And very effectively, too. It's been reckoned that in the five centuries before 1900, only a dozen Europeans had reached Lhasa. Amongst them, as ever, were those indomitable Jesuits, who after the great Matteo Ricci's arrival in China in 1600 were to be a regular feature of the Chinese court in faraway Beijing. Disguised as Hindu pilgrims, in 1624 two Jesuit fathers, Andrade and Marques, made it to Lhasa from India. Later in the 17th and 18th centuries a further handful of Jesuit and Capuchin priests managed to get to the forbidden land, though not always to its forbidden city.

The turn of the 19th century brought an unprecedented, an exponential, increase in the number of foreigners who'd made it to Lhasa. Few Westerners who revel in the idea of an Oriental Shangri-la seem to be cognisant of another of the many dirty episodes of an imperial past, when Tibet's gates were brutally thrust aside in an appalling sideshow of British military adventurism. The Himalayan theocracy was marched upon by the Empire's Indian Army, British Tommies and native sepoys. En route for Lhasa, this campaign, known after its leader as the Younghusband Expedition, with its newly acquired Maxim guns slaughtered untold numbers of medievally-armed Tibetans. The invaders occupied Lhasa and, finding no good reason to be there, suddenly withdrew. Not much has changed in over a century of Russia-paranoia: of St Petersburg's arrival in Tibet which the British were there to rebuff, not a trace had been found. But the lure of Lhasa in the Victorian mind was evidently as strong as it remained in the 20th century and beyond. Edmund Chandler, a journalist who accompanied the invaders, wrote that entering

Lhasa would unveil the last mystery of the East, in this 'unknown land of dreams'.

No catalogue of Western travellers to Tibet could possibly omit Alexandra David-Néel. This daring Frenchwoman bowed to the compulsion to get to Lhasa despite her erudite understanding of the precepts of Buddhism, which she'd studied for many years prior to her assault on Tibet in 1924. Achievement of a material kind, notching up the trophies of high adventure, seem to me to be far from the faith, so it's a matter of conjecture what impelled the grande dame of Asian travel towards the elusive citadel other than the usual compulsions of conquest. Buddhism, after all, exhorts its adherents to strive to dissolve material desires. As we've seen, to prepare herself spiritually for her pilgrimage, David-Néel spent almost two years at the great monastery of Kumbum, the renowned fount of the Gelukpa School. I'm surprised by Alexandra, who from the age of twenty had had years of solo journeying in the East. Her first foray towards Lhasa from Kumbum Monastery saw her in full finery and in an elaborate caravan of carts and yaks and horses which would not have shamed the most well-equipped explorer of the day. The attempt was entirely conspicuous and short-lived. After that, Alexandra opted for the opposite extreme. Shaving her skull, she masqueraded as the half-senile mother of her adopted Tibetan son Yongden. Under her rags she concealed a compass, a pistol (some Buddhist!) and enough cash to pay a ransom. Braving long spells of hunger, snow, ice, the incursions of bandits of the road and always the fear of being discovered, the odd couple eventually reached their goal. In Lhasa for two months and her identity unrevealed, Alexandra David-Néel and her companion did the round of festivals and monasteries and then departed. The dauntless woman spent most of her forty-five remaining years in France, her celebrity ever-growing. In 1968, at the age of one hundred, she applied for a renewal of her passport. For her final journey, not long after, no such credentials were demanded.

Mindful of our own modest but still hair-raising foray into the eastern Tibetan borderlands, there are some truly astonishing accounts by 20th century travellers of these vast, deserted lands. The most dramatic is authored by a survivor of a small expedition which ventured into the northern wastes from Tashienlou (Kangding), in the then Nationalist government-designated province of Xikang. The year was 1940, and the purpose of Andre Guibart and his fated companion Victor Louis Liotard was to identify and demarcate the basins of two obscure rivers. To do this, they had to enter the land of the Ngolos, a loose combination of tribes owing no allegiance to Lhasa and having a strong aversion to strangers entering their territory. I think that they must have been the natives of the high plateau who harried and indeed, terrorised the Red Army on their Long March of the 1930s, graphically described for example in Edgar Snow's epic *Red Star over China*.

'Farmers and herders by day, brigands by night' suited most of the population of wild eastern Tibet. The Ngolo-Setas, however, were murderous brigands both by day and night. The Frenchmen not unexpectedly came under attack and Liotard was killed, along with their cook. Guibart lived to tell the tale *Tibetan Venture in the Land of the Ngolo-Setas*.[5] From Western Sichuan eastwards, on the main 'Tea Road' to Lhasa, a small caravan was lucky if it survived the local highwaymen. Those adventurer ingénues who successfully negotiated the route to Kangding, and further north to Dege Gonchen, and then tried to slip westwards along the main track into Tibet proper were likely to meet resistance from the Lhasa patrols, or even the fate of Guibart and Liotard. The forbidden kingdom indeed it remained.

---

5   London: John Murray, 1947 — English edition translated by Lord Sudley (sic).

RICHARD KIRKBY

Which brings me to the account by another French traveller, and even longer and more erudite bedtime read. On his China travels during the Second World War, Andre Migot, medical doctor and appointed some kind of local commissar by a misguided Nationalist official, stayed first in Kangding. He wrote engagingly and informatively on life in this Wild-West border town, where tea shipments were sealed and repacked for the long journey ahead to Lhasa, and caravans from the plateau headed further east to the entrepôt of Ya'an on the edge of the Sichuan Plain. Already in Ya'an, but not yet in the Tibetan borderlands, Migot had managed to lose all including his trousers to a band of brigands. He was philosophical about arriving in Kangding in rags: once installed there, the (Chinese) Xikang provincial honcho shamefacedly restored some of his losses, including his gold, essential for the road. Other local officials subtly sabotaged his official mission as a government inspector of cooperatives, so he decided to head north. Unlike Liotard and Guibart, who travelled in the strict tradition of geographical mapping, Migot's main thought was to commune *en route* with Buddhist sages in their monasteries, not forgetting the lonely anchorites in their remote caves. But he also had that Lhasa itch, and once in Derge he adopted the David-Néel tactic of scrofulous disguise and headed out with his Tibetan companion towards the gilded deer which top the Potala's monumental heights. A courteous Tibetan aristocrat on a fine stallion, along with his armed escort, quickly rumbled Migot, and his attempt on Lhasa was over. He had no recourse other than to head north through the danger-strewn Ngolo-Seta territory and onwards towards Qinghai. Unlike other intruders he survived: his account, published in 1955 by Rupert Hart-Davis, was, oddly, translated from the French by that supreme wanderer in Asia's Western reaches, Peter Fleming. The proto-spy adventurer of the British empire, brother to Ian

Fleming, engaged in his task with a panache both humourous and enviable.

———∾∾———

I confess that I myself was hardly immune from that mystical lure of Lhasa; fantasy escape was a response anyway to our almost complete confinement to Nanjing of the 1970s, and later to a small town in Shandong. We were permitted limited travel twice a year, but all far-interior provinces were closed areas. In our fevered minds, Tibet had become the epitome of escape and adventure. Our students regarded Tibet as the antithesis, a place of horrors to be avoided at all costs. Back in the mid-1970s, when it came to post-university job assignments, my ex-Red Guard students spoke with very forked tongues when it came to Tibet. As graduation loomed, the more 'revolutionary' of them would post pledges on the classroom wall-chart with assertions that Tibet would be their dream assignment. I couldn't help noticing that those who protested much were likely to land comfy assignments in the growing ranks of the state travel organisation, the *Zhongguo guoji luxingshe*—in some comfortable place in a seaboard province, and as far from Tibet as possible. On one occasion, Nanjing University was brought to a standstill by an official day of commemoration of one of its flock who'd been assigned to the 'Autonomous Region' and been killed in a truck accident. This was seen by the Party authorities as a great opportunity to propagandise the students with tales of heroism in the remote interior, Tibet in particular. On another occasion and at a time when the depredations of the Cultural Revolution were still very fresh, the theme of another short-lived propaganda campaign was the punishment meted out to a Han PLA man. The soldier had taken a pot-shot at a magnificent eagle, regarded by Tibetans as a sacred creature. Great play was made of the soldier's execution, this intended to demonstrate Beijing's firm solicitude for its myriad national minorities and their 'quaint' customs and beliefs.

By the 1980s, whenever a new province was added to the *kaifang* ('open') list, I'd regard getting to it as a personal challenge, though to manage this I had to be able to tack my extramural travel onto one of my official work trips to China. So it was with Tibet. After returning to live in England, in 1981 I'd been something of a go-between role for the nascent Chinese urban planning hierarchy and the comfortable gentlemen of the U.K.'s Royal Town Planning Institute. I'd helped to arrange the itineraries of a number of top-level delegations from the Ministry or Urban Construction and, in particular, from the China Academy of Urban Planning and Design. CAUPD in Beijing had the position of a quasi-planning ministry, and I'd forged warm relationships with its hierarchy when they were leading cadres of the Beijing Municipal Construction Bureau. Indeed, I had particularly good rapport with three of them who were later promoted to the CAUPD. In Sheffield in the 1980s, I persuaded the British Council to fund annual short courses for young Chinese who were learning about the new-to-them ideas of urban planning; it was the CAUPD which made the selections and Sheffield University where I had an honorary lectureship which hosted the three-month courses. An addendum to this: amongst my first group of ten young trainees was the CAUPD'S future director, a position at Ministerial level; in 2019 I was invited to a grand ceremony in China to recognise my efforts to bring some perspective to China's future urban development strategies. While Beijing has universally gone for skyscraper cities and the madness of private car ownership, alongside the best public transport anywhere, at least some of the social and participatory lessons from the U.K. experience were occasionally paid lip-service to.

Back to 1984. When I told the CAUPD people I was intending to get to Lhasa now that the government had made the surprising decision to declare the forbidden citadel open to individual foreign travellers, my friends showed an immediate interest. I'd often met professionals who considered Tibet to be a truly dangerous place even for a short visit. It was widely held that Han constitutions were incapable of coping with high altitudes, and that they could easily succumb to life-threatening *gaoshanbing* ('high-mountain sickness'). So my CAUPD friends were delighted to hear that I would be willing to have a good look at the state of Lhasa, and give them a few ideas on how the planners might go about 'modernising' the place. This hardly seemed an onerous task, especially as my own thoughts were to keep the planners well away from a cityscape which had long managed in its own way without the intervention of hidebound Han planning.

I was thrilled at the prospect not only of getting to Tibet, but having some semi-official business there. With no delay, I got my travel pass stamped and took myself to Chengdu, capital of the great province of Sichuan. I was back in my mother's birthplace, the low-rise city which still awaited its own 'modernisation'. My grandparents' old house hadn't yet been supplanted by a high-rise tower, though the huge Soviet-friendship era Jinjiang Hotel with its nine storeys in a way prefigured the city's future. The Jinjiang remained the only place foreigners were permitted, and after a couple of nights in its full luxury I managed to get myself onto the daily Lhasa flight. In the 1970s, a few Tridents bought from Britain were part of the civil fleet, but our normal experience of flying in China was that very country bus-like turboprop, the Antonov-24, which had conveyed Han Suyin to the occluded city. Not that I had anything against the aircraft, a workhorse first in service in the late 1950s, though after the break from Moscow in the early 1960s I did wonder where the spare parts were coming from.

I was surprised to find myself boarding a large jetliner at Chengdu airport, an Ilyushin Il-62 on its first ever commercial flight to Lhasa. Sailing over the snow-capped mountain ranges of Eastern Tibet at an altitude which seemed only just sufficient to clear them, I had an interesting technical seminar with the four CAAC men who (presumably) left the plane on autopilot while they solicited my opinions with regard to an abstruse section of their flight manual. The general idea in China was that there was Chinese language and 'foreign language', so why was it that I was protesting that I was unable to read Russian, never mind technical Russian? I shooed the puzzled pilots back to their cockpit, hoping they would actually fly the plane. Not so long ago, every pilot of a civil aircraft had been trained in the military on Chinese-made Mig fighters. I'd been inured to the routine when the pilot spotted his destination ahead: the machine was put into what always felt like a too-steep descent, sometimes almost a dive. And now we were plunging towards Lhasa's airport. In truth, what I could see out of my window was better described as a landing ground, as the runway appeared to be more gravel than concrete. One of its boundaries was a wide sweep of river, on the flood plain of which we were just about to land.

The air was crystal clear, the sky was that Himalayan brilliant blue, and from a few hundred metres up, no obvious airport terminal building had shown itself, but what I could spot was a long line of figures spread across the only runway where in a minute or two we'd be hurtling at over 200 kilometers an hour. The aircraft landed a little bumpily and we ground to a halt, and I saw out of my porthole we'd missed the line of figures, though not by far. It's best not to study flight safety aspects before one travels. I been blithely unaware of the fact that here, diurnal winds powering down from the surrounding mountains closed the runway every day at certain hours. In 1984, at 3,566 metres, Lhasa airport was the third highest in the world (now easily surpassed in China at least by the new and crazy Kangding airport, over 700 metres higher).

As for Chengdu airport where I'd embarked, it stood at only 457 metres, hardly a preparation for the blast of thin air which now hit us. It's often said that those who rise slowly towards Lhasa, by the ancient Tea Road which starts in Chengdu, or nowadays by the extraordinary railway from Qinghai's Golmud which was opened in 2006, are likely to adjust to the Tibetan heights far more readily than those arriving by air. The big aircraft was, of course, well pressurised, a matter which I imagined in my technical ignorance might be a help when we landed at high altitude. I've often wondered if it's possible to gradually adjust an aircraft's cabin pressure in order to acclimatise passengers who are otherwise launched without preparation into thin air. As it was, the doors were levered open and I felt a strange force had hit me. I was half knocked sideways, and struggled from my seat and down the steps. The figures I'd seen were now explained: in a cloud of wind-swept dust, a dozen Tibetan women in broad-brimmed headwear were attempting to keep the runway clear, using besoms of bound twigs. Our landing ground looked to be no more than gravel, though in places standard concrete slabs were revealed underneath. How on earth was the massive quantity of cement marshalled for this, which had to be the biggest civil engineering project in Tibet since the Potala was constructed?

There was a terminal building of sorts, a low cinder block

affair. Behind it a CAAC bus had drawn up, and for a few *yuan* I seated myself amongst the twenty or so other arrivals. Leaving the airport precinct, I couldn't miss a huge roadside placard: 'We warmly welcome the comrades from every province for their fraternal aid to Tibet'. The bus set off at speed down the few hundred metres of the airport approach road, and then the fun began. Since first arriving in China a decade earlier, I'd noticed on rare forays into open country that when a road is being renewed, it's not done in manageable sections. Lhasa lay over 65 kilometers distant, and every one of those kilometers was being rebuilt at the same time. I later found out that each one of China's rich eastern provinces had taken on a 'development' project for Tibet, and Anhui was responsible for the new airport highway. For the next three hours, the bus lurched precariously over the rutted ribbon of land adjacent to the road, sometimes leaving it entirely on a loop. Such was the fraternal assistance of Anhui province, according to a sign I spotted, that no-one had thought to rebuild the road in sections.

As we approached from the west and were still at some distance, a cube-like slab loomed up from the plain, the sinking sun illuminating a white edifice atop a cone-like hill. As we neared the Potala, it seemed to rise on its rocky crag almost defiantly from the surrounding plain, somewhat in the way that Edinburgh Castle rises above Castle Rock, I registered a twinge of disappointment rather than excitement. From afar, the Potala mount seemed huge, as it does in every postcard photo. Nearer to, it somehow shrank, reminding me of a typical Evelyn Waugh put-down in his travel book *Labels*. The Egyptian pyramids, the awful Waugh writes, are 'less impressive when seen close'. An initial crusty reaction perhaps, but during my stay in Lhasa and having toured its dark chambers, I was obliged to admit that there was no gainsaying the Potala Palace as one of the Great

Wonders of the World.

The bus deposited me in front of a three-storey brick building with a vertical sign in Chinese at its gate: Lhasa No. 1 Reception Building. Like a lot of these *zhaodaisuo* in remote areas, it was on the cusp of reinventing itself from being a visiting cadres' hostelry to a hotel for foreigners. So far, the entrance hall suggested that it was still the place for the cadres. I was the only foreigner in evidence. I was sent upstairs to a small suite in the standard design of the time—a bed with cotton-padded quilt in a synthetic green-bordered casing, a wonky painted chest of local manufacture and decoration, an upright chair and small table from the same stable, a large floral thermos. It was pleasing that my window gave a direct view of the Potala from the southwest aspect: the sinking sun lit the whitewashed gables in a pink and golden hue. I climbed under my quilt, breathing heavily in the thin air, and slept through to the next morning.

I stepped out into the wide and dusty street and found my breakfast in a wayside café, *youtiao* and strong black tea. Few of the passersby were not Tibetan. Most were urban types, dressed traditionally and substantially, the women in long skirts, cummerbunds and occasionally decorative aprons (*pangden*), with their multicoloured horizontal stripes. The man about town wore a dark robe drawn in at the waist. Most women went bareheaded and the men favoured a felt Homburg, with sometimes a black umbrella against the burning sun. There were the very different out-of-town Tibetans too, yak herders from the plateau, who came in all manner of dress, but generally the sheepskin chuba with, as ever with chuba, the right arm and shoulder free. The wilder characters down from the mountains had their sheepskins stripped down on both sides, hanging from the waist by a piece of twine. Most of their womenfolk, including some very elderly females with dark wrinkled faces, had their thinning hair in multiple braids. Learned papers have been penned on the significance of female hair braiding in Tibet: the ideal is 108 braids representing the Khan Djur, the 108 volumes of the Tibetan holy book. But the manner of braiding and ornamentation with silver, coral, turquoise, also reflects social status, clan, region and fashion. At least in 1984, these traditions had survived the depredations of the Cultural Revolution, and I wondered whether they would be sustained against the winds of 'modernisation' from Beijing. While some of the unappetising practices of Tibet's theocratic feudalism had been forcefully expunged by the Chinese, my instinct was that Tibet's rich cultural traditions would now face huge challenges as immigration from Han Chinese accelerated, with their homogenising, not to say Westernising, influences.

I decided that first morning to wander down to that same river I'd seen from my plane, its waters shimmering on the southern fringe of the city. To the Chinese merely the 'Lhasa River', but to the locals it was the Yarlung Tsangpo, a tributary of what, beyond the Himalayan barrier, would become the Brahmaputra. Incredibly, these waters twinkling over large boulders and gravel would end up coursing through India and Bangladesh before emptying into the Bay of Bengal, almost 5,000 kilometers distant. On the river bank, a man was patching a small round upturned coracle of yak skins stretched over a wooden frame. Another coracle was half-circling mid-stream to the crude paddle of a long-haired youth. Along the bank, some women were beating clothes with hefty sticks. I'd been told by my Beijing planning institute friends to expect a call the day after I arrived in the city, so I returned to the hotel where I found a telegram awaiting me. It informed me that I'd be met that evening by some of the institute's local contacts, and to take my instructions from them. My vague brief had always been to make some kind of qualitative assessment of how the city could be 'modernised'.

I was sought out at the hotel that evening by a contact of the CAUPD who told me that a welcome dinner had been arranged in my honour at a nearby Tibetan eatery, which turned out to be a small and dark chamber just large enough for the standard eight-seater disk of a table. I was surprised that the host was a policeman in his fifties, from his features clearly Tibetan. He was a thickset and jolly, and he bulged from his blue uniform, his oversized peaked hat pushed back jauntily. The other guests were apparently civilians, and apart from my contact they were all Tibetan. I was slightly taken aback by two middle-aged women in traditional dress who were eying me and exchanging amused comments behind their hands. It turned out that my dinner host was either a chief of Lhasa's police or *the* chief. True, I was one of the first individual foreign travellers but it seemed odd that he had got himself involved, and eerily unsavoury. I didn't have the brain left to retreat and it was soon too late, for this strange chortling character clearly intended to get me pie-eyed with strong liquor as quickly as possible. It hadn't occurred to me at that point that high altitude and alcohol can be a deadly mix. The meal was based solely on the yak—not a vegetable in sight in the thick broth, and several dishes involving large and greasy bones, though the food seemed a secondary consideration to the drinking. I quickly felt myself sinking, and all I wanted was my bed. But the table was suddenly cleared and wheeled away, and a ghetto blaster in the corner turned to full volume. It was time to dance. I reeled and whirled with the matrons, with the police chief, who kept insisting on pouring more liquor down my throat. From that evening onwards, my visit to Lhasa became something of a dream. How I got to my bed that night I had no idea. The following morning I couldn't rouse myself and kept my head well under the heavy quilt. When my heavy eyes finally opened, I found myself in a bed and in a room quite unlike the one in the official hostel. Above me was an irregular ceiling of wooden slats. In the corner of the room I could see a painted wooden pillar, its crest a wedge-like piece under a joist, a roughly hewn whitewashed log. When I next awoke, an attractive Tibetan woman perhaps in her forties was standing over me, offering me water in a bruised enamel mug. I had lost track of the hours — sometime later she appeared again with a plate of *momos*, cold and with hard edges. Then it seemed to be getting light again.

When daylight came, I raised myself from my hard bed and staggered to the door. I was surprised to see that I was standing on the upper floor of a building which enclosed a courtyard, with an open balcony. Below me the woman was hanging out washing while singing to herself. I had not the faintest idea how I'd managed to be conveyed to a completely different bed in what was certainly not the hostel I'd booked into. Even now I can't work it out. For the next two days I was treated as an invalid, the woman beckoning me away from the door and back to my bed. But my time in Lhasa was short, merely a week, and I still hadn't visited the city's crowning glory, the Potala. When the woman seemed to be out of the way, I got myself onto the street and headed towards the Jokhang Temple and the Bakhor, the street where clockwise circumambulation is observed by all the citizens of and visitors to the city.

In front of the temple the flagstones were worn concave by centuries of obeisance. Several men and women pilgrims were just then throwing themselves to the ground, wooden tablets strapped to their hands, and raising themselves only to repeat the ritual movement. I took it into my enfeebled head that I should stride past them and this I did, straight through the great doors of the temple. With the idea of gaining a bird's eye view of the thronged Bakhor, when I saw a stone staircase to my right, up I went. I peered over the parapet at the crowds below until a very angry monk with a large stick spotted me and started yelling and rushing my way. It was a crazy thing to do at Tibet's most sacred pilgrimage site and it only happened because I was still in a psychedelic stupor from my strange welcome dinner. The monastery seemed untouched by the 20th century, but how wrong was that impression. Terrible things had been visited upon the Jokhang at the height of the Cultural Revolution, these chronicled by Patrick French in his excellent *Tibet, Tibet: A Personal History of a Lost Land*.[6] The marauding Red Guards had devastated the place and its priceless contents.

Outside again, I joined the tight jostling crowd moving clockwise around the Bakhor. No Han at all were evident. On the crowded street, tall young men—Kham warrior types with red silk tassels tied in their long locks—strode past me with hardly a haughty glance. Half-naked beggars squatted around a white-painted mini-stupa where juniper branches exuded a sweet pungency, while ragged-haired children dodged amongst the tight formation of the moving crowd. After a short while I dislodged myself from it. I was feeling light-headed and had to sit. Luckily there appeared a rough teahouse with stone tables and benches. As I sipped from a stained bowl, two women seated themselves opposite from me, smiling. The younger one, no more than a teenager, carelessly slid her tunic from her shoulders and sat bare-breasted. Her companion said something to me and rubbed her forefinger and thumb together. Even in my half-awake state I could see I was being nakedly propositioned. I moved on, around to the far side of the circular street, where the crowds had thinned and the buildings grew larger and

---

6   London: HarperCollins, 2003.

mysterious.

The following day I thought I was fit enough to tackle the Potala. Yet climbing the stone steps to the entrance was a real trial. It was a curious entrance, a steep wooden ramp on which people were treading down with great care while others waited to climb it. I was waved up by an old man with owlish glasses and a broad-brimmed hat. By the time I'd staggered up the ramp I was exhausted. For the next hour I was thrust along by the jostling throng through dim chambers, in which altars and deity statues loomed in the darker recesses. One was full of light, a great bank of butter lamps laid out before a huge gilded figure of the Buddha. Here an elderly monk resting in a recess muttered 'picture Dalai' as I went by. On and on I went, the route ascending all the while. I eventually found myself on the very roof of the Potala, where a kind of house with many windows stood. This, a notice told me, had been the private residence of the Dalai Lama. The view from the parapets was spectacular, the roofs of the old city and beyond, the sparkling river and far, far away the dun lines of treeless rolling mountains.

Before I left for Chengdu, I fell into an interesting encounter with some educated Tibetans. At a bus-stop I was more or less taken over by a couple of young men wielding a large plastic flagon containing the local barley beer. It seemed impolite to refuse a few swigs. But that was enough to put me pretty much out of it again. I then found myself in a grassy park, which my new companions told me was the old summer retreat of the Dalai Lama, the Norbulinka. Seated cross-legged alongside a group of smartly attired Tibetans, the young men amongst them, I was soon sharing dishes of momos and being plied with the beer flagon. Several large white felt tents with attractive coloured motifs were pitched all around us. I must have asked a very leading question about how these new friends felt about the

Chinese. I remember that a heated discussion ensued. One of the lads who'd brought me there seemed to have decided to learn to live with Beijing's rule. It turned out that he had been one of the 'privileged' youths of Lhasa sent off to the Minorities College in Chengdu. His brother was vehemently of the opposite view. The elderly couple seated next to me, their parents, listened in silence.

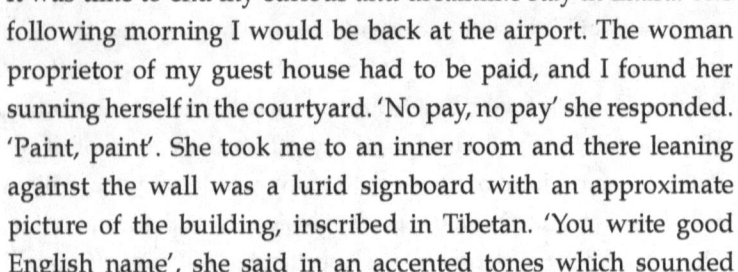

It was time to end my curious and dreamlike stay in Lhasa. The following morning I would be back at the airport. The woman proprietor of my guest house had to be paid, and I found her sunning herself in the courtyard. 'No pay, no pay' she responded. 'Paint, paint'. She took me to an inner room and there leaning against the wall was a lurid signboard with an approximate picture of the building, inscribed in Tibetan. 'You write good English name', she said in an accented tones which sounded more like Indian English than the Chinese version. I set to, and without a blush for the corniness, my sign-painting efforts resulted in 'The Inn of Happiness', all finished in red paint with black borders.

I was now more than ready to leave Lhasa, and to do so entirely without accomplishing the slightest part of the mission which the Beijing planners had set for me. I'd learned nothing of the history of old Lhasa's development, and little of the plans of the city administration. So what actually happened to the ancient city in very few years after my visit? If the wholesale reconstruction of cities in other parts of China was anything to go by, I was certain that Lhasa as it had stood for hundreds of years was unlikely to remain unscathed by Chinese-style modernisation. And this turned out to be the case, rather sooner than I'd expected. It is thought that in 1948, Lhasa had around

600 buildings and a population of around 30,000. Yet by the end of the 1980s, the authorities were boasting that they'd managed to demolish 550 buildings in the city. This was indeed almost all the core of the old city of Lhasa. In its report of 1999, an anonymous foreign conservation group I came across noted that the replacement housing of four storeys was of poor quality, with inadequate water supply and sewerage:

> This description fits most public housing blocks built in the old city, They are built from concrete and stone in mostly uniform design, and have mock Tibetan facades. The battened wall feature is entirely absent. The issue of water supply and sanitation is insufficiently solved. From design, workmanship and materials these buildings are unsuited to the Tibetan climate, as they are hot in summer and freezing cold in winter. An earthquake would spell disaster for the inhabitants as the new houses have none of the protective features of the old architecture.

By the time this report was written, some twenty years ago, Lhasa's population had already increased ten-fold from the 1948 figure, to over 300,000; I guess most of the additional population were not Tibetans but incomers from the east, hastening to this last frontier by the extraordinary extension of the railway from Golmud. The authorities' harsh reaction to protests, some of which have been extremely violent, has done much to destroy any hope of deep social tranquillity in the city, its physical fabric irrevocably torn.

Can I blame myself or just the company I keep? Years after Lhasa, I found in Patrick French's description of the older guard of suborned Tibetan officials that he too was forced at a gathering to drink far beyond his capacity. Was it the jocular policeman who'd somehow spirited the insensible me out of the state guesthouse and into a private hostelry, and if so, why? Whatever had gone on there, my brief visit to the forbidden citadel in the Himalayas amounted, in the end, to no more than indulgent tourism. And even then, I'd been a hopelessly ill-informed tourist and couldn't even bring myself to focus on the excellent Nagel guide book I always carried with me. Furthermore, I'd achieved nothing in terms of my semi-official duties commissioned by the Beijing planning organisation. I'd learned next to nothing of Lhasa's social and political character in the fourth decade of Beijing's rule. And as for those romantic longings for Shangri-La, they'd been entirely dissolved in the haze brought on by a combination of alcohol and high altitude.

V
THE MISSION (1984)

IN THE RUSTY filing cabinet in the garage, I've come across some faded newsprint which escaped the great Cumbrian flood. The newspaper features an account of a London press conference of November 1984, following the return from China of an unusual delegation. I'm billed in the accompanying photo as the group's adviser. The paper also tells that the Thatcher government is still intent on maximum support for the South African apartheid regime, while closer to home in Northern Ireland the right-wing terror of the UDA is going full swing, with, as we later learned, the covert assistance of British intelligence.

But even so, our world then, in 1984, was still a place of hope, of vigorous defence of rights, when trade unions were yet to be defanged, a time when well-paid work was still a reasonable expectation. Manufacturing was still a vital part of the economy, yet to be hollowed out and replaced by the gig routine of bullshit jobs. The post-War settlement of compromise between capital and labour was still in place, and people were prepared to fight vigorously for their rights. These news fragments from another age speak of the coal miners' strike which had yet to be defeated, of the dockers who staged solidarity actions at the ports. With the imaginative, fearless actions of the new feminist movement, the newspaper reports that the BBC had been shamed into scrapping 'beauty' pageants, specifically the Miss World Contest. In 1984, the people were still alive, not yet behaviour-modified by subliminal psyops and endless screen-staring, not subdued as they are now by the commands of a tiny oligarchical elite.

SHIFTING GEARS IN CHINA

If I reflect on the struggles for justice and economic betterment in the five decades in which I've been politically awake, the last four have been ones of overall defeat. In Britain, destruction of the post-1945 collectivist order, such as it was, is by the third decade of the 21st century near complete. Employment rights and opportunities are curtailed, the 'welfare state' disappearing. Out there, neoliberal resource wars rage everywhere, environmental destruction continues apace and it will never be halted without drastic political and economic change. In the poor countries, where the 'development of underdevelopment' (as the great Walter Rodney's termed it) has been the rule for centuries, four billion people lead an uncertain, hand-to-mouth existence.

In 1980, four years before our unusual mission to China, a little booklet with the title *Protect and Survive* had dropped through every letterbox in Britain. 'This booklet tells you', its cover explains, 'how to make your home and your family as safe as possible under nuclear attack'. Using dismantled doors and sacks of clothing, the citizenry was instructed to build shelters under tables (diagram helpfully provided). The absurd *Protect and Survive*, which treated the British public as though they were infants, galvanised hundreds of thousands, then millions into discerning that *protest* and survive was a far more appropriate response to the threat of nuclear war than building a flimsy nest under a kitchen table. This, then, became the popular response to the right-wing government of the United Kingdom (Thatcher's), as well as to those of other Western European nations where a new generation of U.S. nuclear weapons were to be sited. Unlike all earlier land-based weapons systems deployed by the U.S. and its NATO underlings, these were weapons which were designed for unstoppable, surprise attack on Moscow and the countries of the Soviet bloc.

Twenty years had passed since the potential cataclysm of

the Cuban missile crisis. When, during those tense few days everyone feared that the bombs would start to fall, my close friend Martin and I ran away from our boarding school and hid ourselves a few miles distant in a church in a dark valley. From that point in my life arose the first twangs of moral and political consciousness. The library of my Quaker school in Yorkshire subscribed to a little periodical called *Peace News*; I became an avid reader, and soon an ardent pacifist. Yet two decades after Nikita Khrushchev and John F. Kennedy showed enough sanity to defuse the Cuban missile crisis, it was now the raw imperial administration of Ronald Reagan which planned to install the new range of intermediate nuclear missiles in Western Europe. The Pershing II missile was truly an advance in the technology of indiscriminate mass murder. Launched from the U.K., from Germany, from Italy, its creators bragged that the missile could cover 1,600 kilometres in seven minutes and hit with high accuracy, and with no warning, any important target deep within the Soviet Union. A new arms race was signalled by this recklessness. In 1983, after NATO began deploying 108 Pershing II and 450 other cruise missiles in Western Europe, the Soviet Union responded with their new mobile SS20 missile, capable of hitting in a matter of minutes any NATO target other than those in the chief perpetrator's land, the United States.

The first high tide of the Campaign for Nuclear Disarmament had come in the late 1950s. With its establishment-shaking Aldermaston marches, CND's sudden high profile attracted a following inspired by prominent clerics and celebrated figures such as the philosopher Bertrand Russell. Many of the early members had put their trust in the Labour Party, which in the 1960s accepted CND's line of unilateral nuclear disarmament.

SHIFTING GEARS IN CHINA

Then came the 1964 Labour administration under Harold Wilson, which predictably ignored official Party policy and doubled down on an essentially U.S. nuclear arms system based on Polaris submarines. Labour's betrayal, along with the all-out devastation of Vietnam, Cambodia and Laos which provoked a worldwide anti-imperialist movement, eclipsing CND's message and leading to its dormant decade.

Soon, with the belligerence of the Thatcher-Reagan duo and their facile characterisations of East-West relations as the struggle between Good and Evil, with the craziness of *Protect and Survive* which was lampooned in every home in the land, the popular fight-back began. The Cruise missiles were mounted on trucks, and tactical operations required them to periodically leave their bases. Citizens' Cruise-watch squads tracked and harassed their movement along the leafy lanes of Southern England. In 1981, an encampment was set up on the perimeter of one of the United States Air Force bases with nuclear silos in Berkshire. Greenham Common became a rallying point for thousands of women, most of whom had had little previous engagement in political actions. Men, myself included, were welcomed at the site to bolster numbers on big protest days. Meanwhile, CND was being inundated by new members, and the national demonstrations in London drew in hundreds of thousands, even half-a-million. Leaning on the park railings at Marble Arch, I would watch the phalanxes of placard-waving, music-making and dancing protesters as they passed by. The column would often take three hours just to leave Hyde Park and march onto Oxford Street or Park Lane. Inventive banners were held high from every corner of the land. Finally, after three years of struggle, it seemed that the militarists were backing down. Could it really be the case that for once, a massive upsurge in popular opposition had actually coalesced to form a brake on warmongering ambitions? For in

RICHARD KIRKBY

1987 the Intermediate Nuclear Forces Treaty was signed between the United States and the U.S.S.R., and the new missile classes withdrawn by both sides. A nuclear-armed Britain remained, but this was a signal achievement for the European peace movement. After the high tide of 1987, however, the wind was taken out of the great protest movement's sails.

As the great protest movement gained momentum, Sheffield, still the fulcrum of the 'Socialist Republic of South Yorkshire', offered its magnificent City Hall to CND for its annual conferences. As a local resident and active supporter, I was soon drawn into the logistics of these gatherings. CND was coming to be seen by the wider public as no longer an insignificant groupuscule of contrarians; its leaders were becoming nationally known and respected figures. This attracted much attention, not all of it welcome: it later turned out that one Cathy Massiter, an MI5 officer, had by her own later, brave admission been spying within CND over the years to 1985. As far as the state was concerned, if one or two amongst the CND leadership circle had in at some time in the past direct, or merely indirect association with the tiny and almost moribund Communist Party of Great Britain, the movement as a whole was to be tarred with the same brush. The stumbling machinery of state could never seem to absorb a simple reality: that it was possible to be both a peace-mongering socialist and an anti-Stalinist — that is, to thoroughly oppose the powers-that-be in Moscow. This critique was of course on an entirely different basis to that of the Soviet Union's Western antagonists. It was a fundamental precept of the people in my own not inconsiderable circle of peacenik-leftists that the Soviet Union needed regime change, as it's today known. Not the imposition of the nascent neoliberal regime of our imperial masters, but rather a socialist revolution which would install a truly democratic polity. Here, the commanding means of production would remain in state ownership, but under *collective* control. In short, a democratic revolution which didn't need to throw out the baby with the bathwater, as later happened in the 1990s when the international sharks with their 'shock therapy' moved in on a hapless ex-Soviet Union.

So we young New Leftists had no time for the Communist Parties of Western Europe, especially after 'les évenements' as they've been immortalised. France, May 1968, where the riot police, the hated CRS, smashed heads in their thousands but where the unions under CP control led millions of rebellious workers away from what was shaping up to be a pre-revolutionary moment. This, along with the 1968 Soviet invasion of Czechoslovakia, was indeed the year when the scales fell from the eyes of many young radicals. The New Left, which now would forever refer to Western European communist parties as 'tankies', held that socialism in the modern age demanded allegiance only to ideological belief, and certainly not to any country, whether it be the Soviet Union, China, Cuba or any other state which had chosen to place, willy-nilly, 'socialist' or 'people's republic' in its title.

It was clear that the membership represented at the CND annual conferences was inclined to be far more militant than CND's executive, and there seemed to be a constant effort to dampen ardent spirits. It upset me that amongst the leadership there were those who wished to hold it back. Marjorie Mowlam, for one, seemed to be a stalwart of the CND conservative faction. While a lecturer in the Politics Department of Newcastle University, she'd been the flatmate of a close friend of mine; she later visited my Sheffield home so I can claim I knew her a little. Mowlam abandoned her lectureship in favour of the bursar's job at Northern College, a labour movement-supported college for working people known as the 'Ruskin-of-the North'. She confessed that her move was opportunistic and it was going to be a stepping-stone to a safe Labour seat in Parliament. And so it came to pass. As the Blair government's Minister for Northern Ireland, Mo Mowlam was to go on, of course, to achieve sainthood, consecrated by her early death from cancer. It was only later that I discovered, not entirely to my surprise, that Mowlam was a long-time member of that U.S. loyalty group, the Atlanticist British-American Project.

Another unlikely character who used the Labour party and CND as a launch pad for her illustrious career was Catherine Ashton. I well recall her as a rather retiring individual. At the height of CND's resurgence, 1977-1983, Ashton worked in the organisation's London offices; she eventually became its National Treasurer and a Vice-Chair. A good time later, after she had made a useful political marriage and was anointed Baroness Ashton of Upholland, from 2010-2014 Ashton carried the Ruritanian title of 'High Representative of the Union for Foreign Affairs and Security Policy'. A meteoric ascent which brought her to the position of First Vice-President of the European Commission. Ashton's most inglorious moment came via a leaked phone call between her and Estonia's foreign minister. She was told, rightly, that the Maidan killings in Kiev in 2014 were mainly the work of *agents provocateurs*. This didn't stop her, and the whole EU machinery from throwing their weight and — not to mention the hundreds of millions of Euros — behind Ukraine's and viscerally anti-Russia and indeed neo-fascist regime, which had come about through the 2014 U.S.-organised *coup d'état*.

There was one further person, female too, who rose to national prominence through CND. Of her, I retain far happier memories, occasioned by the CND delegation to China. I speak of the movement's chief, Joan Ruddock.

Sheffield played a uniquely important role in Britain's nationwide anti-nuclear movement of the early 1980s, a tribute to the local leadership and particularly to one David Blunkett. Council Leader from 1980-87, Blunkett, now in the House of Lords having served the Blair administration as Minister of Employment and later as Home Secretary, has long left his peacenik reputation behind. Once an MP, Blunkett lurched significantly to the right; he would today no doubt, as Baron Blunkett of Brightside, disavow his views when, as a leading local politician, he was committed to unilateral nuclear disarmament. Under his guidance, Sheffield City Council had put its money where its mouth was, going far beyond the gestures of those numerous U.K. local authorities which had merely declared their territories nuclear-free. Signs to that effect were regular sights in those days at town and city boundaries. The city went far further, voting grants to all aspects of the peace movement. These included a £20,000 annual subsidy towards the Sheffield Peace Shop's rent, the production of a booklet *You and the bomb*, aimed at countering the government's laughable *Protest and Survive*, and to cap it all, a huge one-off budget allocation of £90,000 to employ for five years an official Council Peace Officer.

Sheffield's largesse extended to a number of didactic artistic efforts. The author Raymond Briggs, nationally known in the U.K. for his 1978 children's illustrated book *The Snowman*, watched by millions in its silent cartoon adaptation Christmas after Christmas, went on to produce his own anti-nuclear war film. *Where the Wind Blows* must have had quite an impact when it was released in 1982, reaching parts of the population who had never strayed into this horrific territory. When a stage version was produced locally, Sheffield City Council helped fund it. Additionally and remarkably, the sum of £10,000 (equivalent at the time to two senior council officers' annual salaries) was voted for an updating aimed at general release of Peter Watkins' 1965 film, *The War Game*. This masterpiece of horrific realism about a nuclear attack on Britain was considered by the BBC, which had commissioned it in the first place, 'too dangerous' to show to the British public. For those who considered the post-1950 'defence' posture as nothing out of the ordinary, the Watkins film would have come as a terrific and frightening jolt. Back in 1967 when the film was still taboo, as a member of the Bristol University Peace Group, I'd helped to stage a well-attended showing of *The War Game*.

Numerous films have been produced on the theme of nuclear war, both of the shock-horror commercial genre and of the avowedly anti-nuclear. *The War Game* might be still banned by the BBC, but the year 1984 brought forth a spectacle which, in the pantheon of nuclear war films, has been described as coming closest to depicting the full horror. The extraordinary thing was that the film in question actually received part-funding from the BBC, which then promoted *and* screened it to a startled public. Then, after sitting down himself to watch *The War Game*, Alasdair Milne, the BBC's Director-General no less and a 'safe pair of hands', felt morally driven to support the production of *Threads*. This new creation was all Sheffield. Mick Jackson, the director, was persuaded by local writer (and member of my Sharrow Labour Party branch) Barry Hines of *Kes* fame to cast ordinary locals in the principal roles; dozens volunteered as extras. The filming and simulated death and destruction took place all over the city and its Peak District hinterland, with even Sheffield's famous Town Hall being gutted by the firestorm. In September 1984, the BBC broadcast *Threads* to over six million viewers. Apart from the film's anti-nuclear proselytising, it was a production acclaimed in all quarters for its artistic merit. *Threads* was showered with awards and had no fewer than seven BAFTA nominations. As if to redress their cowardly situation over *The War Game*, official Britain commemorated the 40th anniversary of the U.S. attacks on Hiroshima and Nagasaki by getting the BBC to give *Threads* a second screening. That would be unthinkable today: the BBC in the post-Iraq War era has become a very different animal, and it sticks tightly to its role as a cipher for the British state machinery. In the 2020-21 'pandemic', the BBC supremely acted out its role as transmitter of shady statistics, as official censor of dissenting medical views, many of them from high experts in virology, immunology and the like, including Nobel prize-winners. There was simply no room at the BBC for expert voices questioning the house confinement of hundreds of millions worldwide, the de facto demolition of national economies, the incessant, deliberate fear-mongering. Today, with all U.K. parliamentary political parties in fulsome support of the so-called 'independent' nuclear deterrent, and its insane upgrading through the Trident missile programme, not to mention the war against Russia, there would be the proverbial cat-in-hell's chance of an oppositional film such as *Threads* being tolerated, let alone being financially and morally supported by the state broadcaster. Such is the world we now inhabit.

For our 1984 CND mission we might have taken *Threads* to show to our hosts, though most of the cultural references and the Sheffield version of English might well have defeated a Chinese audience. Instead, we settled on another film which Sheffield City Council had a hand in. One thousand pounds was provided to Scientists Against Nuclear Arms (SANA), a group founded by renowned physicist Mike Pentz along with his colleague, the neuroscientist Steven Rose, both of the U.K.'s Open University. In association with Carl Sagan, the 20th century's best-known astronomer, planetary scientist, cosmologist and astrophysicist, the grant was intended to assist research for a documentary on the climatic consequences of nuclear war. In 1984, as a late convert to the cause of nuclear disarmament, Sagan co-authored *The Cold and the Dark: The World after Nuclear War*.[7] It harked back to the massive eruptions, which began in 1807, of a number of volcanoes along the Pacific Rim, and in the Caribbean region too. The Pacific Rim activity culminated in Mount Tambora, in what was then part of the Dutch East Indies, blowing itself apart. This truly catastrophic explosion is thought to have been the greatest anywhere for a millennium; the huge quantity of volcanic dust propelled into the lower stratosphere formed a barrier to sunlight, resulting in significant lowering of average temperatures across the globe. In East Asia, massive famines and floods ensued. In South Asia the monsoon was disrupted. North America and Europe also suffered poor crops for several years, localised famines even, and widespread hunger and disease. The year 1816 came to be known as the 'Year without Summer', the 'Poverty Year'.

Carl Sagan and his group of concerned, anti-nuclear scientists, along with his colleagues in England, postulated on the basis of a series of experiments that even a limited nuclear exchange would precipitate an event similar to that of the early 19th century volcanic super-eruptions: a *nuclear winter*. Those who weren't amongst the tens, hundreds of millions killed or injured immediately would now confront worldwide crop failures and starvation. The propagandising of just this message was the spearhead of our mission to China. The hour-long documentary which we took to China as the centrepiece of our mission of persuasion was a SANA production on the nuclear winter theme, bearing the anodyne title *A Change in the Weather*.

---

7   Paul Ehrlich, Carl Sagan, Donald Kennedy & Walter Orr Roberts, New York & London, W.W. Norton and Company, 1984.

SHIFTING GEARS IN CHINA

I'm sure that Beijing must have looked on with alarm when the vast West European uprising against Cruise and Pershing missiles was ignited. Uncertain how to react, initially China barely commented on the upsurge of the European peace movement. It was certain that Beijing regarded its members as little more than Soviet dupes — or worse. Gradually though, Beijing came to characterise the opposition to U.S. missiles as mostly sincere, but badly misguided. In early 1982, I was in Beijing on a research visit connected with my work on China's urbanisation policies; I was surprised when a person of influence sought me out and put to me that henceforth Beijing might soon not only adjust its views of the European peace movement, but those concerning the Soviet Union too. Indeed, China's slightly softer line on Moscow was evident at the UN's Second Special Session on Disarmament. Moreover, in late 1983 China agreed to become a fully-fledged member of the global nuclear club by joining the International Atomic Energy Agency. This implied a willingness to place imported equipment and nuclear waste storage sites under international scrutiny. But suddenly thereafter there was a new chill in Sino-Soviet relations, doubtless reflecting a power struggle going on within the Chinese leadership.

'I have pleasure to transmit the following message to you from China's Association for International Understanding', wrote a first secretary of the Chinese embassy to one Bruce Kent. 'The Association welcomes CND delegation of four members visiting China from October 31st to November 15th, 1984.'

The invitation to venture into China was delivered to a man who had done more than anyone to try bring the British public to their senses on the issue of the nation's nuclear arsenal. Monsignor Bruce Kent (as he was before he saw the light) was like no other Catholic prelate. Always well-argued, he performed as an eloquent roving ambassador for CND. It was to him that the Chinese turned when they realised that the best supported peace group in Europe wasn't going to go away. So that was it. At a Council meeting of CND, the invitation was mulled over and approved, with the proviso that China's Vietnam conflict should be raised by the delegation. In February 1979, China had actually gone to bloody war against Vietnam. Four years after the Americans were ejected from Vietnam, the U.S. and China alike were obsessed with the notion that the Soviet Union was going to plant itself in southeast Asia by taking over U.S.-vacated facilities, especially the deep-water port in Vietnam's Cam Ranh Bay.

As someone who was supposed to know about China, David Blunkett had at some point had put me in touch with the office of the leader of the Parliamentary Opposition, Neil Kinnock, who in turn recommended me to his Welsh compatriot, Joan Ruddock, Chair of CND. I was to be the delegation's fifth member, its China adviser. I got down to work and produced a wad of briefing notes on how China had developed its nuclear arsenal in defiance of the Soviet Union's refusal to disclose its own secrets. In my initial notes for the four delegates, I tried to get across the essential geopolitical issues. I wrote:

> Whatever the Chinese say, the prevailing state of the Washington-Moscow-Beijing equation has a bearing on every foreign policy issue (of China's) including attitudes to the nuclear arms race. During the ultimate period of Mao's ascendancy, that is the Cultural Revolution (1966-76), the attitude in China was that the danger of nuclear war was a mere paper tiger. That 'people were stronger than weapons' and even if there were a nuclear war involving China, it was not too bad that two-thirds of the population would die, as

one third would survive and China would still be the greatest and most populous nation on earth.

I went on to review the rabid anti-Soviet Union environment from which China was just beginning to emerge. When I'd lived in China a decade earlier, the barrage of anti-Moscow propaganda was matched by material but tacit support for Western military adventurism. Wherever it imagined the hand of Moscow at work, China would do its best to support the other side, the side backed by the United States. Palestine was one of the few exceptions to this rule. Beijing couldn't easily avoid giving support to the Al-Fatah movement led by Yasser Arafat, whom I saw in Nanjing a couple of times. Here, his fighters were apparently being trained by the PLA.

But how about the Kissinger-fomented *putsch* in Chile in 1972, in which China quietly sided with Pinochet? Then there was the ongoing struggle in Africa against Portuguese colonial rule, where, in Angola, China stood alongside Washington in support of Holden Roberto's very reactionary FNLA. Mobutu, the dreadful dictator of Zaire and an ally of Roberto, had been installed by the CIA and MI6 following their probable murder of the progressive Patrice Lumumba: he was also one of Beijing's favourites. In Mozambique, where the Cubans gave decisive support to those fighting for independence, China did all it could to hinder them. In the chaotic aftermath of Washington's destruction by bombing of eastern Cambodia, the atavistic Khmer Rouge movement came out of their jungle hideaways and took power, heavily supported by China. Incidentally, once 'Kampuchea' had proved its belligerence against Vietnam, the United States and the United Kingdom became covert supporters of Pol Pot's war, the U.K. providing special forces to train the Khmer Rouge fighters in mine warfare. Decades on, mines are still regularly killing and maiming poor rural Cambodians. In 1979 too, following the Iranian revolution which overthrew China's good friend the Shah, the United States was very secretly invited to move their bases, mainly listening stations, from Iran to China's north-western border with the Soviet Union. I could go on. Closer to home, during my Nanjing days I was regularly incensed by the diplomatic warmth, including lavish paid tours, being showered on the most reactionary, pro-NATO and anti-Soviet politicians of Western Europe. Franz-Josef Strauss of Bavaria epitomised these, but Beijing's fawning love of Margaret Thatcher when she came to power in 1979 was, for me at least, the pink limit.

———∽∽———

At a briefing day with contributions from China academic John Gittings, the Oxford Research Group and myself, I had a chance to get acquainted with my four fellow delegates, for in effect I was the fifth. Like Bruce Kent, Joan Ruddock, Chair of CND, was generally respectfully treated in media interviews. Having wet her toes in the swamp of parliamentary politics in 1979, unsuccessfully contesting a Tory seat, in late 1981 she decided on a change of gear and was elected CND's leader. The movement had become too large and vociferous for the mainstream media to ignore, and thus Ruddock, along with Bruce Kent, were regular faces on U.K. news and current affairs programmes. Ruddock in my estimation was the most accomplished advocate CND could ever have hoped for. She exuded charm, took great care with her wardrobe and was on the beautiful side of demure. Most vitally, she was a flawless speaker and one whom I have never in any context seen bettered. Well briefed, Joan Ruddock could speak to the point, and always side-step the little traps set by hostile media interviewers. She's the only person I've ever come across who could complete a lengthy paragraph of perfectly composed and to-the-point argument without a single pause. Her silvery and Welsh-lilted tones permitted not a single 'um', 'ah' or 'uh'. A perfect ambassador for CND, a perfect foil against those of its opponents who would like to characterise the movement as the refuge of inarticulate scruffs with half-baked arguments.

Mick Elliott, CND's treasurer, was the group's fixer. At the time, the tall and sensible Elliott ran Sheffield Polytechnic's students' union. He was also well connected with the Labour Party and the elderly, mainly Communist Party-inspired trade union mafia—the city's original political movers and shakers. As for Roger Spiller, I'd observed this thoughtful and measured person at the Sheffield-based CND national conferences as he circled around the leadership coterie. In fact, he'd soon gotten himself elected as one of CND's Vice-Chairs. The fourth member of the delegation was Janet Bloomfield, already on CND's National Council, and on her way to a bright future in various peace-oriented organisations. Janet was a humorous and somewhat matronly thirty-year-old, a figure within the offshoot known as Christian CND; I was to get on well with her.

The benign-sounding Chinese Association for International Understanding (CAFIU) had first appeared in 1981, joining the long-established Chinese Association for Friendship with Foreign Countries (CAFFC) to serve China's post-Mao order as an ostensibly non-Party NGO. 'Making friends and influencing people' across the globe was its one aim. Like today's Confucius Institutes, CAFIU and CAFFC were post-Mao China's incipient soft power agencies. Diplomacy during the Mao years had been narrowly proscribed: relations were either 'State to State', 'Party to Party', or the catch-all 'People to People'—which in actuality meant the people who approved of the Chinese Communist Party's endeavours in running their country. But now China was catching on quickly to the new demands of successful global discourse.

From its beginning, CAFIU had become the main promoter of China's city twinning movement. As related in earlier chapters, I had something of a key role in the miserable charade, with Sheffield being the first U.K. authority to link up with a Chinese city. Later in the 1990s I did my very best to discourage the marriage between Europe's most rapidly declining city (Liverpool) and Asia and the world's fastest growing megalopolis, Shanghai. I was ignored, of course. The signing ceremony was an excruciating experience, the Shanghai hosts bewildered by an argument between the Lord Mayor and Council Leader as to whether Liverpool or Everton were the best football teams. The Mayor of Shanghai, remember, is a key member of the Central Committee of the Communist Party of China, a person presiding over a population and an economy which even by the late 1990s dwarfed those of many European nations. When Shanghai's illustrious Mayor made his return visit to Liverpool, the old and declining maritime city's coffers were empty. On leaving to go back home, the Chinese entourage was presented with the hotel bill. This was nothing of my doing as Liverpool City Council was, and remains, a law unto itself. I was, however, called to the PRC Consulate in Manchester to soak up the Consul General's wrath.

———∽∽∽———

I happened to be in China on another mission in October 1984 and arranged to join up with the CND group in Beijing. Mick Elliott had, unbeknown to me, written me a number of faxed letters concerning the delegation's arrangements, surprisingly sent care of Britain's ambassador in Beijing. I have one of them before me: it's signed off in a manner somewhat alien to CND's usual informality ('I have the honour to be Sir your Excellencys (sic) obedient servant'). The ambassador elected not to pass the messages on to me: perhaps it was the absence of the appropriate apostrophe that did it. Anyway, the appointed hour had arrived, and on the 1st of November 1984, I got myself to Beijing airport to meet up with the new British Airways flight direct from London. The airport greeting party consisted of a CAFIU interpreter, along with a courtly functionary, a Council Member, who was to accompany us throughout our visit as a kind of benevolent minder. Shi Zhongbeng was his name. We were whisked in three spanking new Mercedes limos to the Wanshou Road State Guesthouse in the city's west. At the routine programme meeting that evening, it was clear that our hosts had done their research and wished to provide at least the bones of a useful itinerary. Auguring well for the seriousness with which they approached our mission, Shi Zhongbeng suggested that we drop the idea of travelling to the far south (Guangzhou, Shenzhen).

The next day we were off to the Foreign Ministry to be welcomed to China by a Deputy Department Director. That afternoon we were given the Party line on peace and disarmament and China's 'no first use' undertaking regarding nuclear weapons; our formidable interlocutor was Ou Tangliang, who'd joined the Communist Party long before 1949, making her a very senior person, even in 1984's terms. Ou Tangliang was presented to us primarily as a politician, a Standing Committee (read 'cabinet') member for every session since the early 1950s of China's law-making body, the National People's Congress. She was also a woman who loomed large in China's foreign affairs circles. I later learned that Ou Tangliang had served the People's Republic in numerous top jobs, from Secretary of the

Communist Youth League in the 1950s, to a ministerial position in foreign affairs from 1978-82. She'd already long retired from her formal political roles, but was yet another senior luminary on CAFIU's Council. Born like my mother just after the end of the Qing dynasty, Ou survived until November 2001, expiring at the age of 105 years.

Acrobatic performances are an auxiliary branch of China's diplomacy, for they impress upon the foreigner the subtlety and ingenuity not merely of the body but of the Chinese spirit. After an evening at the acrobatics had suitably softened us up, the next morning we had a challenging encounter with three senior men from the Beijing Institute of Strategic Studies. My notes:

> The Institute is reportedly under the Defence Ministry and the above personnel (the three) though in civilian clothes, probably have military rank; of the three, Mr Shi Jinkun is clearly the most important, having access to foreign travel and to military commanders of NATO.

And to quote from Roger Spiller's interview with the three military men:

> The people we met in Beijing from the Institute of International Strategic Studies seemed to be the most aware of what happened in the West but their view was dominantly one of support for NATO, and for any action that was taken against the Soviet Union.[8]

So the Chinese Communist Party of 1984 was still very much

---

8   *China Now* 'CND Goes to China', 1985, No.111, pp 6-9.

leaning to one side. Spiller went on to remark that we left our Defence Ministry interlocutors in no doubt that CND fundamentally disagreed with their position. The signs were all very discouraging. I couldn't help noticing, for example, the warmth these military men had showed when Alexander Haig's name was mentioned. While in office, Haig had proposed that it would be a good idea to show Moscow that NATO meant business by firing a 'nuclear warning shot' at them. After his resignation as U.S. Secretary of State in 1982, and in this role having encouraged and funded the death squads of El Salvador and Guatemala, Haig had become a regular visitor to China. At the apex of the military-industrial complex for decades, and NATO Supreme Commander in the 1970s, in China his new role seemed to be that of arms salesman.

Things went a little more our way later in the day. That afternoon a large audience of well over one hundred foregathered at the guesthouse for our *pièce de resistance*, the showing of our nuclear-winter video *A Change in the Weather*. As well as senior foreign affairs think-tank types, representatives had been told to come along from what counted in China as 'civil society': a clutch of elderly CAFIU worthies, official trade unionists, people from the Women's Federation, the Academy of Agricultural Sciences, as well as from the Party media — not forgetting some leading members of the officially approved Christian churches. There were others too: my notes read 'See attached list of luminaries'. Unhappily, it must have been *de*-tached by that flood in Cumbria when our archives were inundated. Still, I can see that following our harrowing film we had a lengthy question and answer session.

Our screening followed by a few questions satisfactorily concluded, we were driven down the great Chang'an Boulevard to Tiananmen Square and the iconic locus of all Chinese state functions, the vast Soviet neoclassical-style Great Hall of the People. It was time for our welcoming banquet, and we were told we'd be hosted by Li Yimang, President of CAFIU. The very elderly Li was presented to us as a former Central Committee member, though still serving on the all-important Central Advisory Commission of the Party. A later excavation of Li Yimang's exploits disclosed that he was one of the military leaders involved with the disastrous South Anhui Incident of 1941, when, during the Anti-Japanese War, Chiang Kai-shek's forces massacred their supposed (Communist) New Fourth Army allies. Li Yimang was now so visibly infirm that he shouldn't have been made to host a banquet in a vast chamber of the Great Hall for strangers from afar. And especially for ones bearing no tribute to the Court of the Communist Party. My surviving menu, incidentally, shows that, if the half dozen cold appetisers are included, the banquet comprised over twenty exotic dishes. When speech-time was called, Li Yimang mustered just a few words from his seat, and Joan Ruddock rose (as ever) to the occasion with a faultless response.

Our first Sunday was put aside for routine tourism, another formidable branch of China's soft diplomacy — the Great Wall and the Ming Tombs. We returned to Beijing to a press conference. Mark Brayne, Beijing correspondent for the BBC, had already recorded two interviews about CND's thrust into China, the first with Roger S while still in London, and the second with Joan R on the first day of our programme. The BBC had done yet another interview for its World Service audience, this fielded by Roger S. It's astonishing looking back that the state broadcaster's controllers considered it quite natural in those far off days for a major civil society movement, one which espoused policies fundamentally opposed by the government, to be repeatedly provided a platform. It reminds me once again how much we've lost since 1984.

The Great Wall Hotel press conference yet again drew in the BBC's Mark Brayne; others who turned up were Hugh Davies (*Daily Telegraph*), M.B. O'Callaghan (*Guardian*), Anthony Barker (Reuters), Mark Baker (*Financial Times* & *Sydney Morning Herald*), as well as a lone Eastern bloc correspondent representing the German Democratic Republic's ADV agency. Though I was an active CND member, indeed chaired Labour CND in Sheffield, as adviser my place was to keep my mouth shut, and I let my four delegates field the many questions, both about the objectives of CND and our pilgrims' progress through China. Despite the predilections of most of these journalists, the atmosphere was friendly and genuinely enquiring.

Later, correspondents from the *China Daily* and Radio Beijing arrived at our guesthouse to conduct interviews with Joan Ruddock. One of our CAFIU people had already smilingly handed me a copy of *Cankao xiaoxi*. This daily 'Reference News' was available on subscription to Party cadres. It was able to publish news and views which wouldn't appear in quite the same form in easily available national and provincial newspaper – all strictly aligned to the Party machinery. As a resident foreigner I'd only very occasionally caught a glimpse of *Cankao xiaoxi*; its big brother, *Da cankao*, was strictly for Party cadres above a certain grade (or actually *below*, as No. 1 grade was forever Chairman Mao's). This daily publication included verbatim, unexpurgated translated reports lifted straight from the newspapers and government reports of foreign friends and foes alike. Senior members of the Communist Party were at all times aware (albeit through the prism of their own political culture) of developments and opinions in the wider world. On 1st November, as the copy of *Cankao xiaoxi* reveals – I now have it in front of me forty years on – CND's stance on NATO's nuclear weapons was spoken of in highly critical terms. It's a brief 500-word analysis which was seen by literally tens of millions of Party and non-Party cadres throughout the land. CND and the European peace movement were obviously being closely monitored by China's embassies. The day after our Beijing press conference, the *People's Daily* also carried a brief, and this time merely factual, mention of the delegation.

We left the capital for the familiar territory, for me at least, of Nanjing. Here the Jiangsu Foreign Affairs people guided us through a programme which brought us to the Nanjing Union Theological Seminary. I wasn't the least surprised that Bishop Ding Guangxun, head of the Party-approved Chinese Christian Society, was on the itinerary; he was usually wheeled out when a certain kind of foreigner arrived. The C.P.C. has a long history of 'united front' work, with itself in the lead of alliances with all kinds of non-Communists-approved religious leaders, members of the eight 'Democratic Parties' which were tolerated (except during the Cultural Revolution) 'under the Party's leadership', prominent non-Party members of the intelligentsia, and so on. The Bishop had been anointed with membership of China's National Consultative chamber; he was also a deputy to the 'parliament', the National People's Congress. And like others we were meeting, a natural for CAFIU's Council. Like many prominent figures of a certain Chinese generation, Ding Guangxun had attended Shanghai's St John's University. Founded in 1879 by American missionaries, St John's became a prestigious institution of the Anglican church for the whole of China. Lin Yutang, the most renowned Chinese man of letters of the 20th century, and I.M. Pei, world-famous architect, were both graduates, as were many others who went on to attain (and usually, later, to lose) high office within the People's Republic. Even Rong Yiren, China's premier 'national capitalist' whose Wuxi home was our temporary quarters after the Tangshan earthquake of 1976, had passed through St John's. In the 1960s and '70s, to be the product of a foreign religious sect's schooling wasn't something to be advertised. The professor with whom we'd worked at Shandong University in the late 1970s had suffered so much from St John's bourgeois taint that he had tried to kill himself by jumping out of a window. He survived, but with a bad limp.

The Anglican Church as such had been brought to an end in the 1950s. Ding Guangxun, however, continued thereafter as the *de facto* head of Protestantism in China, under the state's religious umbrella and bearing the odd name (in English) 'Three-Self Patriotic Church'. Ding justified his acquiescence to state supervision by proclaiming that religious people should have a sense of social responsibility. That, of course, didn't preserve him or his family from the repression of the Cultural Revolution, though such things could never be mentioned to foreigners; I was vaguely aware that his wife, Professor Guo Xiumei, had suffered more than him at the hands of the Red Guards. Like millions of other educated or semi-educated Party cadres, she'd been sent off to labour in a remote rural area. Professor Guo had been a rather transitory colleague at Nanjing University, and from time to time she appeared in our department principally to give us a dressing down in her perfect English English.

In the event, when our delegation arrived for our very ecumenical meeting, the Bishop was away on some business or other. We were met at the early 20th century edifice of the Nanjing Theological Seminary by Bishop Ding's Deputy, along with a man who introduced himself as the Secretary of the China Christian Council. My notes at the time, headed: 'Discussion including briefing by us on Christian CND'. Janet Bloomfield, as I've mentioned, was involved with the offshoot of CND for avowed Christians, and along with the most prominent peace campaigner in the U.K., the venerable Monsignor Bruce Kent (CND's Roman Catholic General Secretary), our hosts might well have been labouring under the misapprehension that CND, this actually very secular movement, was really one of Christians with a (misguided) conscience.

Nanjing's grand banquet was at the Jinling Hotel, a monumental construction looming high over the city centre, at Xinjiekou. The occasion was hosted by a man I seemed to recognise from official events in the late 1970s when he emerged as Nanjing's Deputy Mayor and also its Party Secretary. Now a *renshi* – 'personage', unsurprisingly Liu Feng was yet another name on the CAFIU Council. My first stay in the astonishing edifice, the Jinling, had been shortly after it was completed in 1982. At the time the Jinling, financed in part by a Singapore Huaqiao, an 'Overseas Chinese', was far and away the highest building in the whole of China. I wondered how the army of building labourers drawn in from the villages managed with the demands of a structure which completely dwarfed both in scale and technological wonder anything they'd ever undertaken. The citizenry of Nanjing, and especially the visitors to Jiangsu's capital from out of town, were for the first few years of the new hotel's life to be found in a great crowd spilling over the street, their eyes raised in awe at the multi-storey wonder. The management turned this to advantage, offering 10 *yuan* guided tours; in the revolving restaurant which crowns the building, the open-mouthed tourists would file by and gawp as you downed your gritty coffee. In 1982, the plaster and timberwork in the rooms were crudely finished, with all the marks of peasant labour. But now, two years on, the interiors of our guest rooms were all re-modelled to international standards. The Chinese were already rolling quickly along the road of modern skyscraper construction, a skill in which they would soon be world champions.

SHIFTING GEARS IN CHINA

The following morning, we were at my old haunt, Nanjing University, now a very different place from Cultural Revolution days. I'd been back in Nanjing only once or twice since leaving there in 1977, and this time the air of openness was palpable. In those bad old days few colleagues would risk stepping an inch out of line with a foreigner. Now, just a few short years after the new regime had installed itself, you could actually have a sensible and wide-ranging discussion with academics, which though still limited by what might be sayable to foreigners was nonetheless a breath of fresh air. I went off to find the Foreign Languages Department in the far corner of the campus where our office had been; it was, in Cultural Revolution days, approached through a doorway above which was placed a colour portrait of Mao — presumably to ward off any evil spirits which might come in the train of we barbarians. Now I was able to have an informal chat with some of the new and ambitious breed of students, and almost two decades after leaving Nanjing University I found a couple of my old colleagues in the same offices. I rejoined my fellow delegates to stage another showing of the SANA nuclear winter film. Included in the audience, thoughtfully on the part of the University, were staff and students of the meteorology department. Discussion was limited and it was clear that the subject was entirely new to our viewers. But we were glad to be able to spread the word a little further, and, what's more, to some of China's best educated youth.

We were taken the next day to meet more scientists at the provincial Academy of Agricultural Sciences, as well as the Institute of Application of Nuclear Sciences in Agriculture. The staff had clearly been primed to emphasise China's peaceful use of the atom. The female director of the Genetics Radiation lab presented a slide show of their work, always emphasising the point. On our part, we hammered away again on the nuclear winter theme.

Then we had a short (political) tourism break. First, we were given a pleasant boat trip down the Yangtze, which allowed our hosts to impress upon us the wonders of that surviving icon of the Cultural Revolution, the great two-tier Nanjing Yangtze River Bridge. Later we were taken to Nanjing's Purple Mountain, where we climbed the 392 steps to the mausoleum of Sun Yat-sen. Whether they be in the Mainland, Hong Kong or Taiwan, just about all Chinese agree that Sun Yat-sen is a kind of founding father of China's modern statehood. Thus even during the Cultural Revolution, Red Guards and others proclaiming their purest proletarian credentials saw no problem in paying obeisance at Sun's tomb. I've climbed those steps many times (and the first time in 1973); my Chinese Party friends have always been a little coy about the question of what happened to the body, some hinting that the Nationalists spirited it away when they fled to Taiwan.

After burning off some of those extra banquet kilos on Purple Mountain, we returned to the city for a significant encounter with the officials preparing a new museum to be created in Nanjing to commemorate those hundreds of thousands slaughtered indiscriminately by the Japanese army when it entered what was then China's capital. I think the idea behind this meeting was to demonstrate to us that like the peoples of the Soviet Union, the Chinese know a thing or two about the horrors of war, and even being nuclear armed, their government would do all in its power never to have to use such weapons. Certainly, 'no first use' was a central part of the official doctrine which we heard time and time again. A far larger and hugely impressive memorial hall later replaced the 1985 building, completed in 1995 and designed by China's most prestigious architects. I visited it not long since in the company of my former tutor and friend from my Bristol

University days of the late 1960s—the world-renowned exponent of Marxian political-economy, David Harvey.

After Nanjing, we took the train eastwards to Shanghai for a couple of days of serious discussions, firstly at the Institute of International Studies where we were apprised yet again of the official position on China's nuclear arsenal. Once again, our hosts were keen to press home the point that China's weapons were inconsequential in comparison with those of the four other (official) nuclear armed nations—it was always 'our 5% to their 95%'. The next day we were at the Shanghai branch of the Chinese Academy of Sciences to meet research fellows in the fields of optic fibres, plant physiology and atomic energy. The peaceful use of nuclear energy and China's stance on non-proliferation were the themes once more impressed upon us. Beginning to feel a little cynical about the repetition, we relaxed that night in the Peace Hotel. With Janet B on the guitar and a superfluity of local wine we let our hair down with a sing-song—a raucous quasi-blues in which '95%' was the refrain.

After yet another acrobatics show, and a visit to one of Shanghai's Neighbourhood Committees, we took the overnight train back to the capital. A visit to Beijing University's Department of International Relations gave us the opportunity to explain what was going on in Western Europe, and why the siting of new classes of weapons was such a dangerous and retrograde move. Schooled as they'd been for two decades in anti-Sovietism, the questions from our large audience demonstrated a stubborn scepticism. That afternoon, however, an unexpected item was inserted into our programme, which turned out to be the most significant encounter of our entire visit to China. Twelve very senior scientists from the Chinese Nuclear Association, the Energy Research Association, the Ministry of Nuclear Industry, the Chinese Academy of Sciences, the Nuclear

Dynamics Committee and Beijing and Qinghua Universities were assembled at the guesthouse. The purpose seemed to be to give *us* a stern lecture on the theme of the nuclear winter, as though we'd never heard of it. The way in which the theses of our SANA film were regurgitated back to us was all but comical. Encouraging though, too. It appeared that something might after all have stuck.

As the assembly broke up, I idly picked up some papers which had been left on a chair. One turned out to be a briefing on the background, party allegiances and position within CND of each of the five of us. Re-reading this Chinese document today, I'm amused to discover that Chinese 'intelligence' was as lacking as I'd always hoped. Under my name I discovered things about me which had never happened, Chinese universities where I'd never been engaged. On a more serious note, the accompanying two-page document listed nine briefing points to be used as rebuttals, or at least as hard questions, regarding CND's policies. Point no. 7, for example, asked:

> Why should we have invited CND to visit China? CND currently opposes the British government's nuclear policy. Though we've invited CND to visit China, China supports the independence and unity of the European nations.

The implication was that Western Europe could only guarantee its independence (from the Soviet Union — unsaid) if Britain and France hung on to their nuclear arms and acquiesced to the wishes of Washington. Such was the *idée fixe* of the Chinese state a quarter of a century after the end of its messy alliance with the Soviet Union, and fifteen years since the deathly clashes between the two countries on their Siberian border. This despite

China's Korean War experience, and the devastation visited by the United States upon nations hardly a stone's throw from China. Those resisting vassal status — Cuba, Iran, Venezuela, and now of course Russia and China too — have had to be willing to pay a very high price. It's now over 40 years since normalisation between Beijing and Washington, yet only very recently have the geopolitical rules by which the United States lives and breathes sunk into the consciousness of those at China's power pyramid.

On our penultimate day in Beijing, my annotated itinerary declares: 'We were provided with a wide-ranging presentation on China's political-economy since 1949, and elaboration of current reforms in agriculture and industry, given by a Deputy Director of the State Economic Commission'. Well, you couldn't fault our Chinese hosts — they'd now given us the works. I thoroughly approved of the effort to present the political-economic background, though of course just as in Britain, the 'reforms' China proudly had in train were in reality an invitation to that chill wind called 'the market'.

The final Beijing day was the occasion for a further surprise. Mao's regular exhortation of the 1970s: 'Dig tunnels deep, store grain everywhere and never seek hegemony' (*shen wa dong, guang zhi liang, bu cheng ba*) reflected his simplistic view that China could guard against a nuclear attack in much the way that in the battles of the past his forces had survived conventional warfare. In a vast national enterprise, huge quantities of building materials and labour were utilised to create a network of underground chambers and passages where the population could pursue a troglodytic life after a nuclear attack. Around the campus of Nanjing University were dotted the steel doors to the tunnels which the students and staff had spent their energies burrowing out after the 1969 Sino-Soviet border war. I'd long suspected that just like the U.K. government's *Protect and Survive* foolishness of the early 1980s, there could be little science behind Chinese air-raid preparations. Even worse, above ground housing and urban infrastructure was starved of funds throughout the Mao period, and as I analysed in my 1985 book, *Urbanisation in China* they fell into considerable disarray.[9]

We were never invited to peer under our Nanjing campus, but now in Beijing, we callow and naiive Western anti-nuclear campaigners were to be shown Beijing's civil nuclear defence preparations. We entered the No. 1 Department Store in Beijing's 'Oxford Street', Wangfujing. A female manager guided us to a roomy lift and we descended under the city, though how deeply we had no idea. We stepped out into a wide tiled corridor, its ceiling with ventilation ducts, and were guided along some long passages past thick steel doors with wheel-locks. 'That's a hospital and operating theatre,' our guide announced. Through more steel doors we stood above a large auditorium with banks of seats falling away to a stage. Could these vast burrows withstand 500 tonne bombs, let alone an all-out nuclear attack? How about the sucking out of all oxygen by the inevitable firestorm? Built under every settlement in the country, large or small, this was in all likelihood a gargantuan folly, a crazed waste of scarce resources. Mao's successors apparently took that view, as soon after his death the Chinese media were regaling us with stories about Beijing's overcrowded accommodation for out-of-towners being supplemented by dormitories in the now 'former' air-raid caverns.

Official Chinese hospitality is much about switching foreign guests' moods. Few have failed to be charmed by an assembly of Chinese youngsters: the day's excursion ended in a kindergarten, which couldn't have been further than the

---

9   *Urbanization in China: Town and Country in a Developing Economy, 1949 – 2000 AD*, 3rd edition, London: Taylor and Francis, 2018.

subterranean experience of the morning. After that, we got ourselves ready for the farewell *yanhui*, as the Chinese call their lavish celebratory dinners. We were surprised to be once more chauffeured to the broad steps on the east side of that great neoclassical and pillared edifice dating from 1958, the Great Hall of the People on Tiananmen Square. The company awaiting us comprised the full complement of CAFIU executives, with a few senior Beijing University professors thrown in. The occasion's host, Zhu Xuefan, led us courteously into the building. I noted that his business card was festooned with high official positions: Vice-Chairman of the National People's Congress, Chairman of the Revolutionary Committee of the Guomindang (KMT), for starters. This latter was, and to this day remains, one of the eight parties with a token existence during the bad years; by the early 1980s it was again tolerated, encouraged even, by the ruling Communist Party. Of the eight, the Revolutionary Guomindang is in fact by far the most prominent, today with a membership well into six figures. Claiming the mantle of Sun Yat-sen's original Nationalist Party, and dominated by high-ranking 'intellectuals' (some of whom were known to me), I think it's fair to say that this grouping isn't entirely without influence.

Perhaps just in my honour of my years in the province, the Great Hall finale was staged in its Jiangsu Chamber, a space dominated by a huge painting of the Yangtze River Bridge. In de-mob mood, we saw off a couple of dozen dishes of delicate southern cuisine and raised our glasses of strong sorghum liquor until defeated.

The following day, and after yet another BBC interview, we were on our flight back to London. Just one further duty called: a press conference was staged at a Bloomsbury hotel. Worn out by two weeks of solicitous hospitality and meetings, not to mention the jetlag, we nonetheless managed to put together a statement which summarised our meetings and then cut to the chase:

> The Chinese government holds to its 1964 unilateral declaration that it would never be the first to use nuclear weapons or to use nuclear weapons against a non-nuclear state or nuclear-free zone. As the USSR has subsequently made a similar declaration, CND calls on NATO, the U.S.A., Britain and France to make a similar commitment. China's earlier stance was that they would only be prepared to take part in any nuclear disarmament negotiations if the U.S.A. and USSR had already made a reduction of 50 percent in their nuclear arsenals. They would now accept 'substantial reductions' as a precondition.

So much for CND's efforts to spread the word eastward in 1984. Forty years on, and China remains a nuclear-armed state, though no longer one of just five in the world. Israel, India, Pakistan have been added to the original list, raising the stakes so much higher. The Soviet Union is long gone, and the Warsaw Pact with it. But not, very much not, NATO, led by an ever-aggressive United States. Had not the U.S. vowed to destroy five nation states in seven years? Since our 1984 mission, an almost ceaseless series of imperial wars have been waged, with utter destruction wrought on Afghanistan, Iraq, Libya and Syria. None of these conflicts seemed to risk escalation into nuclear war. Not so with Obama's 'pivot to Asia'; according to John Pilger in his documentary, *The Coming War on China*, the United States has half-circled China with dozens of missile bases. The Trump and Biden administrations, in thrall to that military-industrial complex against which Eisenhower warned so very long ago, have stretched tensions to new heights. Meanwhile, China has significantly developed its nuclear missiles and particularly its anti-missile technologies, and by all accounts is capable of efficient defence and, in the worst-case scenario, of a belligerent response to any attack. Moreover, the hostility between China and Russia has long since evaporated. What was inconceivable in 1984 was that the relentless U.S. pressure on China would bring Beijing and Russia together in a tacit mutual self-defence pact, a matter which one fervently hopes will give pause to the war parties of the West. And this chapter was almost all written well before the present proxy war between the United States and Russia — and by tacit extension with China too, in Ukraine.

VI
TURTLE SOUP (1989)

IT ALL STARTED to fall into place at London's great Olympia exhibition hall. Some bright spark had decided to stage an export fair of Chinese goods, and there I encountered Lily Wu, a woman of poise and soft-cheeked beauty, though she must have long since seen her fortieth birthday. It was late Spring of 1989, and the for the moment, the lively scenes of protest in Beijing and the warming weather of London seemed to offer a world of promise. But not, apparently, for Lily Wu, who seemed rather short on deals.

I wandered the almost deserted aisles of the exhibition and thought to myself that the few bemused natives peering at the displays weren't there by design at all. It was just somewhere to go to get away from the Spring showers. As I loitered along, trying to look sufficiently detached to deter the stall holders from pouncing with offers I'd have to refuse, Lily engaged me with a smile and the slight bow of the cultured Chinese. I glanced past her at her stall—an eclectic display of glass phials of anonymous minerals, yellowing plastic containers of patent medicines with their usual promises in that quaint English which is the preserve of Chinese advertisements, devilish-looking electronic gadgetry for acupuncture, woven bamboo baskets, and ...little trays of blue-black rock. Despite myself I was brought to a sudden halt. Lily registered my gaze and mouthed the single word *banshi*. Yes, 'stone slabs' indeed, but ones with a special significance.

In my Sheffield office, where I had the unlikely task of connecting the rusting industry of the north of England with the up-and-coming Chinese economy, I'd been sought out by Alan and his blinged-up lump of a son, Darren. Alan's working life had begun as an entrepreneurial recycling merchant, or what we used to call a rag-and-bone man. Moving on to bigger things, Alan bought an old flatbed truck, and got himself a yard in a corner of central Leeds which the council seemed to have forgotten. By the early 1980s, the crash in British manufacturing meant that all over the north, hundreds, maybe thousands of 19th century mills and factories were being razed; Alan would grab anything with a scrap price, from roofing lead to cast iron railings.

Yet in the transformation of Britain's landscape from industry to hackneyed consumption, the late 1980s was also building-boom time. Mock 19th century homes with their patios and porches, 'heritage centres' and supermarkets aping medieval chapter houses were springing up all over. The new fashion was for slate roofs, and the meagre output of the old quarries in Wales and the Lake District just couldn't supply enough. So those in the know, Alan included, made sure the wrecker's ball only started to swing once the slate had been carefully rescued from the doomed mills. As others got in on the game, Alan found that he could join a faster league by importing slate from places like Spain.

Even that wasn't going to meet the huge demand at the right price, and by the time I got there, amongst the jumble of Alan's Steptoe-yard were several coarse wooden crates bearing most exotic markings. Unlikely though it was, some importer was getting their hands on the cheapest and best hand-cut product, all the way from China. Scrap dealers abhor middle-men: they head straight for the source. As for our Alan, he would go one better. Forget about simply buying foreign slate—he would trounce the competition by buying his own slate mine. In China! And the person to make this happen was, apparently, myself.

Lily was excited. Her first potential customer in two days and he was talking big. Her little bits of black and grey *banshi* (for Lily knew no English) came from the largest and finest deposits, she assured me. Indeed, back home she had a certificate from a famous German geologist, the famous Mr Gu-luo-se-man, who'd declared her slate heap in the mountains of Shaanxi province to be the best in the world. She could arrange everything. We only needed to come. The deal was ours. Back in Leeds, Alan and Darren scrutinised Lily's samples and declared themselves happy men.

In no time at all, a determined party of slate hunters was winging its way to Hong Kong. Alan, son Darren, their friend Paul, and me. Hong Kong promised to be something of a cultural experience, for none of my travelling companions had ventured overseas, unless you count a couple of trips to the fish and chips and tankard beer of the Spanish Costa resorts. I didn't quite know how to handle our lads from Yorkshire in the perfumed crush of downtown Kowloon, and when they dived into the nearest thing to a British pub and began to confuse their jet-lag with high pressure beer, I thought it all for the best. At least we weren't propelled, as I'd feared we would be, towards the sleazy and unrewarding clip-joints of Wanchai.

My experiences in getting from Hong Kong to the China of Mao were vividly engraved. In those days, you'd take a slow train from the very tip of Kowloon to the border, and trip over a lightly guarded bridge to the other side where China's handsome five-starred flag stirred in the breeze. After a leisurely lunch, you'd then proceed with the obligatory guide towards Guangzhou, and after a night's rest in a soft bed with mosquito net it would be onward to the north.

By the late 1980s, with air services between Hong Kong and China's larger provincial capitals, all this was in the past. Indeed, our destination of Xi'an had several flights a day, for it was the location of China's new and magnificent tourist attraction, the subterranean terracotta regiments of the Qin Emperor. On the four-hour flight to the old military field at Xi'an, our little band was tagged onto a tour group of elderly folk from Taiwan, for the first time returning to the province they'd fled forty years earlier. I ignored my slate men and made friends with these interesting old timers. During my earlier times in China, only those 'Taiwan compatriots' who'd declared for Beijing had been allowed into the Mainland. There, they'd be regaled with lion dances, drums and cymbals, and all the exaggerated fanfare reserved for political prodigals. But now anyone from Taiwan was welcome for their money, and all they could expect was regimented tourism and envious glances. As the aircraft coursed over sparkling paddies, huge silvery rivers and dry hills towards China's northwest, the Taiwan contingent offered around their favourite dried beef snacks, while plying me with tales of life before the 'Communist bandits'.

Xi'an airport hadn't changed a lot since my first visit, sixteen years earlier. Yet the atmosphere in China promised to be unrecognisable. Already in this year of 1989, the year of Tiananmen Square, for some weeks mass demonstrations had been staged throughout the country. And by pure chance, we'd arrived in Xi'an on the most prescient protest date in the Chinese calendar. The Taiwan-based Nationalists and their Communist adversaries agreed on very little. But both sides commemorated the greatest, the most significant marker of China's modern nationhood. We'd entered China on May 4th — seventy years to the day since Beijing's youth had rallied to denounce the insults heaped on their country at the close of the First World War. Then, the Western powers and their Versailles Treaty had ejected the defeated Germans from Shandong, and shamelessly handed over the province to the Japanese.

Now, on May 4th 1989, the China that greeted me boded ill. As my new Taiwan companions handed in their health declarations and shoved their way through a ramshackle barrier, I was pulled to one side by a member of the border police.

'Do you have video?' he asked officiously. Unusually, I was carrying a couple of these suspect items, as an engineering company back home had asked me to do them a favour. They had a potential sale in Xi'an, and I was to pass on some technical tapes. The stern-faced officer in his new-style braided uniform with a funny high-peaked cap took the video tapes, gave me a receipt and said he'd deliver them to the hotel within a day. I rejoined my travelling companions in the bustling concourse just at the moment that a worried-looking Lily appeared.

With introductions out of the way, Lily whispered nervously in my ear. We were likely, she was saying, to be held up at the airport for quite some time, as protestors had surrounded the city centre where our hotel lay. 'It will be dangerous', Lily assured me. So there we sat, until Lily and I agreed on a plan. Instead of the limousines lined up outside, she'd get hold of an old locally made minibus, and we'd hide ourselves behind its drawn curtains and get ourselves into town. An hour later, we were being deposited at the entrance of that massive 1950s complex built by the Russians, the Xi'an Hotel.

I'd never witnessed the Chinese in rebellion and was impatient to get out and observe the action for myself. But without my companions, who'd have no idea what they were getting into. The slate men had accepted my mumbled explanation for our unorthodox journey from the airport—every so often the air resounded with roars of a distant crowd and I'd mentioned something about a football mob. I hared off in the direction of the noise, but was brought up by a familiar Yorkshire yell: 'Hey, where'er you off to, son?' I'd been rumbled, and waited crossly for my three companions to catch up with me. A hundred yards from the hotel, we turned into a large square, partly grassed over, where the roar was magnified tenfold. In a large expanse of green in front of a new office complex were gathered some thousands of chanting demonstrators.

Pushing my way into the nearest knot of protestors, I found myself amongst students from the famous Jiaotong University. The throng had surrounded a grand hall in the centre of the square and, according to the students, within and effectively under siege were the provincial chiefs. The demonstration was good-humoured, and I indulged in a little banter, fielding the usual barrage of questions about myself. These young people seemed conscious that the outside world was watching China and its unprecedented street dramas. A Westerner speaking Chinese always brought a crush of inquisitive onlookers, and the usual buzz went down the line of 'What did the foreigner just say?'

Flying in to this spectacle was all very exciting. But I'd temporarily forgotten that protests or not, this was still China, and it wasn't long before my tactless presence had come to the notice of less well-disposed onlookers. Suddenly my mini-crowd dissolved and I was staring up at a large, blue-uniformed policeman.

'What are you saying to these people?' he barked at me in perfect English. 'Who are you? Give me your passport.'

I declared also, of course, in English, that I was no more than an innocent businessman and that my passport was with the Provincial Public Security Foreign Affairs Office, as our host Madame Wu intended to take us tomorrow morning into a restricted zone.

'That cannot be true because I am the Chief of Security in

Xi'an's Foreign Affairs Office, and I have never heard of such a thing. And I am the only person to issue a special travel pass for foreigners.'

As I tried to convince him that at this very moment Lily Wu was probably searching for him to deliver our passports, I realised that I'd put my foot in it. My camera had been shoved into an outside pocket but the strap was dangling out and the policeman spotted it. Lunging at me, he grabbed the instrument, and with me still hanging onto the strap raised his trophy to the gathering crowd of onlookers.

'You have been taking photographs. You must give me the film.'

I could see that I wasn't going to get away with this and let go of the cord.

'You have the camera so please get the film yourself,' I brazenly replied. This turned out to be unfair to the poor man, as he couldn't work out how to click open the film compartment. The crowd had encircled us again and looked on derisively. The policeman was becoming flustered.

If this were to go on any longer, it would have become a matter of face, and things might go badly for me. I grabbed back the camera and ripped out the film, tossing the ruined celluloid into the air. At this the crowd erupted in mirth, closing round the officer. I thrust through them and legged it. From a distance my friends had observed this little drama, and I yelled at them to keep pace with me back to the haven of our hotel compound. This wasn't a good start; I was in a state of high anxiety, terrified that my foolish indiscretions might have fouled the chances of getting our travel passes. But I'd reckoned without the power of Lily. After a tense supper, our hostess appeared with four passports, each with an insert authorising special entry into the military zone of the Qinling Mountains. The great slate day was just a few hours away.

We were roused before four the next morning and descended the hotel's curving stair to the lobby, where Lily awaited us with two characters in dark glasses whom we hadn't seen before: security men. Outside in the cold, vehicles were puffing out steamy fumes. I assumed that the shiny and well-shod Toyota Land Cruiser would be for Lily and her foreign guests, while the hangers-on would make do with a battered Chinese minibus, a creature which all Chinese know as a 'bread-bus' due to its loaf-like shape. This one I appraised with jaded eyes: as usual, some of the sliding windows were just jagged panes through which torn lace curtains hung. I was astonished when Lily and her two cohorts climbed into the cosy, well-sprung Land Cruiser, and her honoured foreign friends were waved into the uninviting bread-bus.

Naturally the moment this trip was announced I'd done my best to find out exactly where we'd be heading. Lily's reply was invariably: 'Not far.' Just outside Xi'an.' And soon we were racing south through Xi'an's deserted boulevards and into the semi-rural outskirts, on a pancake-flat loess plain, our driver with his foot hard down in an effort to follow the faster vehicle ahead. Peering down the aisle in the pre-dawn gloom, I could just detect the outline of a formidable wall of mountains. I decided that just as Lily said, we had to be almost at our destination, which would be some quarry against the nearside of this natural barrier.

Reaching the foot of the mountain wall, our two vehicles started to climb a zigzagging and increasingly precarious route. The whining engine of the bread-bus drowned out any thought of conversation, and I concentrated on shielding myself from the icy mountain blasts. After an age of hairpin bends we were at last at the summit, and as the gears eased off, I clambered forward and asked our driver how high we'd climbed. *'Hen gao'* – 'very high', he chuckled as he lit up yet another cigarette, oblivious to the jerry cans of spare diesel slopping by his side.

Not to worry, I told myself, our destination had to be just down the other side. It was time for breakfast and I delved in the cardboard box supplied by the hotel. Inside was the familiar foreigners' packed meal of pickled vegetables, a chicken leg, curly white bread, and a hard-boiled egg crowned by a crumbly slice of dry cake. My companions took one look and then tossed their boxes out of the window. I was beginning to wonder how I'd manage to maintain them in anything like a placid state.

Meanwhile, the Land Cruiser had taken off and was winding through the hairpins far below us. Away we careered in chase and by the first screeching corner our driver had shoved the gears into neutral and perhaps was calculating the amount of diesel he would be later selling on the side. By the next elbow we were chasing along at tyre-screeching speeds, and in self-preservation I wedged myself between a seat frame and a couple of ten-gallon fuel cans and prayed that the valley below would rise up quickly to meet us. Overladen trucks lurched and rolled as we hurtled by them, horn ablaze.

By and by, every few hundred yards, shaggy haired mountain children stood by the road wielding thick hose pipes of bamboo, jets of water arching over the tarmac. It took me a while to work out that the pipes were gravity fed, their upper ends dipped in torrents which then tumbled through culverts below the road. Their purpose was even more mysterious, until I saw ahead of us a truck parked by the roadside and water being played on their steaming brake drums.

'Bloody 'ell! 'Ave you seen that,' was the comment from my friends. My own thoughts were merely a silent prayer to the gods of the Chinese brake-lining industry.

We'd descended into a long U-shaped valley where the road

ran in a gradual gradient beside a rushing river. After an hour or so the valley widened and the road and river curled around it more lazily. On the exposed sandbanks, small knots of men could be seen sifting through the gravel.

'Look, they've got to be panning for gold. Get the driver to stop!' yelled Darren.

'Oh yeah — let's have a slate mine and a goldmine too,' I muttered under my breath. But the Land Cruiser ahead forged relentlessly on, and our driver wasn't to be diverted from his manly task of keeping pace. Another hour passed, and by now the sun was reaching for its highest point. My companions were becoming restless, and wry comments were in the air. I pretended not to hear, fixing my gaze through the window at the rushing landscape.

'Thought you said it would be a short trip to't slate mine,' Alan turned to me accusingly.

'I've only told you what Lily's told me,' I returned plaintively as we hurtled onwards.

Darren, who'd climbed into the front seat the better to observe the gold prospecting, suddenly screamed back to us, 'Hey, there's another bugger right ahead of us — surely we're not...'
He covered his eyes with his hands and I realised that he wasn't just putting on an act. Right enough, ahead in the broad valley floor loomed another mountain wall, even more fearsome than the first.

'No, it'll be OK. We'll be turning off soon down some track, and then we'll be there,' I said to myself. Not likely. Once more the engine began to grind and we were heading upwards to the first of a succession of hairpins and back into the mists.

This time the relentless Land Cruiser had allowed a stop at the summit, where a waymark declared that we were now at almost two-and-a-half thousand metres. We fell out into thin air swathed in a freezing fog. Lily had produced an expensive fur coat and was pretending to savour the view. Alan and Darren glowered at her and shivered in their thin jackets. By now I was getting annoyed myself: it was time to put the screws on Lily.

'Please tell me how far it is to the slate mine,' I addressed her grimly. Lily smiled her sweetest and most innocent smile and for the first of many times that day mouthed the words, '*Kuai daole*' — 'Nearly there now'. I gave up, and gazed out at the mountain peaks which all around us pierced the layer of whirling clouds.

Our anticipation made the second great descent even more unnerving. The unmistakable stench of overheated brakes soon wafted through the bus, and risking my neck by looking out of the window, I was sure that I could actually see sparks coming out of the rear wheel. We pulled off the road by a fire-douser, who for a few *fen* gave our wheels the bamboo hose treatment. Now we needed to go even faster to catch up, and with a few more hair-raising switchbacks we were soon down in another great U-shaped valley, following another fast-flowing river.

My companions had given up complaining and seemed to have resigned themselves to whatever transpired. Limbs at all angles, they were catching up on their sleep. It was now well past midday and I settled into a daze, my watch showing two o'clock, two-thirty, three — we charged relentlessly onward after the Land Cruiser.

Then something new. Around a bend, a settlement of some sort announced itself, and in a couple of minutes we were at busy market crossroads. Scattering the peddlers' handcarts we pulled into a walled caravanserai-type compound. Lined up to greet us was a whole posse of rustic-looking local cadres, with whom Lily was already conducting an animated discussion.

This was no chance halt and I felt a rising anger that Lily had kept me in the dark. When you venture onto someone else's patch in China you have to play the role of humble and obedient guest. With a sinking heart I understood that what little measure of control we'd had with Lily was now to be wrested from us by these new hosts. Lily turned to me and made some introductions. I must have looked appalled, for Lily took me on one side to explain.

'You are the first foreign friends these people have ever seen and they want to give you very special treatment,' she said in a tone of finality.

'But how about the famous German geologist, your friend, who'd been here recently to check out the slate?' I wanted to know.

'I am sorry,' confessed Lily, 'I have not met Mr Gu-luo-se-man myself.'

'But when was he here?' I insisted.

'I did not bring him to see the slate,' Lily stated flatly.

'But his scientific analysis of the slate mountain?' I insisted.

'I was told he wrote about that in an American magazine, in 1929,' was Lily's sheepish whisper, as she turned with an exaggerated little bow towards our new commanders.

'What the bloody 'ell's going on now, lad? Let's get on to 't slate, for Christ's sake,' said an angry looking Alan.

My exchange with Lily had been in Chinese and it was lost on my companions. I had no intention of enlightening them. There was no doubt about it. The local chieftains were obliged to subject their important guests to a fulsome round of Chinese hospitality. It was clear from Lily's demeanour — alternately stern to us and charming to the officials — that there was to be no quick departure. We were ushered into a low building within the courtyard. Here the local chieftains, all politeness, signalled us to be seated around a large, unadorned disk of plywood. At that, Lily, her underlings and the locals just disappeared. For the best part of an hour we were left in the company of three plaited-haired peasant lasses, who plied us with hot towels, saucers of aromatic peanuts and bottles of a watery local beer. They watched over us with studied indifference, while I kept wondering how they'd deal with the ogling that came from Darren's direction. Meanwhile, the beer was greedily drunk, but the anaesthetic effect that I'd hoped for failed to appear. With every glass my charges seemed to be a little more agitated. But there was no way I could even start to explain what we were doing, plonked around at a huge round table at four o'clock in the afternoon, eleven hours into our journey and with not a whiff of slate.

Just when things were beginning to look very awkward for me, Lily and the town cadres returned, red-faced from their own pre-prandial drinking session. Seating themselves, our new hosts gestured towards the doorway, animated not merely by alcohol but by some unfathomable pleasurable expectation. Through the plastic lattice screen came one of the serving girls, her arms stretched around an enamel washbowl, the kind of thing which you'd find on a wooden stand in any country hostelry. The vessel was centred carefully before us, and the beaming pride of our hosts was matched by the appalled countenances of the slate seekers. Swimming in isolated splendour in a circle of watery liquid was an entire turtle, head, tail, flippers, carapace and all.

A man in his fifties with tight blue jacket and a reddened face took the chief host's seat—in China always easy to distinguish as it's in the 'safest' spot opposite the main entrance. He fell upon the bowl with his chopsticks, and flicking over the carapace started delving in the innards. Before Alan, Darren and Paul knew it, their saucers were filled with a cocktail of small bones, cartilage and bits of stringy brown flesh. Thankfully, at that moment a couple of the waiting girls thrust into the little room to deliver a large pile of steaming *mantou* and little plates of spinach. At least there was something to appear busy with. But of course, as soon as the first morsels had passed their lips, the obligatory speechifying began. In turn, the four local cadres delivered their effusive welcomes, addressed as much to Lily as to her foreign captives. As ever, the toasts concluding each speech demanded another tot of the local clear spirits, and after a short while even the special guests were suitably befuddled and standing on cue for each toast.

'What the fuck *is* this stuff, lad?' enquired Alan as he downed another glassful. The thing about Chinese *baijiu* — white lightning as I call it — is that if you can get through the first two or three glasses it becomes a pleasant and unstoppable experience.

I couldn't fail to notice that the cadre's superlatives were directed towards Lily as much as to me and the slate men. More than once, I heard praise being lavished on one 'Deputy Secretary Li'. Emboldened by the drink, I politely addressed Lily:

'Madame Wu, may I ask you who this Deputy Party Secretary Li is?' Herself having supped beyond the point of Chinese modesty, our Lily declared loudly that Mr Li was none other than her father.

'And what does your respected father do?' I enquired. In a theatrical whisper, Lily mouthed 'He is the deputy governor of our Shaanxi province.'

All was now falling into place. Lily's unlikely promises of unhindered business deals — the one hundred percent purchase by foreigners of mineral rights was certainly beyond anything I'd heard possible — and her ease in insinuating foreign devils into a restricted military zone meant only one thing. Big connections! So our Lily and her old man, deputy boss to a province larger than many nations, were planning to be pioneers in the exciting new game of entrepreneurialism.

The rituals of drinking and toasting continued unabated

amongst the four locals and Lily. I'd played this particular game many times before but now I could only think of the mounting wrath of my Yorkshire crew. Lily's enthusiasm for her local cadre band was slackening. The day was dwindling. I spotted her peeping at her diamond encrusted timepiece before rising to a fulsome toast to the town's leaders, their families, their extended families, to Deng Xiaoping, to our fine business prospects together. I enthusiastically chimed in with my own platitudes and a final *ganbei*, and this time Lily and I remained on our feet in a clear signal that the merrymaking was at an end.

Leaving behind an empty turtle shell sitting on an upturned washbowl and a room spattered with tiny bones, our hosts steered us back to the minibus, and a moment later we were reversing out of the compound gates.

The motorcade had more than doubled in size. The town officials had mustered a black Russian saloon while their lesser brethren rode in a couple of Beijing jeeps, the sturdy vehicle with a robustness only matched by the flimsiness of its interior furnishings. Off we sped in the same general direction as ever, on a metalled road with the dashing river to our right in the broadening valley. Through the windscreen I spied yet a third sheer valley end. The backlash from the liquor was already creeping in, and I detected a new mood of sullen resignation amongst my charges. But not far out of the town, something new happened. Our jeep-pathfinder sheered off the main road into a side valley. After a few hundred yards the rough way became a stony grassed path and we drew to a halt.

As our party started out on foot, the sun still played brightly on the sloping valley floor but was dipping alarmingly towards the nearest escarpment.

'Soon be there,' smiled Lily for the thousandth time.

From time to time we passed a rough cottage, each one

roofed in great slabs of grey-blue stone. Never before in China had I seen anything like this. The three professional slate hunters looked interested and cheered up a little. We strolled onwards and upwards. The landscape put me in mind of an English dale, except that our little party was now joined by a gaggle of shaven-haired Chinese youngsters who chaffed around us. Alan, Darren and Paul walked in silence, their usual collective demeanour of disdain now one of growing expectation. The advance knot made up of the local cadres and Lily came to a halt. Ahead was a rough gate and the end of any path. A grassed-over hillock the size of a small Egyptian pyramid loomed immediately in front of us. Lily turned triumphantly to the slate men of Yorkshire. This was it! This is what the famous Gu-luo-se-man had discovered. We'd finally arrived at that pot of gold at the end of the rainbow.

Alan's face fell. He clambered over the wall. To my amazement, one of our cadre companions thrust a large hammer into his hand. Alan climbed up a few yards and started to violently scrape the ground free of grass and shrubs. His efforts revealed nothing but dark earth, and a few chips of rock. He turned to us with a groan.

'This lot must be bloody joking,' he exclaimed. 'Where's the mechanical digger? We need a jack hammer, at the very least! What the bloody 'ell do they think we can learn from this?'

I felt an urgent need to disappear. The sun had dipped behind the slate mountain and a chill was in the air. Shuffling over to Lily's side I told her in no uncertain terms that the only thing to do was to stay the night back in the town. Then we could come out again and conduct more thorough investigations, preferably with a fully equipped team of workmen. Darren and Paul caught on to what was passing between Lily and me, and loudly seconded the motion. Lily's usual benign expression this time failed her completely. A frozen-faced 'No, it is impossible' was all that would pass her lips. By this time, Alan had hopped back over the gate, and I could see he was in the kind of black mood which would soon have him waving his hammer right in Lily's face.

Once again, I pleaded with Lily to arrange some local accommodation. 'Just one night would do!' I repeated. Apart from anything else, dusk had now fallen, and the prospect of a twelve-hour drive back to Xi'an in darkness had unnerved me. Though the inclination of the Chinese official on occasions such as this is normally to equivocate, Lily's 'No' continued to be firm and clear.

'But why not?' I pleaded. 'These local bosses are really friendly and I'm sure they'll have room in their *zhaodaisuo*.' I was referring to the guest house for visiting cadres and out-of-sight banqueting which every self-respecting work unit possessed. Lily looked contrite. 'We cannot stay out here overnight because your special travel permits only allow us one day, and absolutely no nights,' she told me—though given her powerful father it seemed more likely to me that she wanted home comforts rather than some barren dormitory.

'But why, Lily?' I choked. 'Didn't you know how far this place is from Xi'an?' There was no response, but it suddenly came to me: Lily herself had never strayed into these parts before. Even worse. Her acquaintance with the business of slate, or for that matter any business, was as remote as the Qinling Mountains.

Just as I was resigning myself to the horror of the mountain switchbacks ahead, not to mention the retribution of the slate-men, the chief local host withdrew from his jacket a sheaf of handwritten notes. Now he launched into another speech of welcome, a cataloguing of the virtues of his patch, the economic progress past and foreseen, and the unchallengeable place of *his* slate mountain within the great pantheon of slate mountains. As he began an involved explanation about the construction of a railhead some eighty kilometres distant, just to handle the great slate exports as they trundled towards England's shores, I noticed Darren and his dad edging around the circle.

During the lecture, the drivers had inched their vehicles up the grassy track and parked just down from us. I could see the Yorkshire slate delegates had now positioned themselves as near as possible to the luxurious Land Cruiser. At some mutually understood signal, they made a concerted dash towards the vehicle, leaping into the back and slamming shut the door.

It was every man for himself. Lily proved herself no slouch either. She grasped the hand of the astonished, stuttering chief and slipped into the front of the Land Cruiser alongside the two security men. The driver indicated the vehicle's tailgate, stuffed though it was with coils of oily rope and a couple of sacks of some local produce, no doubt picked up in the town to be sold on back in Xi'an. There was just enough room to squeeze in crosswise with my legs tightly bent at all their joints. Within seconds, all the vehicles except our forlorn bus were occupied and we commenced a tricky retreat, in reverse gear, towards the grassy turning place some hundreds of yards below. When each had completed the manoeuvre, the convoy sped off back towards the town.

The locals squealed through the gates into the township HQ. Our own two transports were about to peel off and head out of town, when a robust cadre, his cheeks burning from the afternoon's exertions, knocked sharply on our driver's door. The tailgate was flung open and onto my cramped legs was hoisted a heavy yellow cardboard carton. As I shifted it into a more possible position the clinking of glass revealed a large cache of the local beer. We were off. At least our long odyssey over the two mountain peaks would be well deadened by drink.

The journey back to Xi'an was a haze. Yes, there was the fear of never arriving alive, the excruciating pain in rump and knees from my posture in the back of a bucking vehicle, the disjointed refrains of the Yorkshire dialect drinking anthem, *On Ilkley Moor B'aht'at* coming from the front, not to mention the intense desire to urinate. This time we didn't need those peasant lads with their bamboo hoses to cool the wheels, for every half hour the four of us would roll out and relieve ourselves on them. But the alcohol worked its magic too, and we seemed to be back in Xi'an in no time at all. By three in the morning we were snoring between starched hotel sheets.

Descending that grand, red-carpeted stair to the breakfast suite some time near midday I was met by the frosty stares of my clients. The cancellation of my consultancy fee was the first small matter raised. More pressing was an announcement from Darren that I was due for a good old pounding. This, apparently, was how matters were settled in his world of business. Darren's father nodded in angry assent. I glanced at Paul, always a little more the diplomat, and was comforted by his wry smile. After all, it wasn't going to be his slate mine, and maybe, thought I, he could see a little of the funny side of our wild goose chase.

'Now come on, Darren, we'll have to sort this out back home, won't we?' Paul generously offered. Darren scowled and promised to rearrange my facial features at a later date.

And what of Lily Wu? She'd made herself scarce, and with nothing else to keep us in Xi'an, I set about persuading the threesome that things would turn out more hopeful at the meetings I'd arranged with the sophisticated slate traders of Beijing.

I retreated to my room to pack. On the bed was a package that hadn't been there when I left for breakfast. The envelope bore the characters *Shaanxi sheng gonganting* – Shaanxi Province Public Security. Within were two empty video cases, and a tourist brochure in English wishing me a most happy and relaxing sojourn in Shaanxi, the cradle of Chinese civilisation and a new business partner to the world.

There's a postscript to the ill-conceived journey into the mountains of Shaanxi. Quite unexpectedly, I did manage to climb back into the slate-men's favour by solving a strange matter of Chinese face. A few months after the slate debacle, the Leeds mob got in touch to ask whether 'hand-made' bricks were available in China for export. Under the eagle eyes of town hall conservation officers, these things were in great demand in the U.K. for building and restoration projects. Our domestic brickworks seemed only capable of mass producing the smooth, uniform bricks which were useless.

'All Chinese bricks are 'hand-made' as far as I'm concerned,' I responded. I'd often observed how the wet clay was formed into wooden frames at the ubiquitous Chinese brickworks. A few enquiries sent to Anshan produced favourable replies. Soon a shipload of Chinese bricks had been loaded on a Chinese freighter en route for England.

But Dalian Port Inspection Bureau wasn't having any of it. 'If we send these bricks to foreign friends, China will lose face! They're not modern bricks, they're rough and uneven and not up to export standards.'

But that was the whole point. As far as the strange foreigners were concerned, they were just the ticket. I arranged for a typical, rough and ready British 'hand-made' brick to be sent off to Anshan, who took it down to the port authorities at Dalian.

'If that's what they want, they can have as many as they can pay for,' was the response. For the first time in history, plain Chinese terracotta was soon arriving in vast quantities on our shores to the acclaim of town halls, and to the great profit and pleasure of a gaggle of Leeds scrap dealers. The slate mine now forgotten, I got my fee.

VII
INTELLIGENTSIA (1996)

Z*HISHIFENZI*: in its literal translation, the Chinese term for 'intellectual' is quite comical, at least to me. 'Elements with knowledge' are the stars of this chapter, especially one particular element named Shen Guanbao.

The Economic and Social Research Council (ESRC) had advertised a new programme with environmental overtones, and along with a well-known ecologist from Liverpool's geography department, I put in for a major slice of the action. Ian B and I were surprised to find that we'd landed the largest grant in the entire programme a quarter of a £million indeed. China's urbanisation process had entered a new phase. Tied to novel global outsourcing networks and a spatially horizontal supply chain within China, the country's myriad townships were suddenly the focus of frenetic manufacturing activity. The global factory system was simply being parachuted onto China's fragile rural terrain, onto a workforce which had no industrial experience. Long unchanged rural landscapes were being torn asunder by this untrammelled industrialisation, water courses and soils polluted, village air thickened with fumes.

Our plan was to conduct a project centering on environmental perception. The research would be a first for China, where measuring opinions had long been beyond limits to Chinese researchers, let alone foreign ones. We would choose three research locations, broadly east to west across China. Our hypothesis was, that in rural townships of the eastern provinces, which had experienced the post-Mao industrial transformation earliest and most intensely, there would be signs of a backlash. People would be questioning the tearing up and re-configuring of the traditional human and natural environment, the pollution of air, water and land and the sweeping away of a timeless agricultural tradition. They would be beginning to regret their unalloyed enthusiasm for 'modernisation' and becoming nostalgic about their former, more grounded and less frenetic and polluted way of life. By contrast, those in the interior provinces where rural industrialisation was only just getting a grip would be in the throes of modernisation fever, yet beginning to awaken to the knowledge that their environment was under adverse pressure. By even further contrast, those in the peripheral (and poor) provinces of the far west — places like Gansu and Xinjiang, where modern industry had rarely been seen — would welcome with open arms just about anything that brought non-agricultural employment and wage incomes. The pollution, the destruction of nature, would be far from people's minds. These, then, were the notions which our ambitious study would set out to test, by asking a lot of people a lot of searching questions. This isn't the place to describe how we fared in what turned out to be a long and involved project. The tangible outcome was a book.

It was a decade earlier that the People's Republic had started its gentle foray into Western seats of learning. Often from institutes under the Chinese Academy of Sciences (CAS), researchers were despatched to Western Europe and North America as 'visiting scholars'. Their receiving institutions were intrigued by the possibility of linking up with a nation with which there had been no substantial academic discourse since the 1930s. Fees were almost never charged by the U.K. universities. By and large, the exotic new migrant — the Chinese visiting scholar — was accorded an enthusiastic welcome and given the freedom of the campus. With no obvious projects or objectives to pursue they were allowed to hang around laboratories, ask questions, sit in on lectures, all with never a mention of money.

Today (or at least in the early 2020s before the Great Alteration), if you were to walk the couple of kilometers from Sheffield's hilly middle-class suburb of Broomhill towards the city centre, the count of Chinese students would be in the dozens, maybe low hundreds even. By the time you got past the red brick University administration building and continued on to Division Street, you would notice that almost every shop, restaurant, café displayed signage in Chinese. All this began very quietly forty years ago: when in the early 1980s I was living in Sheffield, a mere four citizens of the People's Republic resided in the city. In a mid-Victorian terrace house opposite the massive Hallamshire Hospital the visiting scientists from China lived their distinctly odd lives. First of all, at that time any Chinese being sent overseas, even on a brief delegation tour, would be mandatorily outfitted by a team of ancient tailor-survivors in Beijing. A standard grey two-piece suit was the uniform, cut on distinctly ancient lines and reminiscent of the British 'de-mob' suits of the post-1945 era. The Sheffield foursome wore these religiously at all times, along with those matching appurtenances of 19th century costume (and not seen in China for a generation), the collar and tie. Cut off from the lives of their University colleagues as well as from any non-PRC Chinese in the city, fending for themselves (PRC men are surprisingly adept at cooking) and nervously trying to relate to the strange foreign world, the four middle-aged men from China Academy of Sciences research institutes found our household their only safe haven. Occasionally they came over for an evening of *jiaozi*, of course always as a foursome. In fact, they were enjoined never to leave their premises singly, and I never saw them do so.

As time went on, the Chinese Embassy's new Education Section based at Ealing in West London encouraged the scattering of their citizenry in the U.K. to try making friends (and influence) people. I was told a deadly secret by one of the four, a physicist from the Institute of Optics: 'Our Embassy is now giving us some extra money every month because then we will be able to make friends with our Taiwan compatriots here and even buy them drinks.'

Whether that ever happened I doubt, as apart from their be-suiting in Beijing, everyone selected to go overseas as a visiting scholar had to spend some weeks in the capital at a special induction school. Rather ironic today, with China in an extreme but autarkic form of getting-rich-quick, back then lectures warnings of the 'sugar-coated bullets' of capitalism were on the menu alongside language classes. And severe strictures on deportment in front of foreigners, too, so that China's face wouldn't be lost. Always there were dire warnings about the drinking habits of Westerners. I couldn't help noticing when living in China in the 1970s that amongst the foreign language learners, the English pub was talked of in wide-eyed whispers. It was always presented in Chinese texts as a Hogarthian den of iniquity. For years after the visiting scholar business began, I'm certain that no PRC citizen in the U.K. was ever to set foot in a public house.

The immediate attraction for a university department's hosting of a Chinese visitor soon became clear: an invitation was likely to be extended to departmental bigwigs to make a return visit. All that was expected was a few off-the-cuff lectures (delivered to most appreciative audiences), followed by a round of banqueting and sight-seeing. This is the pattern of events a couple of years before I arrived at Liverpool, when my department had played host to a visitor from the newly formed China Research Academy of Environmental Science (CRAES), an outfit under the equally new Ministry of Environmental Protection. The senior academics of my Liverpool department had duly collected their visas and headed off to Beijing for the VIP tour. Chinese officialdom does know a thing or two about winning friends and influencing people. No doubt the two Liverpool professors sipped at their little glasses of fiery banquet *baijiu* amidst affirmations of undying friendship and promises of a bright future in joint research.

No foreign individual or group could conceivably conduct fieldwork in China without a local partner, who would act as guarantor of conformity to all regulations. In politically neutral fields, fieldwork collaboration with foreigners was becoming acceptable to the Chinese authorities. For example, Liverpool colleagues were involved in projects on the geomorphology of the Northwest's *loess* lands, But it was a different matter for the social sciences, which simply hadn't existed during Mao's time. Now, in the mid-1980s, they were just beginning to emerge under tight state supervision. But social science *fieldwork* in China remained altogether in its infancy. In disciplines relating as ours did to sociology and anthropology, obvious difficulties lay in our path. Furthermore, in these areas, there had been a few notorious false starts in this area in the early 1980s, principally in research partnerships with un-self-aware U.S. academics. But I remained blithely confident that something could be worked out, as I had over a decade behind me of nurturing personal relationships with China's top planning and environmental echelons. Surely it would be easy to persuade some of my friends to partner our environmental perception project? Unhappily, though, Ian B and I were prevailed upon to limit our search for a research partner to my Liverpool University department's tenuous friendship with the aforementioned CRAES, an outfit which, quite unsuitably, lay firmly on the science rather than the *social* science side of environmental studies.

To Beijing we then went, to meet Wu, the CRAES man who'd been in Liverpool. His research centre, such as it was, consisted of a two-storey structure of badly mortared red bricks on a muddy lane on the northwest fringes of the city. We were expecting to see at least well-equipped laboratories and lecture rooms. But CRAES was so new that it hadn't advanced beyond a skeletal state. In retrospect, it was clear that the nascent outfit was speculating that the largesse of Liverpool would put some flesh on the bones. The usual round of banqueting and sightseeing of Beijing's 'scenic spots' led rather directly to the suggestion that it would be necessary for their leaders to come to Liverpool to work out the details of the research collaboration.

Weeks later, Wu and a couple of his Party bosses arrived for a return match. I knew things were going to go badly with CRAES when, after an official University reception and exchange of formal gifts, Wu came to me with a complaint. The Party Secretary's wrapped gift from the University was smaller in dimensions than the one presented to Wu.

'You have made the Party Secretary lose face, and he is very angry,' grimaced Wu.

It was useless arguing against such absurdity. The fact was that the man had received something (I forget what it was now) of far greater value than his underlings. Should I have wrapped up the official's present like a set of Russian dolls, just to save his ridiculous face? Concluded with Wu were some rather basic discussions on our research proposal and methodology, and to all intents and purposes there was some agreement. Wu's job now was to return to China and locate three suitable research sites across the great breadth of the country in which to test out our hypothesis.

We waited in Liverpool for news, but weeks later, nothing, so we thought it essential to get ourselves back to Beijing. After all, the ESRC demanded strict adherence to schedules. But once in CRAES's odd backwater, it soon became clear that we were being taken for a ride.

'I have arranged with Dongying County in Shandong Province that we should do all the research there,' Wu proudly announced. I once lived in Shandong and had a rough idea of the location of this place. Anyway, the proposal that we should do all the fieldwork, the interviews, in a single eastern county bore no resemblance to our project design.

'I have already made contact with the leading comrades there,' Wu smiled winningly, 'and they would like to invite you to visit them.'

However, Wu went on, it would be most convenient if our budget could stretch to the purchase of a CRAES car for the purpose of the research. A suitable one had been found for only 180,000 *renminbi*.

RMB180,000? A car? Ian and I looked at each other and making some non-committal response we returned to our hotel — and to Liverpool.

As it happened, I had a very firm contact in Beijing's new environmental ministry, and if we needed to find out more about this Shandong county, my friend Liu Chunyu would be the man. After Sheffield and Anshan signed up to be twins, Liu had been sent to Sheffield's Department of Environmental Health for a year to learn how Europe's Steel City had managed to clean up the foul red dust which is the byword of every steelworks town. The focus was the giant Anshan works described in a previous chapter. Liu and I became close friends, bosom pals almost, and he was often round at our Sheffield home cooking *jiaozi* with us.

When the Ministry was formed, Liu was co-opted from Anshan municipality to head up one of its divisions. So I sent him a fax, our means of communication in those pre-internet days. Liu informed me by return that most of the dozens of counties of Shandong didn't possess a single environmental protection officer, so everything in a considerable area of several million population was unregulated and the environment unprotected. The county which CRAES had selected was not merely a provincial model of environmental rectitude—it was getting a name as a national paragon. It had attained this because the government had assigned the county no fewer than four environmental protection officers. Clearly, a series of Potemkin villages could offer nothing revealing to our intended research project. Further, the whole idea, as CRAES well knew, was to select our three research sites on a macro-regional level: one in the undeveloped far West, one in the somewhat developed inland provinces and one in the over-developed coastal region.

After a few angry but entirely fruitless exchanges with Mr Wu, Ian and I decided that we had no other option than to terminate our discussions with CRAES and strike out for a new Chinese research partner.

After we'd retreated from CRAES, two things happened. The bad news first—in pretty much a conspiracy between the other university in Liverpool (John Moores), which stood to gain (and was to do so), and a certain professor at Liverpool's arch-rival institution in Manchester who happened to be chair of the ESRC's grant-giving committee, Ian B and I were thoroughly stitched up. On the excuse that we had (with the ESRC's authority, no less) changed our Chinese partner organisation, our massive grant was withdrawn. This was a major blow, not only to our activities but to our esteem as academics. Only through my good standing with a number of organisations, including the British Council, did we manage to accrue sufficient funds not merely to continue but to complete our research in China with flying colours and produce a reasonably creditable book at the end of it. [10] Our fieldwork was expensive, demanding the deployment of a home team of four, as well as half a dozen in our Shanghai University partner team. Enough cash would have to be in the kitty to cover numerous international flights, our team's travel subsistence to the far ends of China, and much more.

The second thing that happened was rather more pleasing. We fell in with a new research partner, the best we could have ever wished for, and his name was Shen Guanbao. I'd first met Shen when he gave a seminar at London's School of Oriental and African Studies. He was in London for a year and was the first holder of a fellowship established at the London School of Economics more than a generation before, specifically for a Chinese social scientist. The conflict in Europe, the civil war in China and the Communist victory meant that the fellowship had never been taken up until Shen Guanbao appeared on the scene. He agreed to meet us and, with the minimum discussion about schedules and finances, agreed to partner the project.

With the dawn of the post-Mao order in the early 1980s, Shen had become the very first and favourite protégé of an elderly Professor, an ancient scholar who not long before had made a triumphant return from the 'cow-pen' of his internal exile. Fei Xiaotong was in the 1930s one of the tiny number of Chinese elite scholars who had any interest at all in the mud and mosquitoes of village life. In his native Jiangsu province, the 'land of fish

---

10   Richard Kirkby, Ian Bradbury and Guanbao Shen, *Small Town China* Burlington VT: Ashgate, 2000.

and rice', he descended to those rice roots, to coin a phrase, to conduct a study of the economic and social conditions of the local peasantry. He then turned up in the late 1930s at LSE, and studied for a doctorate under the renowned Bronislaw Malinowski. Fei's thesis was converted into a ground-breaking book—an academic's answer to Pearl Buck and her perceptive novels of Chinese village life. I'm fortunate, in owning a rare first edition. [11] In his preface Malinowski writes:

> I venture to foretell that *Peasant Life in China* ....will be counted as a landmark in the development of anthropological field-work and theory.... Our attention here is not to a small, insignificant tribe but to the greatest nation in the world.

Unhappily, but hardly unexpectedly, the Mao system looked unkindly on the bourgeois social scientist, and after a bright start in the People's Republic, Fei's star was quickly cast in the deepest of shadows. It was the Anti-Rightist Movement of 1957 which actually did for him. For the next 22 years little was heard of Fei Xiaotong. But along with the hundreds of thousands who had survived downfall and sometimes exile, in 1979 began the slow process of Fei's rehabilitation. By the early 1980s, Fei's star was again in the ascendant; showered with honours and awards by the global community of anthropology, he was soon appointed director of the Institute of Sociology at the newly created Academy of Social Sciences. A professorship was also created for him at Beijing University.

With the 'Four Modernisations' as the new crusade in China, the Communist Party by this stage of post-Cultural Revolution

---

11 Fei, Hsiao-tung, *Peasant Life in China. A Field Study of Country Life in the Yangtze Valley*. London: George Routledge and Sons, Ltd, 1939.

life had every reason to restore honours to the educated classes it had long shunned. By the end of the 1980s, as a luminary of one of China's 'Democratic Parties', Fei Xiaotong was elevated to the Vice-Presidency of the Chinese People's Consultative Conference, an advisory committee of wise (or perhaps tame) men and women which is often described as a kind of House of Lords to the law-promulgating National People's Congress, the NPC. His new role as 'politician' didn't stop there: Fei soon found himself promoted to the deputy chairmanship of the key standing committee of the NPC. I guess this was a gesture designed to impress the educated non-Party constituency, for I can't imagine that he wielded much influence. The Communist Party, in its new modernising phase, needed the outward-looking intelligentsia on board, and who better as a confidence booster than this amenable old fellow with his foreign acclaim and foreign doctorate? Thus in the space of a few years, and in the eighth decade of his life, Fei Xiaotong rose from disgraced bourgeois academic to become one of the pillars of China's establishment, *de jure* if not *de facto*. The irony is that it was under Deng Xiaoping's direction of the 1957 Anti-Rightist Campaign that Fei was thrust into two decades of disgrace, and it was under China's post-Mao strongman, the self-same Deng Xiaoping, that he was not merely rehabilitated but elevated to one of the highest sinecures in the state machinery.

Fei's seminal work based on his PhD bears the title *Jiangcun* – 'River Village'. The actual river village was in his native Wujiang, a resource-rich county of Jiangsu province. The real name of the place is Kaixianggong. There, half-a-century after his first sojourn in the village, Fei set up a research station which re-established academic work focusing on the dynamics of rural life in post-Mao China. The previous two decades had seen the strict application of migration controls, effected through an urban rationing system, as well as through various measures of surveillance. It had also given heavy emphasis to the production of grain crops. Now, in the early 1980s, with the breaking up of the rural people's communes and the threat of mass migration to the cities, potentially creating what China's authorities in any age have always feared—mass disorder or *luan* as it's known. There was an urgent need, then, to anchor hundreds of millions to their rural loci. In the early 1980s, Fei Xiaotong himself was responsible for coining the essential slogan of the day: *litu bulixiang* ('leave the soil but don't leave the village'). This meant, essentially, a rapid diversification towards non-agricultural activities—rural industries and services. It seems that Professor Fei's role, supported by surveys and investigations launched from his revived Kaixianggong research base, was indeed to propagate this new and not unreasonable national model of urban containment.

With the generic title of *Xiao chengzhen da wenti* ('Small Towns—Big Issues'), in 1984 a series of books was published under Fei's name. Like all traditional grand masters, for that is what Fei Xiaotong had become, it was his acolytes who actually did the work, including the drafting of his reports and books. And chief amongst these acolytes was none other than our Shen Guanbao. Following Fei's resurrection from oblivion, Shen had become the old man's very first doctoral candidate and pretty soon his amanuensis. Shen's assigned role was to manage the research in Kaixianggong, and write it up too. The publications bear his master's name, but never Shen's.

It turned out that Kaixianggong was not far from our most easterly research station: Ian B and I later spent a day with Shen at the Kaixianggong outpost—the day that we were to meet Fei Xiaotong at the celebration of his 85th birthday. As we shall see, we never got to it.

SHIFTING GEARS IN CHINA

As China opened up, many Western social scientists saw it as the last great frontier for fieldwork research and a happy hunting ground where they could burnish their reputations. After Beijing and Washington finally came together in 1979, there was a honeymoon period in which American scholars were lavishly indulged in China. Some notorious indiscretions ensued, and by the mid-1980s the Chinese authorities were keeping foreign researchers on ever-tighter reins. Opinions, even on such matters as environmental degradation are, of course, dangerous. As I mentioned earlier, no-one conducted research in China without a local partner, and Shen's (and indirectly, Fei's) backing was the best protection anyone could wish for.

Little by little, we fathomed Shen's highly unorthodox past. On the whole, my Chinese contacts and collaborators were reluctant to say much about what happened to them during times of political repression, especially the Cultural Revolution. But often assisted by strong liquor around a rough table after our day's survey work together, Shen would talk. As a political reprobate who, very unusually, had been sent into rural disgrace not once but twice during the Cultural Revolution, Shen had a great deal of hinterland. Here was a man who'd entered Shanghai's prestigious Fudan University to study physics, but ended up in exile on the mudflats of Chongming Island, a neglected lozenge lying off the mouth of the turgid Yangtze. Then, in the mid-1970s, when his University had been reopened, he was found guilty of a second 'mistake' (nature undisclosed—perhaps the 'counter-revolutionary' May 16 movement?) and was sent back to live with Chongming's smattering of poor farmers and fisherfolk. Shen's stories of life in the wilderness were numerous and often tragicomic. After his second spell of exile, he decided that delving into Chinese society, especially the lives of the vast rural population, was going to be a more rewarding field than physics.

Somehow, he managed to switch to the newly revived discipline of sociology and get himself into the Institute of Sociology of the Chinese Academy of Social Sciences run by none other than the rehabilitated Professor Fei.

I warmed to Shen's eccentricity, rarely seen amongst China's long-cowed intelligentsia. He was no stranger to China's increasingly evident underclass, to its low dives even. He once told me that he'd even spent a lot of time amongst the novel breed of prostitutes who infested the China-Burma border. He could drink with the best of them and the diplomacy of tobacco—a vital element of male schmoozing—was second nature. Unlike most academics, who stuck rigidly to social boundaries and all the social proprieties, this small, bespectacled man with even boyish features framed by an unruly mop would strike up conversations with just anyone around him—with the next table in a greasy chopstick café, in the airport queue, anywhere.

Shen Guanbao, originally of the famed Fudan University, was now operating with a group of social researchers based at the new Shanghai University. In this position, Shen edited a popular journal, *Shehui* ('Society'), which widened the public debate on many fronts long taboo. To our project, Shen brought a ready-made group of field researchers from Shanghai University's new Sociology Department. It was the mid-1990s, and a sign of the times for China's official news media was the birth of the radio phone-in, and even rather stilted TV chat shows. Our Shen had worked his way into becoming the host of a highly novel live weekly prime time 'social issues' show broadcast by Shanghai's Dongfang TV station. This went out to an avid audience far up the great Yangtze Basin.

'Only about 300-400 million people,' Shen grinned. In a China where power was becoming just a little defuse, Shen Guanbao had somehow risen to become one of China's first ever Public

Intellectuals. Once, Ian B and I arrived on the Moscow to Shanghai flight and were whisked by Shen in the TV station's limo straight to his studio, where he proceeded to interview us live, in half-Chinese, half-English. The hot topics were things like whether China should go for mass car ownership, and the semantics of fashion. I blush even now at the memory, for after twenty hours with Aeroflot and no sleep my Chinese lips spouted incoherently. Ian B did rather better sticking to his only recourse of English.

Our fortuitous link-up with Shen meant that our work based in three regions of China, two of them technically closed to foreigners, let alone to their social investigations, was only possible because of his relationship with Fei Xiaotong. The august professor stayed very much in the background: the only time we were to get within a few metres of him was an odd and unexplained encounter on a remote road in the far West of China. Maybe Fei had been on some kind of inspection tour in this, the remotest part of Gansu. Perhaps the weighty NPC grandee had been up to Dingxi County (our Gansu research base) to brief our Party interlocutors on what to offer us. We shall never know, but it was certainly a weird encounter. Fei Xiaotong was embedded in a convoy, himself in a smart *mianbao che* ('bread bus') charging along in the opposite direction, on a little used country highway. We were just rounding a bend when the air was filled with the raucous klaxons of the Chinese police. Our driver quickly pulled into the roadside dust, and we awaited whatever it was that was coming around the corner. As the convoy with its police outriders passed us and began to pick up speed, we noticed Shen waving at a disappearing figure in the minibus, who was raising his hand in salute.

'That was Professor Fei Xiaotong,' Shen announced mysteriously. With no further explanation we boarded our vehicle and went on our way.

Later in our project fieldwork we were back in Jiangsu, in river town territory. Wujiang had become one of China's richest county towns, and the area itself was amongst the most affluent, in per capita output terms, of China's 2,000+ counties. The local Party cadres were making hay. Fei Xiaotong was celebrating his 85th birthday in this, his home town, and Shen and we too were invited to bend our knees to the great man. We took time off from our programme and installed ourselves in this supercharged town, where the local Communist leaders had evidently already transformed themselves into mini-capitalists with their chauffeured Mercedes and great black Audis. Our hotel was the usual elaborate tower complete with post-modern Doric columns, swathes of polished marble, and the young service staff, sons and daughters of the local peasantry, nattily got up in spotless uniforms. We were in Shen's hotel room for a pre-party drink or two, and Shen very deliberately proceeded to put himself into an alcoholic stupor. He just lay prone on his bed and moaned incoherently. Without our man there were no birthday greetings for Fei, and we never did get to meet him face-to-face.

Later on, this inexplicable sabotage became explicable. It wasn't that Shen thought it a bad idea for Fei to meet *us* in the flesh. The stalwart Qian Wenbao, one of our project team whom we'd brought from Liverpool, explained the next day that this was a ploy on Shen's behalf to deliberately miss the party. Chinese culture has no problem with the drunken state — it's a perfectly 'normal' thing, and a sign even of great depths, of the true poet. No shame attaches. Moreover, just like the rare case of people in the East 'running amok' and even killing people while in that temporary state, when under the influence the drunk can be entirely excused from all his bizarre actions.

But why, in this instance, did Shen use the ploy? The answer was that he'd recently fallen out with his master. Fei desired Shen to park himself indefinitely at Kaixianggong, and get on with more of the same research which had proved so welcome to the higher-ups. Shen Guanbao had other ideas: he wanted to stretch his wings and fly, which was what he was doing with all these exotic visits to Liverpool (and elsewhere overseas, too, as his fame spread), which our research budget enabled and financed. There were further attractions — Shen had become besotted with one of the Shanghai University team who invariably accompanied him on his U.K. trips, and who shared the ex-council flat which we rented for Shen near to our Liverpool University campus. I had huge sympathy for his neglected wife, who in rather a traditional manner made an effort to co-opt the third person in their relationship. Whenever Ian and I were in Shanghai, we would be invited to the family home for a meal; Shen's paramour was always welcomed along to these dinner gatherings and treated almost as a younger sister by Shen's poor wife.

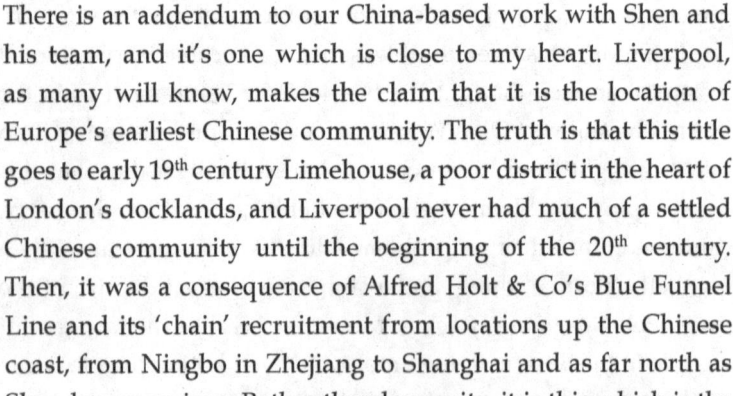

There is an addendum to our China-based work with Shen and his team, and it's one which is close to my heart. Liverpool, as many will know, makes the claim that it is the location of Europe's earliest Chinese community. The truth is that this title goes to early 19th century Limehouse, a poor district in the heart of London's docklands, and Liverpool never had much of a settled Chinese community until the beginning of the 20th century. Then, it was a consequence of Alfred Holt & Co's Blue Funnel Line and its 'chain' recruitment from locations up the Chinese coast, from Ningbo in Zhejiang to Shanghai and as far north as Shandong province. Rather than longevity, it is this which is the distinctive feature of Liverpool's Chinese community. It was to lead me, along with Shen Guanbao and Li Ling, to conduct a most interesting social investigation. And important too, because outside the People's Republic, it was the very first time that Chinese social scientists had embarked on a societal research project.

From Sydney to San Francisco to Singapore, before the 1980s almost all the global Chinese diaspora stemmed from south China, principally from Guangdong province. In their millions, the British empire transported indentured Chinese labourers to wherever they needed them, from the rubber plantations and tin mines of Malaya to the sugarcane fields of the Caribbean.

In the first half of the 20th century, many Chinese settlers in the British Isles, and in North America after the railroad rush of the 1860s, gained a living by opening laundries. As a child, I used to see these around the place: there was one in York somewhere near Walmgate Bar. Chinese laundrymen were a feature of many British shipping lines, and indeed, in the Second World War they were to be found on every Royal Navy vessel. An amusing personal aside is that when my very English maternal grandparents had to leave China in the midst of the nationalist upsurge of 1926/7, Quaker philanthropy helped them to start the Home Service Laundry in Derby. This enterprise steamed on until the 1960s when it was overtaken by launderettes and dry cleaners. What else could you do if coming from China?

Then came a far less diffuse wave of Chinese immigration than those which had arisen because of the shipping trade. By the 1960s and 1970s, every city in Britain was settled by a community of Cantonese and almost every town, too, had a few Cantonese families. The new migrants were chiefly from Hong Kong and often from the villages of the colony's New Territories; of course, it was no longer laundries but restaurants, and soon takeaway outlets, with which the new Chinese residents became firmly identified.

Apart from the non-Cantonese character of most of the early Chinese residents of Liverpool prior to the migrants from Hong Kong, it's the scale of the Chinese presence which is striking. From 1939, the city's port kept a register which listed over 20,000 Chinese seafarers as irregular residents. After the atrocity-laden Japanese invasion of China in 1937, British antifascists had been involved in a broad campaign to boycott Japanese goods and shipping. To this end they'd established good contacts amongst the Chinese seafarers in different ports. The story can be found in Arthur Clegg's fascinating account.[12] A Chinese Seamen's Union was formed; despite wartime restrictions, in early 1942 its members who happened to be in port staged a protracted strike to protest their pay, and their compensation for injury and death. Compared with the British, the Chinese seafarers received paltry sums. The strike was largely successful.

Following the Second World War, hundreds if not low thousands of these men were stranded in Liverpool, many being summarily deported after overnight police raids. Spouses and young children left behind, and were forever bereft. The Liverpool shipping companies had blacklisted those who'd taken part in the strike, and certainly they were amongst those forcibly removed from the city after the war. Men who escaped the deportations continued to work on the Liverpool vessels; with China's Second Civil War raging and, after 1949, the West's embargo of the new People's Republic after 1949, they found themselves unable to return to their native places in east or north China. So several hundred Chinese seafarers quietly made their home in Liverpool, a good few employed by the shipping line

---

12 *Aid China: a Memoir of a Forgotten Campaign*, Beijing: New World Press, 1989.

as it chugged on towards its final collapse in the 1970s. By the 1990s, unbeknown not merely to us academics but also to most of Liverpool, some several dozen now elderly survivors of the wartime community and the Blue Funnel Line's sinking were still in the city, as were their next generation of part-Chinese Liverpudlians, almost none of whom spoke anything but English.

In the aftermath of the 1981 inner-city riots in London's Brixton and Liverpool's Toxteth, town halls started to take an active interest in their resident ethnic minorities. In Liverpool as everywhere it was the new contingent of Chinese settlers from Hong Kong which became the officially recognised 'Chinese community'. In Liverpool, the shabby restaurants in and around Nelson Street became the core of their Chinatown and the focus of the local council's attention. By the 1990s, I was a member of a consultancy team which was engaged to brighten up the streets of the enclave, giving them (dubious) character names; my Chinese team in the University and I, along with a local architectural practice, saw to the construction of the largest, most lavish Chinese ceremonial archway (*pailou*) ever built outside China. My first task, amusingly, was to go to Liverpool's arch-rival Manchester and measure their Chinatown archway donated by their twin city of Wuhan. Liverpool's *pailou*, of course, had to be bigger and better. Embedded with 200 terracotta dragon heads, it stands at the top of Nelson Street, in all its proud glory, the *pailou* is probably the largest such outside China.

With the Hong Kong influx of the 1960s and 70s, the dwindling band of non-Cantonese in the city—from Zhejiang, from Shanghai, and as far north as Shandong even—were sidelined, forgotten by history. And not merely by officialdom: they were marginalised by the Cantonese newcomers themselves. I do recall my surprise, shock even, when I first discovered during my time in Hong Kong in the 1970s that intolerance to the point of racism existed between 'north' and 'south' China. Acid remarks were by no means one-sided: my friends from Shanghai and Nanjing would refer to their Cantonese cousins as *Nanfang manzi* – 'Southern monkeys'. This deep north-south antagonism is based on more than linguistic separation (most 'Northerners' find the Southern dialects, and especially Cantonese, impenetrable). There are deep roots: as far back as the Second Opium War (1858-60), or the later Boxer War, for instance, in their hatred of their distant Qing dynasty rulers the Cantonese frequently sided with the imperialists from the West. This tendency survives today in the susceptibility of Hong Kong youth to taking up cudgels against Beijing.

To me, the study I was about to embark upon, with Shen Guanbao and his partner Li Ling as the fieldworkers, was significant. Years earlier, when I was a student at the Architectural Association, the sociologist Richard Kuper lectured us on something pretty obvious – but something which our privileged mindsets had not hitherto registered. He reminded us that almost all social science enquiry is conducted by the elite upon the non-elite. I still vividly recall his pyramid on the blackboard, with an arrow pointing downwards from its apex to its base. Western anthropological research on the poor benighted masses in the colonies and ex-colonies was all too familiar. During my Bristol days a typically colonial-minded professor of sociology would lecture us on the 'quaint customs' of the Nuer, or the Trobriand Islanders. Ever since becoming involved with the new breed of Chinese social scientists, I'd been harbouring an itch – to get them to burrow into the occluded corners of our own society, and in a decisive way turn that downward pointing arrow on the pyramid 180 degrees so that it pointed from the base to the apex.

So what exactly was this research project? The opportunity came unexpectedly, after a chance conversation with Ian B, in which he mentioned that his partner had a colleague, ethnically half-Chinese and yet Liverpool through-and-through, whose father had settled in the city after the 1939-45 war. One of the Blue Funnel Line survivors, no less. We learned that these retired mariners would meet and socialise, in the food plaza of the Council's St John's Market, to them perhaps a pale imitation of the traditional Chinese teahouse,. There they would pass a few hours each Monday. reminiscing and exchanging news. This turned out to be the fertile ground which I'd long been seeking. I primed Shen Guanbao and Li Ling and one Monday sent them along to the market. They returned that afternoon, full of enthusiasm.

'The old men were really happy that we'd 'found' them, 'Li Ling remarked. 'They felt they were just lost in Liverpool and that everyone had forgotten them.'

'They were amazed to be approached by Chinese people in Liverpool who could speak their own dialects,' Shen added.

The great thing is that our research partners were not only trained in the sociological method; their language abilities were just perfect. The Shanghainese spoken by Shen Guanbao and Li Ling is closely related to the neighbouring east Jiangsu dialects, though the feisty Zhejiang Ningbo tongue could present them with a few problems. In the following days we discussed what role we could play in bringing this small community with their exponentially grown Liverpool families (for most married or re-married locally) out of the shadows. The lives of each of the men had been extraordinary — plucked from East China in the 1930s and 40s, serving in the war when half the Blue Funnel Line's ships were sunk, being stranded in a foreign place where language and culture were alien, and then marginalised by other more vocal Chinese groups.

We set about discussing the viability of an oral history project, and the notion was gently introduced to the venerable fraternity over a couple more Monday mornings at the 'teahouse' in the St John's Market. The idea was enthusiastically received and indeed sold itself: twenty-nine of the men volunteered to take part. Standard procedures for oral histories with all the protocols were worked out; to ensure no sensitive lines were crossed, I set up a steering committee drawn from local interest groups, this including the 'official' Chinese community, the Liverpool National Museum & Galleries and a few other worthy organisations. The interviews took place in the confidential environment of my office, tape recordings were transcribed and then translated, and the data divided into two sets, one going back to China with Shen and Li Ling. In short, Li Ling soon became the author of the Chinese language account of the project. Published by a reputable Chinese academic press, in timeworn tradition it bore only Shen Guanbao's name. What Li Ling hadn't bargained for was that over the next decade and even beyond, she became an honorary tour guide for those old men and their (younger) families. Now they were out of the shadows it was time, after more than half a century, to make a return visit to their homeland.

When I departed Liverpool University, I took with me the complete seafarers data archive. Many other projects have intervened in my life since, and to this day I and, in particular, an accomplished colleague from London University are still working on the English language publication. But since this will be a kind of history book and I am no longer subject to crazy academic performance targets, the pressure to get the thing done is mild. But it will be done, thus filling an important gap in Liverpool's 20th century history — and honouring the lives of a group of Chinese uprooted from their culture and exiled on very foreign shores.

RICHARD KIRKBY

Some time after our work together had concluded, perhaps 2003, I visited Shen in his Shanghai domain. He proudly showed me how he was using some of his foreign loot, courtesy of the Liverpool connection, to modernise. For China's new middle class, hardwood parquet floors were very much the in-thing. Shen also showed me his new attic room, reached by a rudimentary ladder. More extraordinary by far, while still holding down his post at Shanghai University, and still operating somewhat at Fudan, Shen had announced that he was also now the *de facto* boss of a private university financed by China's most celebrated manufacturer of *gaoliang* booze — the Maotai Company from distant Guizhou.

'Why them?' I asked Shen as he rather unsteadily drove his new company VW Santana around the lavish campus of this new university which had colonised a huge tract of farmland within the north Shanghai ring. Shen explained that his employers wanted to have a presence in the big city and impress the Shanghai Party Committee with its munificence, and hence make even more money. Later, Shen declared that he would be taking over the running of another private university, this time in Sanya on the large tropical island of Hainan, 2,000 kilometers distant. He became one of China's new breed of long-distance weekly commuters.

No death is timely, but Fei Xiaotong had had a good innings, and in the People's Republic of the late 20th century he'd soared to undreamt of heights. Unhappily, his ever-youthful amanuensis outlived him by only a few years. But for a peasant lad, twice-exiled Shen Guanbao also touched the stratosphere. His peripatetic, unsettled work and relationships, his dedication to hard smoking and hard liquor were all refreshingly uncharacteristic of an intellectual class known more for its timidity. But they also did for him. Shen Guanbao's untimely demise came as no great shock to me. I was sad, but glad too to have known and enjoyed a true Chinese eccentric of the modern age.

VIII
THE HEIST (1996)

FOLLOWING OUR TIME with Shen Guanbao at the Spartan research station high up on Gansu's loess plateau, Beijing promised some rest and recreation, even a bit of gentle tourism. At the very least, we'd anticipated a long *baijiu*-fuelled dinner that Beijing summer's eve. The day after next, Saturday, we would be heading for Irkutsk ('technical stop' as the mysterious Aeroflot announcement always had it), then Moscow and finally Manchester — courtesy of the Russian airline's lumbering new weekly flight linking Moscow with the Chinese capital. All that was left on the list for Friday was a visit to the Embassy to meet our British Council paymasters, and a date with the Ford Foundation's new China director. An opportunity to sniff out new research funding was always to be seized.

The Aeroflot way via Moscow wasn't one we would have chosen; it was the only option for our cash-strapped team, and always a journey into the unknown. Because we had no transit visas, passengers like us who had to wait a night or two for their onward flights had to file out of the airport flanked by soldiers (who every time demanded a pen from me) to be confined in a crude hotel block standing in a dense birch wood. Large numbers of African travellers, awaiting transport to remote capitals which no other European airline would serve, were always hanging around. Some had been imprisoned in the block for a matter of weeks. Worse, between connections, in the chaos of bandit-capitalist Russia, the hub-and-spoke Moscow airport had an unpleasant habit of spinning off a good part of one's luggage.

On one occasion, so we were told on the quiet (and amusement) by our friend and partner Shen Guanbao, his University Party boss Old Liu whom we'd invited to Liverpool for a bit of naked schmoozing, was relieved of a small bag of gold jewellery he'd intended for his Shanghai mistress. The airport concourse was a place where distrait passengers were running hither and thither searching for their lost luggage; in particular on one trip through the airport, there was the quiet hysteria of a Scandinavian doctor whose vastly valuable cargo of medical equipment intended for some African hospital had evaporated. We used to joke that the Moscow airport baggage handlers were most likely resting in the VIP lounge in their Armani suits, awaiting their flights to the Bahamas.

At the Academy of Social Sciences and at Fudan and Shanghai Universities, Shen seemed to have built up quite a power base, and his acolytes seemed to be everywhere. Think Master and Grasshopper in that 1970s David Carradine mystical series *Kung Fu*. We'd been met at the station by one of Shen's very own Grasshoppers, the 30-something year-old Huang who had been one of the first Fudan postgraduates to benefit from Shen's pioneering guidance in the new social sciences. Now Huang's duty was to serve his Master, to carry his bags and to arrange our accommodation in Beijing. He'd booked us in at a new hostelry known as the Sheke Binguan — 'Sheke' being in this instance the Chinese contraction of 'social science' and Binguan the usual word for a hostel for a special clientele, in this case visiting researchers of the Chinese Academy of Social Sciences (CASS). Before the establishment of this latter organisation one year after Mao had died, it was impermissible to step beyond the prism of 'Marxism-Leninism-Mao Zedong Thought'.

So what of this Sheke Binguan? Parachuted into the average Chinese cityscape since the Great Helmsman went to see Marx there've been at least four generations of new buildings. China's market madness demands a constant tearing down and raising up, so as to capture ever-rocketing land values. But back in 1994, on the edge of this crazed property boom, it was still possible to create a three-storey building within a few minutes of Tiananmen Square. No doubt a thirty storey point-block now occupies the site, but back then the newly built Sheke was modest, redbrick, pitch-roofed, European gables. There it was, a home-from-home for the itinerant researchers of CASS, and the few like Shen Guanbao who had the connections, the *guanxi*.

Remarkable services were on offer at the staid academics' new resting place in the capital. The Sheke had the usual facilities of a small *zhaodaisuo*, but I decided that in its short life it had morphed into something like a knocking shop for the intelligentsia. And the infestation of young and not so young women of the night (or day, apparently) was not, as Shen later claimed, a mere convenience for 'research'. Shen once told me with a straight face that he'd sought out a young woman of the profession down in Yunnan's borderland and spent a day or two closeted with her in a hotel—hands-on research which had never been seen in Mao's day. Half-a-dozen times in our first Sheke night the thin plywood door reverberated to a gentle but persistent fist. I was too exhausted to bother opening it, unlike innocent-abroad Ian B whose manners were always far better honed than mine.

'Does this gesture mean anything in particular to the Chinese?' he asked me at breakfast, as he flapped his arms in an empty embrace. I let him in on the surprising and incongruous secret. It was clear that the Sheke's management had found an ingenious way of lining their pockets in the 'it's glorious to get rich' China of Mr Deng Xiaoping.

That morning, we'd wandered up to Tiananmen and pondered whether to revisit the Forbidden City. But it was a lazy day and we perambulated through the ancient *hutong* of downtown Beijing, returning to the Sheke for an early afternoon nap. Shen had business somewhere in the capital, and we'd agreed to await him and then find a place for a fine supper. He would return at 3 o'clock and we were to meet in the lobby. Gentle sunshine suffused the wide pavement outside and at the appointed hour I stepped out to enjoy the street and wait for our friend. Dangling from my wrist was a shiny black leather man-bag in which nestled passport, our Aeroflot tickets for Saturday, a wad of travellers' cheques and some three thousand U.S. dollars I'd picked up from my watch dealer friend in Shanghai (why watches and Shanghai is not a matter I should go into just here...). Thoughts of security never entered my head, for though I knew that China was now far from being a land where petty crime was rare, the notion that foreigners might be victims was outlandish and unthought. Stealing from or otherwise molesting a foreigner was, all Chinese citizens knew, a dangerous matter and likely to be a capital offence.

The Sheke stood a few yards from an intersection of two broad boulevards. Over the road, on the corner, stood a modern building with a restaurant along its ground floor frontage. Wisps of barbecue smoke wafted over from the *shashlik* sellers who'd set up on opposite corners of the crossroads. In recent years thousands of young men from Xinjiang had flocked to the cities of the east to make probably quite good livings selling lamb kebabs (as well as commodities more exotic) on the streets. All over the world the most recent migrants are blamed for acts of lawlessness and the Xinjiang youth in China's eastern cities were no exception; on several occasions my sympathy for the underdog had found me defending their rights to locals who should have known better.

Three o'clock had come and gone and though getting a little

itchy, for we had plans for a full afternoon, I continued with my flagrant vigil outside the Sheke. Finally, two hours late, Shen turned up, his disarming smile dissolving my annoyance, and we agreed to his idea of stepping over the road and taking our dinner in the concrete slab of a restaurant I'd been eyeballing most of that afternoon.

Passing through the columned portal— postmodern flummery had hit China's cities hard in the early 1990s—we found ourselves in a long, cavernous chamber with three long parallel lines of tables, one against each of the walls and one down the middle of the room. The place was empty, the thirty tables with their greying cloths untenanted, and the half-dozen demurely dressed waitresses seemed hardly in welcoming mood. Now, the normal procedure when rare foreign diners appear is to seat them in full view of the open entrance, advertising the high life ('wow—foreigners') offered by the establishment. I found it odd that one of the surly young women beckoned us into the heart of the chamber, well out of sight of passers-by, and insisted that we take one of tables in the central row.

Three of us and four chairs, so onto the spare chair, masked by the tablecloth, I slid my bag of treasures. Shen ordered bottles of Beijing Snowflake and set about the serious business of debating the menu with our waitress. This done, we settled into our beers in warm anticipation of what was to come. We hardly noticed that four more customers had arrived, and like us were directed to an inside table just beyond ours but along one of the side rows. I recall noticing out of the corner of my eye that no sooner had the foursome been seated but they were calling over the waitress and asking if they could move to another table on the opposite side of the chamber. Perhaps I just thought 'Fengshui nuts' and they think they'll get indigestion in the wrong seats'. Whatever, their request was an easy one to grant and the four men rose as one and crossed over, past our middle table, to the other side. Instead of taking to their new seats, they merely marched to the entrance, were waived out with a knowing smile from the reception desk, and were gone. Odd, I thought.

Our dishes arrived and we were set about an unhurried feast. Our stomachs lined, Shen decided to order more beers. At last it was time to pay. It was only then that I felt for my little bag under the tablecloth and found nothing but an empty chair. Shock, horror, disbelief that something as vital could be lifted from me right in front of my very eyes. It wasn't obvious how the theft had been accomplished until I remembered the manoeuvres of the four men who'd arrived shortly after we did. The matter becoming clear. The restaurant staff were obviously in on it.

Shen marched over to the desk and demanded to use the phone. 'I've telephoned the Chaoyang District police HQ and they're sending someone over,' he explained. Night had come on and as we waited for the police to turn up, suddenly the lights were dimmed and Cantonese love songs started blaring. The half-dozen waitresses had cast off their white jackets and blue trousers, applied layers of powder and lipstick, put their hair up and were transformed into cheongsam-clad ladies of the night, parading in a gaggle near the entrance to bow in the all-male night-time clientele. The tables were soon all taken.

Meanwhile the heat of the day had suddenly transformed too, into a vast evening thunderstorm, lightning flashing and windows rattling. Through the now closed doors came a hooded figure draped in a heavy olive-green cape, dripping wet. One of the women unwrapped him and a podgy man in his thirties was revealed, dressed in a blue police uniform. The man drew a peaked cap from within his tightly buttoned jacket and set it carefully in the approved manner. The girl pointed to our table, and soon we were being introduced to Officer Lu, who took the fourth chair and made a show of straightening out his notebook while Shen started to describe what had happened. It was a slow and painful business, for clearly Officer Lu had only a basic grasp of writing. After the third request on how to write a certain character, Shen was losing patience. 'Give it me and I'll write up your report,' he said. The policeman, with no sign of embarrassment, passed over his notebook.

'We must go to the police station and these foreigners must report to the Chaoyang District's special officer who see to the affairs of people like them,' announced Officer Lu. Meanwhile, the storm outside had intensified, and the pelting rain and the crash of thunder was now matched by raucous screeching of the night club's speakers. At the far end of the chamber tables had been shifted and dark figures could be seen shuffling unenthusiastically to Cantonese rock.

'You can ride in my Beijing jeep,' he told us. Outside, we found his conveyance, with its canvas cover, parked hard up against the doors. We were soaked as we clambered aboard, Shen in the passenger seat and Ian B and I on the rear bench seat. As we surfed through the flooded boulevards of downtown Beijing I was surprised to find that the protuberance grinding against my thigh was Officer Lu's weighty service revolver. We swung through a pillared gateway into a large compound, at the head of which stood a long building of two storeys. Dim lights came from a few of the windows but the place had an air of abandonment.

'You need to find Officer Jin who is in charge of foreign affairs here,' Lu told us. We descended into the murk of the compound and the jeep took off out of the gates. Officer Lu clearly thought he'd done enough for these troublesome people and now others could take up the strain. We entered the building, no-one there to stop us, and soon we were wandering down a slimed concrete passage, past dusty brown-lacquered doors with no sign of lights. Mid-way we came to a door from which raised tones emanated. Shen opened it. Sitting at a low table were four men in singlets, playing cards. They showed no interest in the fact that strange aliens were wandering the police building at dead of night. Perhaps one of them said 'look upstairs'. In any case, that's where we found ourselves on another long greasy corridor with many doors off, one of which seemed to be occupied.

We knocked and entered the brightly neon-lit room. There were a couple of desks facing each other and piled high with books and papers. On the left-hand wall was a tall wardrobe, the top of which was similarly decorated. On a dusty table on the other side of the room a TV was blaring. The place was deserted—or was it? Lying on an old sofa amongst dirty grey cushions was a woman in a long, baggy black silk skirt. Suddenly realising that she had company, the woman rose to her feet and looked quizzically at the foreign beings who'd intruded on her entertainment. She was tiny, in her late fifties if a day, and peered at us through her black-dyed straggles of dyed hair. Was this unlikely person just the official we were seeking?

'These foreign friends have been robbed, and we were told to report to the Chaoyang District police's foreign affairs officer,' Shen said uncertainly.

'That's me, and I'm Officer Jin, the lady replied in Chinese. Well, what to do next? Officer Jin had turned her attention back to the TV, where the soap's denouement seemed imminent.

'Ah-hem, 'coughed Shen. 'Have you got some forms to fill in, perhaps?' Officer Jin grimaced and woke to her duties; dragging a chair over to the wardrobe, she balanced on it and started riffling through the unruly pile which crowned it. She tugged at some papers and an avalanche crashed to the floor. 'There', she proclaimed, grabbing a sheaf of forms. The officer retreated to one of the desks and placed her spectacles on her nose.

'I.D. cards,' she demanded in the only language known to her.

'But these two are foreigners and as you know, as the person here in charge of foreign affairs, foreigners have passports, not Chinese I.D. cards,' Shen explained with a patient smile, as to a child.

We went painstakingly through the forms. 'Visa and visa number,' Officer Jin demanded triumphantly. 'These foreigners have lost their passports so they don't have their visa numbers anymore,' responded an increasingly impatient Shen.

'So what do you want from me?' she asked with a gleam of triumph.

'Just a letter saying we reported the theft to you, with all the details of what was taken,' Shen replied with great forbearance.

An age passed before Officer Jin pronounced herself satisfied with her work.

'Go to the foreigners' public security department tomorrow and talk to them,' she suggested, handing Shen a single sheet with her handiwork signed off with a large red seal. We were dismissed. Outside in the deserted compound, the rain had ceased and first light was almost dawning over Beijing. It was three in the morning and we were surprised to find a taxi which returned us to the Sheke.

———∽∞∽———

The following day was taken up by an extraordinary round of visits, pleadings and nail-biting, all designed to get us onto that Aeroflot flight the next morning. If we missed it, we'd have to wait around for another week or make other arrangements which, given our dwindling project budget, were out of the question. The morning started at the British Embassy, where we joined the clamour of petitioners waiting for the doors to open. Once inside, by a miracle one of our British Council friends happened to pass through the crowded waiting room, and we grabbed him.

'No problem,' he breezily assured us. 'I know you two and I'm certain of your identities.' Ian B and I wrote down our personal details and the man disappeared through a security door. No more than half an hour later, he emerged waiving two temporary passports. Not something to be expected these days of the misbegotten suspicions and identity fraud. Next stop was the nearby American Express office to report on the travellers' cheques. All done and dusted in a matter of minutes. On we went in another taxi to a narrow street on the west side of the Forbidden City. The Foreigners Security Bureau was housed in a traditional grouping of courtyard housing, hidden from the street by a high wall. Men in the blue uniforms of the People's Armed Police were much in evidence; there were few smiles and nothing to tell us how to proceed. Eventually we were shooed into an office where a grim-faced policeman was clearly unhappy to have his morning reverie interrupted.

'What do you want?' he asked with a scowl. I explained what had occurred.

'Give me your passports,' he commanded. He hadn't listened. 'So, you have new passports but no visas to show me. Without visas you've entered the People's Republic illegally,' he said with a triumphant grin. But no joking was intended. The man slipped into a back office and out came an older officer, equally grim-faced.

'You have no visas and must pay a fine of 100 yuan,' he said with apparent anger, as though we'd deliberately flouted the laws of the People's Republic. 'After that you must pay 150 yuan for new visas,' he said with a scowl. We had other fish to fry at the Aeroflot office, so it seemed wise to pay up and get out of the place before he thought up new obstacles.

Another taxi ride and this time towards the east along Chang'an to the Aeroflot offices, situated on the ground floor of an office building on the boulevard. From that point in the day — mid-afternoon — it was a battle of wills with Olga, Svetlana and Mikhail — and finally the elusive Boris whose job it was to actually issue us with new tickets. *The final problem was with Aeroflot — lack of humour, bureaucratic quirkishness and adherence to the book,* my diary notes. We didn't much fancy having to stay in Beijing for another week until the next Moscow flight, and with the burden of new tickets to buy as well.

'What is your *maska*,' shot back Mikhail after we'd explained the problem. This meant nothing to us. Yet this *maska* was the key to all, Mikhail made clear. There was nothing for it but to go to the nearby Beijing-Toronto Hotel and see if its business centre would help us wheedle some international calls. For a price we found that this was now possible in 1990s Beijing. Diana at Regent Tours back in Bristol thought she knew the problem, assuring us she'd work on it.

Back to Aeroflot. 'It is Friday and this office will close at 6pm for the weekend,' Svetlana informed us with what seemed a glint in her eyes, as though *not* serving customers would be the crowning triumph of the week. The next couple of hours were nail-biting — no *maska*, none that was until the stroke of 6pm, when we heard the telex start chattering. Saved by the bell. My diary entry:

> The telex may have signalled an end to our problems, but getting the tickets in our hands was yet another one. Now we were in the inner sanctum with chain-smoking Boris (thin, peaky-faced, in airline pilot shirt,

gold-rimmed glasses). Shen and I wanted to relieve the enormous tensions of the day but Boris replied *nyet* when we asked to smoke. He takes half-an-hour poring over documents and occasionally grunting/snorting a query in Moscow English. He struggled with our final destination: 'What is man?' he shot at us until he realised it stood for Manchester. Finally all was done and all was well — even Boris managed a small smile.

That night we decided to celebrate in style with a grand dinner, Shen offering to pay. We chose to go back to one of our favourite eating spots at Shatan, a little café run by three sisters. 'No, that's far too cheap,' objected Shen. But we pointed out that he'd have a chance to meet the old lady from Shaanxi who ran a junk shop over the road from the café. Shen had spotted a Han dynasty farmyard complete with clay sheep — what the Chinese know as *mingqi*, an artefact placed in the grave of a rich farmer to help ease his path into the underworld. The woman had offered him the 2,000 year-old creation for the price of a meal in a posh restaurant. So it was to the three sisters that we went, and Shen got his farmyard.

The next morning our struggle with Aeroflot resumed, but only for a minute or two. The great Ilyushin airliner was boarded from the rear, a flight of stairs leading up to the passenger cabin. At the bottom of the steps stood two redoubtable female stewards, whose task it was to relieve passengers of their hand luggage and place it on racks by the stair. I was having none of this, as my bag contained irreplaceable research results and a Toshiba laptop (I still have it — a museum piece). I was chased up the stairs by a screaming steward who had hold of one end of my bag, trying to wrench it from me as I then coursed down the corridor to find my seat. Once again saved by the bell. The pilot was in a hurry to get to Irkutsk and no sooner had I sat down than he gave the order to cabin staff to strap themselves in. My assailant let go of the bag, I tucked it under the seat, and the aircraft started taxiing.

Prostitutes, thieves, black market antiquities—China was suddenly starting to look more like a normal country. Not since my anxiety-laden departure some 17 years earlier had I been quite so happy to be leaving Chinese soil.

IX
KANGDING (1999)

THE ELDERLY *taijiquan* practitioners, out before dawn, were already heading for their breakfasts. By the time the cab inched into the enclosed compound of the Xinximen bus station, Chengdu was suddenly a city in daytime mode

'No, you can't buy tickets to Kangding for tomorrow unless you can show me your *baoxian*, your insurance certificate', the bus station clerk shot back in tones normally reserved for naughty children. On no other journey anywhere, let alone the insurance-averse East, had I ever heard of such a notion.

'Where do you get them from?' I addressed the careworn male face through the aperture in his smeared glass pane.

'People's Insurance Company', he muttered, with a dismissive wave towards the compound gates. We found the office a few hundred yards up the road. Our ten *yuan* certificates did the trick, and with tickets for the next morning's bus we were all set for the fabled Kangding.

Maybe we needed insurance. Over the past couple of weeks, I'd been vaguely aware of a hole in my right trouser pocket. With all those little travellers' sewing kits I'd lifted from hotel bathrooms it could have been put right in no time. On the morning of our journey, we managed to out-sleep our alarm. As we tore along a corridor to the lobby of Chengdu University's guest-house, my lovely apple-green pendant, a parting gift from Louise's Hong Kong *fengshui* godfather, must have escaped. I was instinctively naked without my talisman, but there was no going back. We were late and there would be no more Kangding-bound buses that day. Outside the University gates three motor-pedicabs lurked, and we were soon phut-phutting towards through the wakening streets. Louise reflected on the loss of my lucky jade.

'Perhaps the idea is that jade must suffer, and then you don't have to,' she wryly remarked. 'Though you're meant to be a historical materialist, not a superstitious hysteric,' she threw in for good measure.

———∞———

Kangding, or Dartsedo as it's today known in Tibetan, was always a key staging post on the caravan route between Tibet and China. In 1939, the town had been elevated by the Nationalists to become the capital of a new, contrived province named Xikang. In 1950, the incoming Communist-led government wasted no time in dismembering the upstart province, the western part mostly going to what it termed the Tibet Autonomous Region, the northern to Qinghai province, bits of the southern to Yunnan. A large chunk of the eastern part, including Kangding, was merged with neighbouring Sichuan, by far the largest Han Chinese province by population and area. So Xikang was no longer, and Kangding itself had become merely the administrative centre of a special prefecture—the Garzé Tibetan Autonomous Zhou of Sichuan province.

Throughout China from the early 1980s on there'd been little restraint on internal migration, and in their millions adventurers from the crowded coastal provinces had heeded Beijing's call to 'go West'. In Qinghai province as described in the first Chapter, I'd found large numbers of Hui from the unforgiving lands of Ningxia and Gansu provinces. These 'Chinese Muslims' were vigorously reasserting their traditional role as economic intermediaries between the Han and the minority folk of the far

West. Visiting Lhasa in 1984, it was noticeable that many simple eateries and much petty trading were already in the hands of Han Chinese. In the case of the vast territories around Kangding, the Garzé region, we were to find on this journey that a distinctly Tibetan character was still very much in evidence. It wasn't merely the altitude and the inhospitable terrain which repelled invaders but the irascible and downright dangerous reputation of the locals too.

So the wilderness to which we were heading hadn't needed an influx of eastern migrants to gain its lawless frontier image. This part of south-east Tibet is the territory of the Khampas, who in large part even today care neither for the rule of Beijing nor, historically, that of Lhasa. I'd come across the Khampa youth on my earlier trips to Qinghai and Lhasa— haughty, loose-limbed giants, their long jet-black braids interlaced with strands of red silk. Some wore ornate daggers at the waists, and you got the feeling that these weren't merely for show. It was mainly Khampa warriors whom, in the early 20th century the invading British Indian Army could only subdue with the aid of the deadly new Maxim gun. Half a century later, in the Tibetan rebellion of the late 1950s, it was the youth of Kham who were the shock troops in the hopeless battles against Beijing's PLA.

Not surprisingly, it was from this region that, in the 1950s and '60s, the CIA lifted large numbers of young fighters to training camps in the mountains of Colorado, later to drop them back into Tibet to harass the People's Liberation Army. The CIA Khampa military unit established on the Nepal border was up to 2,000 strong. All this ended only after U.S. President Nixon's arrival in Beijing in 1971. The Chinese government made it clear than any rapprochement would require an end to the CIA campaign. In the still-ongoing U.S. campaign to roll back the Chinese revolution, even that supposed paragon of peaceful resolution of conflict, the

14th Dalai Lama, was by his own admission on the CIA payroll. Some say he remains a servant of U.S. interests. But it was his brother who acted as the chief liaison with the United States in their not-so-covert guerrilla harassment of Beijing's rule.

Straddling the major caravan route from China to Tibet, the bandit-infested reputation of the region goes back a long way. Even halfway through the 20th century, foreigners entered it at their peril. Take the heart-rending account of Frenchman André Guibart, whose surveying expedition into the region north-east of Kangding met with an ambush in which his fellow explorer, along with their hapless Han cook, were murdered. Guibart escaped by the skin of his teeth, the hair-raising time on the high plateaus of Eastern Tibet later recounted in a book.

He memorably observed that the locals might quite happily be herders and farmers by day, only to transform into thieves and cut-throats by night. Even in Kangding, then known as Dajianlu (aka Tashienlou) to the Chinese and Dardo to the Tibetans, no-one was safe after nightfall:

> Robbers abound in this frontier town, making frequent night incursions into gardens and private houses. It is not good to be found in the streets after ten o'clock at night. It is quite common at dawn to find people stabbed and entirely stripped of their clothes.[13]

Lawless Kham featured too in my own mother's palace of China memories. Eighty years before our own journey, to escape the Sichuan summer her family had taken the same route along the

---

13   Guibart, André, *Tibetan Venture,* London: Readers Union/John Murray, 1949, pp24-5.

SHIFTING GEARS IN CHINA

Chengdu-to-Lhasa 'Tea Road' towards Kangding, ponies for their servants and luggage and coolie chairs for mother and her brother and sister. From the Europeans' summer station high above the great gorge of the Dadu River, the infant who was to become my mother wandered off one morning, to be taken by wild-looking Tibetan horsemen. She was returned the same day to the bosom of the family; a ransom was quite certainly paid, though her parents always brushed the matter aside. Quakers were not meant to compromise themselves in this manner. Her recounting of this incident is amongst my first childhood memories.

Kangding with its air of a frontier town lies at the elevated altitude of 2,560 metres, but to get there from Chengdu on what today's maps mark as Route 318 you're confronted by the great barrier of the Erlang Mountains. We'd completely failed to research the journey, and the vicious climb up from the Sichuan plain to that pass even now sends shudders down my spine.

―――∞∞∞―――

It was half-an-hour before we were meant to be departing Chengdu, capital of the great Sichuan province and my mother's home until 1926. The oil-saturated yard which served as the city's bus terminus heaved with vehicles of every size and vintage. Yelling drivers revved up engines as their mates kicked tyres. Anxious passengers watched as their bags were lashed to roofs. Through the fumes and coursing crowd we came across a vehicle with the two smudged red characters for Kangding displayed on a white plastic board inside its windscreen.

'A 16-seater IVECO,' I remarked with some relief―a sturdy minibus of European origin, put together in Northeast China under a Sino-foreign joint venture. As related in an earlier chapter, my sorry experiences in Liaoning with British captains of industry came to mind: almost two decades had now passed since the Chinese had first moves to get hold of Western capital and technology *en masse* and on the cheap. From their standpoint, the joint venture device served perfectly, but the British wanted to play the game by different, more conventional rules. The IVECO was a revelation. We'd been long been inured to the domestically made *mianbaoche* 'bread bus', cobbled together on a chassis unsuited to China's roads, let alone to the country's erratic driving habits. With its high centre of gravity and lethal windows of un-toughened glass, the minibus which took us to work every Nanjing morning always put us in fear of our lives.

A couple of young men were leaning proprietarily on the IVECO's bonnet— our drivers, no doubt. With his thin black moustache in the style of the traditional gangster of Mao-era films, the smaller of the two was mean-looking. His uniform was dirty long-sleeved shirt and brown Dacron trousers, with the customary nylon ankle socks finished off by scuffed shoes. Exchanging grunts with him was a large young man of similar age, smart in his blue jacket, and certainly more amenable-looking. The Nasty One and The Nice One.

Both were pulling hard on expensive Phoenix Brand cigarettes, while they sipped tea from screw-lid jars wound around with plastic wire, the indispensable accessory of Chinese on the move. We'd missed breakfast, so grabbed a couple of beakers of tea from the old woman fanning her briquette stove by the ticket office. Louise also gave 5 *fen* to another matron who was pushing through the waiting passengers with a basket of jasmine buttonholes.

'Forget your jades: this is all the good luck I need,' she said with a wink.

Disdainfully ignored by the drivers, our bevy of fellow travellers was by now jostling around the vehicle's door, anxious to secure the best seats and get going. Standing out amongst them was a statuesque young woman in the long red skirt and black cummerbund of a Tibetan, her braided hair tied up around her brow, her deeply burnished cheeks redolent of the high plateau. Though I'd been twice before into Tibetan territory, the sight of exotic 'national minorities' amongst the drabness of the Chinese crowd aroused in most foreigners a frisson of excitement, and neither of us was immune. Accompanying this handsome Tibetan woman was a thin man of middle age, also tall and deeply sunburned, whom we took to be her father. For his trip to the big city he'd chosen his best Han-style uniform of grey Zhongshan jacket and peaked cap. But beneath his jacket he wore a shiny black leather waistcoat, a defiant touch of difference.

Exotic in a quite different manner were two highly painted ladies in their early twenties. The drivers were certainly taking an interest and I wasn't alone in noting skin-tight, revealing blouses and miniskirts. A sight for sore morning eyes. In 1970s China, when it never paid to stand out from the crowd, I'd lived amongst a subdued and dully-dressed tribe. The two young women ostentatiously waved their long black cigarette holders, and sizing up the weird foreign beings, they lapsed into fits of giggles. Never, ever in the China of Mao would such a brazen display have been possible. But as described in the previous chapter, in the years since the Chairman's departure, from time to time I'd come across this novel breed of Chinese womanhood. We surmised that the two young women would be going west to seek lucrative business opportunities. In quick measure we dubbed them The Two Harlots.

As people watchers and reality seekers, Louise and I relished the thought of being at close quarters with such promising company. For me at least, the very idea of a long distance road trip alongside Chinese companions was still a novelty. Louise was no novice: a few years earlier, on museum collection trips hunting for interesting textiles, she'd spent days crushed in country buses crossing the remote regions of Guizhou. She found it hard to imagine how a couple of decades earlier such an everyday activity as a country bus journey had been forbidden to foreigners.

The drivers were grinding their cigarette stubs underfoot and had decided they'd kept us on our toes long enough. We joined the fray for the best seats, which as far as we were concerned had to be near the back of the bus on its safe, kerb-side. Others had the same idea, and we were deftly elbowed onto a double bench on the opposite, the danger side of the vehicle. Nothing to be done about it and we took stock: right in front of us were the Tibetans, and over the aisle the Two Harlots. The other passengers looked like petty functionaries and traders rather than toilers of the soil. One amongst them seemed out of place—a middle-aged man with that delicate pinkish skin which is the mark of the urban Sichuanese. He was neatly dressed, wearing glasses and had the air of a real intellectual. The man had stationed himself on the back seat and seemed preoccupied by a newspaper. We decided he was The Professor, a title which he retained despite his later absorption in a sheaf of what appeared to be children's comics.

Moments after seven, engines spluttered into life and a dozen vehicles jostled for position near the compound gates. This was our drivers' first challenge: the IVECO took the lead and pulled sharply out onto the quiet streets of the city. A couple of seats near the front remained empty, and a few hundred yards beyond the bus station, out of sight of the red-arm-banded inspectors, we screeched to a halt and in hopped two more passengers. With cash and cigarettes handed over, it was clear that the bus company wasn't going to be benefiting from these supernumeraries. Half an hour later, on the fringes of the great Sichuan plain, three more un-ticketed characters flagged us down, and for a sixteen-seater we were now blatantly overloaded. Down the narrow centre aisle were extra loose-covered seats of a dun hue which hinged out and filled the space, and now I had a new neighbour rubbing shoulders to my right. I was to suffer his sharp elbows throughout the journey as he spun around to chat with his friend.

The Nice One was at the wheel and we headed steadily west towards that long-imagined mountain barrier which fringes the Sichuan Basin.

'It's great that our driver seems to know what he's doing,' remarked Louise. Always the worrier at the start of a long journey, my response was 'Maybe, but The Nasty One looks like one of the usual hot-heads.'

We settled down as the bus sped smoothly along the wide highway westwards, until our nerves were violently disturbed by the Tibetan girl, who ripped open her sliding window and vomited energetically. A good part of her effusions were destined to stay with us: they flew straight through Louise's window and onto her T-shirt. The girl's father proceeded to comfort her with a bottle of fizzy liquid and a bag of greasy dough sticks. Predictably, every hour or so came a repeat performance, which meant keeping our window firmly closed. The sweet stench was soon shrouded by acrid smoke from our chain-smoking companions.

No matter. The IVECO sped happily along through the fertile Chengdu plain with its characteristic half-timbered hamlets. Had it not been for the tall bamboo groves waving serenely in the breeze which ringed each farmstead, the architecture of medieval England would have come to mind. From time to time the road was barred and men in plain clothes would argue with our drivers, usually until cash was handed over. Unofficial tolls in these law-bending, get-rich-quick times? Before midday and perhaps 150 kilometers on, we entered a sizeable town and swung into a roomy compound boasting an elaborate but dead concrete fountain. The centrepiece was a two-metre statue of a diaphanously clad female, Tang dancer style. The fountain's putrid pond swam with bits of those soft yellowish loaves, half bread and half cake, which travellers all over China had adopted as up-to-the-minute 'foreign-style' snacks.

I'd been following the route closely on my *Sichuan sheng jiaotong jiance* — a surprisingly detailed road atlas of the province. In my first years in China, city bus maps had been readily available for a few *fen*, but that was it. Everything else was supposed to be a secret, even to the locals. I relished this novelty of knowing where I stood in that great Sichuan landscape.

While our fellow passengers headed off towards a low building, a smoking stove-pipe tacked onto its outside wall, I walked back to the gatehouse to see where we'd landed. Traditionally, a Chinese walled compound displays vertical wooden name boards at its gate: 'Ya'an Town Ganzhi Autonomous District *zhaodaisuo*', the boards announced. An 'autonomous district' in the Chinese administrative system means one where historically, one of China's 55 non-Han ethnic groups was in the majority — though migration of the past decades have often now made them a minority in their own lands. Our destination of Kangding was the capital of this administrative division, so we felt that progress was being made. As for the city of Ya'an, in 2008 and again in 2013 it was to fall victim to shattering earthquakes, the notorious Wenchuan 'quake featured in the widely acclaimed Chinese film *Aftershock*.

By the time I got back across the yard our party had disappeared into the low building, and following, we found ourselves in a dimly lit windowless chamber which put me in mind of the medieval monastery kitchen in Umberto Eco's *Name of the Rose*. In the centre was a cooking range of whitewashed brick, where elderly Tibetan matrons were stirring oversized iron vessels, around which licked dirty flames. Our fellow passengers were spread about the cavern at makeshift tables—upturned oil drums. A woman beckoned us over to her cauldron where unidentifiable animal parts in a grey sea dived and surfaced again to her wooden paddle. Our fellow passengers were well into their repasts and some were already slurping the last drops of liquid, clearing their throats and lighting cigarettes. Justice was only half done to our own greasy bowls and we retreated to the yard to salvage a snack from our rucksack of dry biscuits and sweet Sichuan oranges. We were watched by some smiling new arrivals—a family of Tibetan herders in their extravagant fur headgear and sheepskins, one arm out in that characteristic Tibetan style. 'My first Tibetan-looking Tibetans,' remarked ethnographer Louise.

Our companions were now outside and heading for the latrine block. Again, we were the stragglers, The Nasty One giving us a small piece of his mind as we clambered back on board. Soon we were back speeding along an open road, devoid of traffic apart from the occasional heavy truck.

Mr Nasty had taken over the helm, and as anticipated, the ride became ever more wearing. I can never settle back and accept that I'm at someone else's mercy, and usually 'do' the driving myself, a tiring habit which only makes the road more stressful. Now, after a short stretch of passable two-lane highway, some twenty miles beyond Ya'an the road suddenly deteriorated into a single track, and became a non-road.

It seems that when China's rural arteries are to be rebuilt there's never a staggering of the operation— both lanes are attacked at once and for miles. As described in Chapter 4, I'd first come across this routine some fifteen years before on the

60-odd kilometer stretch from Lhasa airport to the city. Why this happens is a mystery; maybe such displays of road-building as total warfare inhibit the authorities from clawing back already-committed budgets. Whatever, now, for the next four hours and perhaps 100 kilometres we pitched and rolled over mud ramps and spoil heaps, hanging onto our seats to prevent being thrown with concussive force at the vehicle's ceiling. Naturally, the Tibetan youth proceeded to lose her Ya'an lunch.

The highway repairs came to an abrupt end and for the next hour or so we were on a good surface which rose steadily up the broad valley. Eventually, we approached a second largish settlement—Tianquan, according to my map book. All went smoothly until the outskirts, where we came up against a huge queue of trucks. Perhaps imagining that his foreigner-conveying vehicle carried priority, The Nasty One wove in and out of the stalled convoy, tilting us at dangerous angles on the mud-rutted roadside, occasionally lurching through someone's front yard, scattering pigs and chickens. The Harlots found these manoeuvres laudable and clapped Nasty's every antic. But finally, even he had to concede defeat. It was already after two and we were stuck on a new concrete bridge swarming with smartly uniformed paramilitaries wielding walkie-talkies. Something mysterious was definitely going on, but no-one seemed to remark on this unscheduled encounter with the *Wujing*, the reassuringly named People's Armed Police.

An hour later, wailing klaxons rose to a crescendo and round the bend charged a convoy of police vans followed by four new Toyota Land Cruisers with tinted windows. Half-a-dozen minibuses brought up the rear, conveying the lesser officials, who gazed out impassively at the chaos they'd caused to the up-traffic.

'It's over twenty years since Mao died but the *laobaixing*, the old hundred names, still seem to put up with the arrogance of officialdom,' I remarked to Louise. Who the Land Cruiser bigshots were, and why they were heading away from the Tibetan foothills, we were only later to discover. Once at our destination, we found that preceding us had been a delegation led by none other than China's Premier. He'd journeyed from Chengdu to Kangding to show his solicitude to the long-suffering Tibetans. There, he attended the grand re-opening of the Lhamo Tse Monastery—a place we were later to visit in order, fruitlessly as it turned out—to engage with the abbot.

At last we were on the move again, the ever-rising valley transformed into a messy industrial landscape. We motored on past a cluster of cement works and smoky smelting operations, a primitive fertiliser plant and then a large hydro-station with huge pipes descending from the mountainside. All testament to Chairman Mao's *San xian* ('Third Front') policy, which meant that for twenty years from the mid-1950s on, the lion's share of China's industrial investment was despatched to the impregnable interior. The details were only revealed to the world after he was gone, something which I analyse in my 1985 account.

The gradient was now steeper and soon we'd left the valley of factories far behind. Already it seemed like a very long Monday when the bus pulled up at a roadside bamboo and reed shack, suspended over a gorge. We piled out, stretched our legs, hawked and spat with the best of them, while peering over the edge of the precipice. It was the scheduled after-dinner loo stop, and one by one our passengers crept into the shack and re-emerged doing up their belts and zipping their trousers. The Harlots squealed their horror but obediently disappeared together. Coming out into the bright sunlight, they waved us in with obscene gestures and raucous laughter. The flimsy structure had no floor. Instead, two substantial but slimy bamboo poles were our footrests.

Between them was a drop of hundreds of feet. In my time in China, I'd met with a range of lavatorial experiences, but never anything like this. The unnerving height was well compensated by an absence of those rich odours and writhing maggots which are a feature of most country privies. Our high-wire evacuations successfully and satisfyingly performed, the drivers shooed us back towards the vehicle, only pausing to address us for the first time.

'When are you going back to Chengdu?' Mr Nasty enquired in thick Sichuan dialect.

'We're staying in Kangding and heading back to Chengdu on Friday,' I responded. A wry smile spread across his face. 'Friday won't be a good day to come back,' he shot back, pointing at the ravine with his cigarette stump. He then launched into Sichuan dialect, too thick for me to penetrate, though the gist seemed unmistakably 'You ain't seen nothing yet if you're returning on Friday'. Before I could interrogate him further, Nasty had leapt up into the cab and slammed the driver's door.

We were off again on the endless climb. Until late afternoon, we drove up a fair concrete road, which all of a sudden evaporated. We were at the foot of a massive mountain, and the only way ahead was offered by a narrow and stony track. I checked my watch: it was already half past four and no sign of Kangding. The minibus ground into first gear and lurched onto the 40-degree incline, hard against a continuous cliff face. To our right was an ever-deepening precipice. This went on for minutes, then endlessly, until it seemed as though there was no other life either before or after. Forced to steer around the occasional stalled truck or negotiate one of the many torrents and their deep rifts in the track, we would roll terrifyingly onto the edge of the chasm. Things eased up a bit when we entered a sea of cloud which swirled eerily around the blackened trunks of the dead pines clinging to the rocks far beneath us. Disease, acid rain from the industrial valley we'd passed through? Every so often, we made out roadside shelters roofed with tarpaulins, scrawled signs at their entrances proclaiming tyre repairs and water. These habitations were, ominously, furnished with seats salvaged from vehicles which, we realised, had gone no further. At one o'clock, we halted and out of the mist in some pre-arranged rendezvous a third member of the incongruous Harlot tribe hopped aboard. She was happily accommodated on the plastic-sheathed engine manifold which bulged between the drivers.

Her sisters were both snoring through their painted lips. They weren't alone. Everyone but we and The Professor, now absorbed in one of his comics, had dropped off. I'd often observed that the Chinese traveller invariably lapses into slumber. The gaping ravine a few inches from our wheels was enveloped in dense cloud, and what was out of sight was out of mind. Fatalism and exhaustion were tempting anesthetisers, and I envied the slumbering Louise, who as ever had taken in her stride the treacherous journey. But it wasn't always to be thus.

After two hours of contorted ascent, the track abruptly levelled off. We were approaching the pass of Mount Erlang, which my *Jiaotong jiance* map booklet marked at just under 3,400 metres. Long before the extraordinary railway into Lhasa, two overland routes led towards Tibet's capital from China proper — the Qinghai Golmud route which the railway now parallels, and this, the far more important southwest route, the old Tea Road. Bearing in mind that even today's shrunken Tibet is as large as Western Europe, Lhasa, according to my reckoning, was still a week's ride away. And here we were, defeating the greatest barrier separating the Sichuan Basin of the Han Chinese from the Tibetan Plateau. Beyond us to the west, lay the gorge of the Dadu River, the fabled Bridge of Luding where a decisive manoeuvre of the Long March took place in 1935, as well as Kangding itself. In the growing dimness we could make out a snow-capped peak far, far beyond the Dadu gorge; scrutinising my *Jiaotong jiance*, I realised that this had to be the great Minya Konka, at almost 7,600 metres above sea level one of the world's greatest and most majestic peaks.

In 1939, the Russian-born Peter Goullart had left Shanghai bound for Kangding, on a mission to set up a headquarters of the industrial cooperatives movement. This was being promoted by the government in the interior, where the Japanese invaders couldn't penetrate. He tells of leaving Ya'an on foot, and then climbing the ferocious heights just described, inadequately clothed and shod because bandits had made off with almost all he possessed. Goullart's *Princes of the Black Bone* certainly puts our own journey in perspective:

> I was wakened at dawn as this was to be, the porters told me, a difficult day for we had to cross the first great range of mountains through a pass called Tahhsiangling. High stone steps, hewn out of rock, led up and up the brush-clad slopes and we walked slowly, pausing every five minutes to gather breath. On and on for hours until we reached a cluster of smoke-begrimed huts where only some bean curd and a few eggs were available. In some places the stone steps ascended in a huge spiral, and I had the sensation of climbing a stupendous ziggurat.[14]

Reaching the summit, I thought we might at least have halted for a few moments to mark the conquest and stretch our legs. But no,

---

14 Goullart, Peter, *Princes of the Black Bone*, London: John Murray, 1959, p6.

Mr Nasty was now intent on hurtling off down the other side of the mountain. A chaos of seemingly laden washing lines emerged from the fog, which we quickly registered as the prayer flags of grateful travellers. A definite signal that we were entering a region whose Tibetan population needed to show no inhibitions about their culture. This timeless Buddhist adornment of a mountain pass was doubtless the spectacle which had met my mother's eyes all those years ago; I envied her that sure-footed pony which had borne her to these heights.

'I'm sure my grandparents would have walked the whole way up,' I said to Louise, reminding her of a passage in my mother's memoir which mentioned her parents' aversion to being carried when the going got hard. Their refusal to use their litters upset their team of bearers no end: far from welcoming the Quakerly gesture, the coolies regarded this behaviour as losing them a great deal of face.

If the ascent to the pass on Mount Erlang had been hair-raising, the way down offered no relief. This side of the mountain was clear of cloud; snaking beneath us on a treeless brown landscape we could make out several dozen straight stretches each capped by hairpins. At least this side lacked real precipices, though any slip would mean a fall of scores of metres and certain death. I prayed for the sensible driver to take over, but Nasty wasn't having any of it. This, after all, was his fun, a chance to show his mettle. Downwards, ever downwards we careered towards the silvery, snaking Dadu, ten kilometres of road and two or three thousand metres below. In the time-honoured way of Chinese drivers, the gearbox was shoved into neutral, the brakes assigned the task of defence. When the stench of burning brake pads began to waft into the passenger compartment, it was time for the Chinese remedy, one to which I'd been introduced when with my slate men, and described in Chapter 6. With a pebble-scattering flourish, we pulled off the road at one of the occasional pit-stops. Here youths lounged on their salvaged truck bench seats awaiting business. Our driver argued for a minute about the fee with a barefoot child. A ten-metre length of hollowed bamboo was then trained onto our wheels, which fizzed and steamed like a kitchen wok.

Some way further towards the valley floor, for no apparent reason the bus pulled over. A gnarled old woman appeared from nowhere with a basket of tiny peaches which became ours for a five *yuan* note. Suddenly from behind a rocky outcrop a smart blue pickup glided up alongside. The three aisle passengers seemed to know what the game was. They were soon smiling up at us from the open back of the pickup. Mr Nice announced that 'just for a few minutes' he needed three more volunteers. Surprisingly, The Professor packed away his comic and followed the three aisle passengers. The Two Harlots soon joined him, leaving their bags and giggling loudly at the manoeuvre.

Round the next hairpin, for the third time of the descent we skidded to a halt. This time it was a tree-trunk roadblock. Two stern-faced officials in oversized blue peaked caps slid back the door and conducted a fruitless head-count. Denied their fines, off we sped. It wasn't until we finally reached river level and the town of Luding that the logistics of the subterfuge were clear. Awaiting us in the main street was the same pickup, and after a small wad of notes had passed between hands, its rear occupants — minus the Professor — were restored to us.

'Where has the *xiansheng* (gentleman) gone?' I asked young women.

'That was his brother in the truck,' one of them replied. 'How else do you think he got a free ride from Chengdu?' They're our best customers in Ganzhi,' she added coyly. And the two of them burst into peals of laughter. Some professor...

SHIFTING GEARS IN CHINA

In the depths of the Dadu gorge, nightfall was suddenly complete. Like many Westerners enthralled by stories of the Long March and the rise of the Communists, my introduction to the momentous events of the 1920s and '30s was Edgar Snow's classic *Red Star over China* published in 1937. Snow's account has lately been drawn into question, attacked even as no more than an assemblage of Communist Party-serving myths: there is no greater questioning than that surrounding the epic episode of the Luding Bridge. But here, according to the account told to Snow when he got to the northwest redoubt of Yan'an, the braves of the Red Army heroically clawed their way along the iron chains of the bridge under withering fire, putting paid to the warlord allies of the Nationalist forces, and their gun emplacements on the far bank. The thousands could then continue on the great strategic retreat to the interior, known forever after as the Long March. Had they failed to cross the Dadu, superior forces coming up from their rear would have massacred them, and China's modern history might have turned out rather differently. The revisionist history claims that the whole episode had been quite blown out of proportion. But this was 1999, and I was an unsullied adherent of the Official Version, and Luding was going to be one of the highlights of our tortuous journey. But we crossed over the unseen Dadu on a modern concrete structure, and as we sped on I could only just glimpse the outline of the ancient and myth-laden iron suspension bridge.

Outside Luding we finally lost our decorative young women to their business in the town. Our depleted vehicle set off on the last leg of the journey, and with dusk gathering we were just anxious to get to Kangding and find a place to stay. All I could tell was that we were on another uphill stint, by no means as steep and twisty as the dreaded mountain, but relentlessly rising. Our destination, three hours ahead, was a grinding 1,200 metres above the valley of the Dadu.

———∼∼∼———

Night had long fallen when the IVECO dipped off the road into a muddy yard, with a low modern building with green framed steel window frames to one side which appeared to house a ticket office and canteen. We made out a knot of magenta and ochre-robed monks in the light of a dim lantern, idly there we imagined just to see what the daily Chengdu transport might bring. They greeted our Tibetan duo with bows and double handshakes, and then turned their attention to us. Worried that I might give offence, I was unsure whether to tackle them in Chinese. No problem. One of the monks responded jauntily in the same tongue.

'Go up this big street,' he said, 'and at the top you'll see a monastery on your left. Just beyond, on the right, is our Ganzhi Prefecture *zhaodaisuo.*' In case of any confusion, his companion produced a pencil and inscribed the name of the Kangding guesthouse for officials in my notebook. Ten minutes later we'd trudged up the main street of the town, down the middle of which tumbled a wild mountain torrent, and were arousing a young woman from her slumbers at the reception desk of a three-storey concrete building with a compound full or Land Cruisers. Perhaps mistaken us for official guests, the woman assigned us the *ganbu* (officials') suite which bore the outrageous tariff of 180 *yuan* daily — the equivalent to an entire month's wages of any government servant in these parts. Our quarters consisted of huge bedroom with satin-covered bedstead, a spacious living room complete with the usual hard-packed sofa, as well as a glass-topped writing desk. Attached was a capacious and sparkling bathroom. Perfection!

Back in Chengdu, we'd made friends with the staff of Chengdu

SHIFTING GEARS IN CHINA

University's Museum, and we'd been sneaked behind the scenes to explore the stored collection. Amongst the long-neglected shelves of pot shards and pieces of unidentifiable bronze, I found labels and bits of notebook in the hand of my grandfather John Rodwell. Over half-a-century earlier he must have played a part in the formation of this museum when it belonged to the former West China Union University. Now, working for the museum was a Tibetan woman, Nyima Lhamo, who befriended us in an almost conspiratorial manner, as though we too represented 'the other' in the ocean of Han Chinese. As *de facto* curator of the place, it was she who'd got us into the stores. She let us know that a good friend in Kangding was none other than the abbot of the newly recreated Lhamo Tse Monastery, the place that China's Premier had just visited, and which is known to the Chinese as the Nanwu Si.

'The abbot who the Chinese call Duo Chu is not really in charge of the Monastery,' explained Nyima Lhamo with a knowing smile. 'In fact, the abbot's leader is a young boy who is a Living Buddha.' So, we surmised, Abbot Duo Chu was more like a regent. Or perhaps the real authority lay altogether elsewhere.

It was late afternoon when we walked to the north of the town, being drawn towards Lhamo Tse Monastery by waves of amplified chanting. It was, we later learned, the third day of the *kaiguang*—'opening of light' being a literal rendering of the ceremony of consecration. We entered the high ochre-painted walls through a great gate and found ourselves in an expansive courtyard, to the middle of which groups of monks were seated cross-legged, in untidy rows. Many had little hand-bells, others wielded *vajra*, and the chant suffusing the air was the recitation of Buddhist sutras.

A well-dressed, brightly lip-sticked and indeed attractive Han woman in her fifties approached us. 'My name is Holly

Wang,' she announced brightly—and somewhat surprisingly in English. The woman gave the impression that she had some sort of official capacity as she persisted in asking our business. In return, we enquired as to hers. It seemed incongruous to find such an urbane Han amongst this throng of devout Tibetans.

'I'm a Buddhist, and I'm from Zhejiang province and I'm here to join in the *kaiguang*,' Holly Wang explained. 'And I'm going to stay at the Monastery a long time.

'Why is that?' I enquired.

'Something has happened in my life and the monks will put it right,' she said wistfully. We told Holly that we were looking for the Abbot and, she seemed unfazed, offering to take us straight to him. With our new friend, of whom I have to say we were already a little suspicious, we wandered around the office cells of the monastery until we found a rotund and harassed looking Abbot Duo Chu in a corridor. He seemed to be impatiently telling a monk to do something or other. Holly Wang muttered a few words of Chinese and we handed over Nyima Lhamos' letter to the man, which he took with something of a grimace. Perhaps by sending Holly to us as a forbidding emissary, he'd thought that it would be easy to get rid of these alien nuisances on his patch. But now that the connection with Nyima Lhamo had been made clear, our *guanxi* had been established and we couldn't be so easily dismissed. As he scanned the letter, he shifted from leg to leg, and wouldn't look our way. Holly Wang stepped in, as if to save faces on both sides, and more particularly to get us out of the Abbot's presence.

'The ceremony will start now in the Great Hall and now we must go,' she said sternly.

'Come tomorrow at 10 o'clock,' the Abbot mouthed in Chinese as he hurried off in its direction.

We were soon caught up in a good-natured crowd of pilgrims,

each holding onto the chuba (gown) of the person in front, and leaving our shoes at the entrance we were propelled into the cavernous space of the Monastery's Great Hall. We followed our guide as she tiptoed around the dense mass of cross-legged pilgrims, they gazing up at us as if it was the most normal thing to see a couple of Westerners in their midst. Once seated on the concrete floor, an air of hushed expectation descended on the lofty temple with its huge brocaded wall hangings. Before a kind of altar, wisps of smoke emanated from huge bronze incense burners arrayed around it. And above the altar was a daïs and throne.

A stir went through the congregation as a curtain was parted and a procession of yellow-hatted elders entered. Behind them waddled a richly be-robed child of perhaps eight years old. The little Living Buddha, no less. Two of the monks stepped forward and lifted him bodily onto the gilded lotus throne, and a resonating murmur of approval coursed through the assembly. Suddenly the air was rent with clashing of cymbals, the sounding of trumpets and the pounding of drums, followed by monotone chanting from the monks. The ceremony had commenced.

Squatting beside us, Holly Wang had decided to give us something of a running commentary.

'This beginning part is about expelling all the ghosts here,' she whispered. We hoped she wasn't referring to us -- the *Yangguizi*, the 'Ocean Devils' as we would have been called a couple of generations earlier.

Meanwhile, the crowds around us had relaxed and broken into gasps of expectation as young monks tripped amongst the congregation with pails of *chang*, that Himalayan barley-based beverage for celebrations and funerals. As I'd discovered at that raucous party in Lhasa (Chapter 4), to the unaccustomed, at high altitude the tipple can be dangerously inebriating. The assembled crowd murmured in happy anticipation, grimy bowls appearing from the depths of those long Tibetan sheepskin gowns for every season, the chuba.

The little Living Buddha's attention to his devotions was obviously limited, and now he was casting sneaking glances towards the two strange beings amongst the congregation and smiling coyly. One of his guardians noticed and to the amusement of the crowd, tried quietly to admonish him, But the child was finding us more entertaining than the wavering incantations of the monks.

There was plenty going on and lots to look at, but as the ceremony might be going on for hours, we thought it best to beat a retreat. Outside in the inner courtyard another odd encounter: an old man with walnut face, who at first we took to be a monk in plain clothes, accosted us and struck up a conversation.

'Where do you work?' he surprised us by almost shouting in passable English while tugging at my sleeve. I mentioned Liverpool and its university.

'Oh — very famous,' he proclaimed as though he'd made an intimate study of the rankings of England's seats of learning. Unprompted, the man then launched into his life story, all in rapid-fire Chinese.

'I was an orphan, beggar, until I joined the *Gongchandang*, Communist Party, to be a soldier. They sent me to get educated in Changchun in the Dongbei,' he spilled out. After more in the same vein, he began to speak in hushed tones and money seemed to be mentioned. Now thinking the man was a pilgrim mendicant, I got out some *renminbi* and tried to slip them to him, but he brushed my hand aside and began to speak agitatedly in Chinese about some obscure matter. He spied something or someone over our shoulders and abruptly took himself off, leaving us puzzled and none the wiser. Perhaps, we later thought, he'd been sent to interrogate us by the Abbot on the strength of a dubious claim to speak the foreigners' tongue.

I glanced at my watch: it was six o'clock and dusk was falling, and there seemed to be no point hanging around any longer. We headed for the great portal of the monastery, intending to be back again the next day and hoping to discover a more relaxed reception.

The next day—my diary marks it as Thursday 17 June—at the appointed hour we made our way to Lhamo Tse, but there was no-one to greet us in the time-honoured manner of the East. We could only hang around in the great courtyard hoping for developments. On its far side, a few minutes later we caught sight of Abbot Duo Chu, his back to us, assisting one of his elderly confrères up the main steps. We glanced upwards and found that the balcony skirting the upper floor housing the living quarters was crowded with onlookers. Monks and pilgrims alike had emerged from their cells to witness the discomfort of our outlandish selves.

'Quickly, where's the camera—this'll make a great photo,' Louise whispered. But as I grabbed it from my shoulder bag, an ancient lama raised his hands in admonition. Three men in Han outfits then sidled over to us and asked if we too were Buddhists. Above us on the balcony we spotted Holly Wang, but oddly she failed to return our waves. Had she been reprimanded for befriending us the day before? Was she on a mission of her own?

Our promised encounter with Abbot Duo Chu now seemed to have drifted away, and things were becoming uncomfortable. We decided to leave, and headed for the great entrance of the monastery compound. Once outside, we loitered on the dusty path, reluctant to withdraw completely. There an old lama surprised us by addressing us in a friendly manner of the 'where do you come from?' variety, until Holly Wang and a fresco painter, who'd told us of his ambition to get to San Francisco (of all places), appeared together outside the portal. Our erstwhile pilgrim guide was no longer the friendly presence of the day before.

'The Abbot is too busy to see you,' she announced in Chinese. She then turned on her heels and was off.

Oddly, a group of lamas then emerged from the monastery, one of them clutching an up-to-the-minute Japanese camcorder. From a few yards distant and grim-faced, he started to film us. Obviously more of a security man than a monk, and all of a part with Holly Wang's change of mood.

———∞———

It was still early days in the re-emergence of long-suppressed religious practices in China and with all eyes on this great monastery in the wake of the Premier's visit, officialdom was in a nervous state. So we decided the following day to give up on Lhamo Tse and its unhelpful, not to say hostile and suspicious lamas, both genuine and probably not so genuine. There were other monastic orders in the city awaiting us. Indeed, right opposite our *zhaodaisuo* was the Gelugpa sect monastery, the 17th century Anju Si, compact and ancient-looking and built around a sloping cobbled court, looking every bit the caravanserai, which of course it was too. We marched through the arched gate but a young monk appeared from behind a massive prayer wheel and barred our way. From his robes he drew a rolled-up *thangka*.

'Two thousand *yuan*', he kept saying, in Chinese. We demurred, at which he frowned and waved us away in a 'clear off' gesture; we turned back towards the street distinctly unimpressed by Kangding's monastic piety. To change the unpromising rhythm of the place, that afternoon we climbed up to a kind of park above the town, passing rows of *mani* stones and ending up in a Chinese-style pavilion where an old fellow, apparently the caretaker, restored our faith in the locals by bringing tea and sitting with us awhile as we gazed at the far snow-clad cone of Minya Konka, which though still distant soared high above the foreground peaks.

Next morning, we went off to the third monastery of the town, Dordrak, which the Chinese know as the Jingang Si — a redoubt of the Red Hat School of Tibetan Buddhism. Here, the atmosphere was almost welcoming and we soon joined a group of pilgrims from the ancient metal-working centre of Derge, far to the north in the wilds of the Hengduan Mountains. The most charming of the women had beautifully plaited braids, intertwined with numerous coral and turquoise strands. She seemed to be taking a particular interest in me; I was quickly convinced that I'd met the self-same person a few years before, on the long flight of steps leading up to Lhasa's Potala. After all, for some richer Tibetans, long pilgrimages were still a way of life. Back home, I dug out my Lhasa slides and when I compared photos this turned out to be the case.

The woman beckoned Louise over to the bank of huge prayer wheels, while I did an Oriental squat outside with the menfolk. Delighted by Louise's apparent fervour, the pilgrim group invited us to join them in the main chamber of the temple. Here they adopted a shuffling gait and we joined their little column; ever the anthropologist, Louise got out her notebook to list the configuration of deity statues around the space, but was told off by a man in a red tea cosy-like hat who must have been the temple keeper.

Eventually we emerged from the gloom. To the right of the chamber was another, smaller one, to which our new friends now beckoned us. The entrance was covered by a heavy yak hair drape with a black skull at its centre. This was the chamber of wrathful deities of pre-Buddhist Bon practices. The interior was dark and forbidding, and it wasn't until Louise had followed our guides in making rather energetic prostrations towards a terrifying deity figure that we were allowed to emerge from the little house of horrors.

———∽∽———

Friday had come around all too soon and it was time to head back to Chengdu. Before the sun rose, we trudged down to the little bus station for our 7 o'clock departure, to find the same two drivers and the same minibus.

'Bloody hell, what do we do now?' was my pointless reaction. There was no other way out. Kangding had to wait another decade before it got its airport. My son William, at the time resident in Chengdu, much later told me how he flew into what was to become the world's third highest airport. At 4,280 metres above sea level, Kangding's is beaten in the height stakes by two others, both in Tibet.

We set off from the town, coursing down the endless valley of with its tumbling river to our left, the freewheeling vehicle reviving that familiar feeling that I was going to die and there was nothing I could do about it. But all went well a far as the gorge of the swirling Dadu and soon Luding: now we had a clear but transitory sighting of the ancient bridge of Long March fame. The valley floor also afforded a clear view of the road up to the dreaded Erlang Mountain pass, which snaked up the opposite mountainside. As far as the eye could see was an unbroken line of tiny trucks was evident, which if one watched carefully were either slow-moving or motionless.

'Remember Mr Nasty's remark on the journey here?' Louise remarked.

'"You ain't seen nothing yet!" I seem to recall,' said I.

'Well, this must be it,' Louise rejoined. But what was actually in front of us was still a mystery. We crossed the raging Dadu on the modern concrete bridge and the minibus started grinding up the mountain. So far so good—no obstacles in sight. After a few hundred yards we drew to a halt. I recognised the pull-in: it was where we'd had our illicit passengers restored to us when we'd been hurtling down from the pass. And just as then, a smart pickup sidled up with three people squatting in the back. The front-seat passenger was no other than our old friend the Professor. Our supernumeraries were back with us again and we felt quite part of the old club. I stepped down to admire the view, though my eyes were drawn instead to the driver who was kicking the tyres. They were entirely bald, smooth as boiled eggs.

'*Luntai hen buhao.*' 'The tyres are really awful', I exclaimed in horror. Mr Nasty merely laughed in my face, shouted the familiar refrain '*shangche*' ('all aboard'), and we were back to the crush of legs and luggage, gears grinding up the ever-more tortuous incline.

It wasn't long before we hit the back of the convoy which we'd spied from the valley below. The trucks were those modern and robust products of the great Changchun No. 1 Auto Plant, established with Soviet aid in the 1950s. These though were all recent models, cabs painted a pleasant eggshell blue, drivers' doors bearing stencilled names in Chinese and Tibetan showing their *danwei*, their work-units. Every truck was loaded well above their cabs with huge logs, massive tree trunks. With their centres of gravity raised so dangerously high, those vehicles crawling up the incline were lurching and swaying alarmingly. A wonderful challenge for Mr Nasty, who managed to work his way around half a dozen trucks until we reached a point where the convoy was stationary, almost blocking the road. Here, the cabs had all been abandoned, their wild-looking Tibetan drivers seated cross-legged in little knots on the track-side, for all the world unconcerned with anything but their conversation, their snacks and their cigarettes. Manoeuvring around the stalled trucks was going to be our brainless driver's *tour de force*. Naturally, he chose to do so on the precipitous side of the road rather than on the inside, bank side. We managed to get by maybe three dozen of the over-laden monsters before the track narrowed further. This merely gave Mr Nasty the opportunity of a stellar performance. With one set of wheels on the cusp of the precipice, the minibus rolled and pitched to the cheering of every one of our danger-oblivious fellow travellers.

By now I was just about quivering in my seat from anger, rather than from fear. 'Anquan diyi, bisai dier,' I started yelling from the rear of the bus. Any Chinese beyond their teens would have immediately recognised that I was parodying the Cultural Revolution slogan forever heard at sporting events: *Youyi diyi, bisai dier* — 'friendship first, competition second'. The adapted version I was yelling was 'safety first, competition second'. Rather than add their voices to a plea to respect life and limb, this reminder of the very passé slogan was a cause for hilarity. The other passengers merely cheered on Nasty with added gusto. We arrived at an impasse. A truck had slewed across the track and there was nothing even he could do about it. Louise and I had had enough. We grabbed our bags and slid open the door and decided to walk. How we were to get back to distant Chengdu we never gave a thought.

'We've got a job to do, anyway,' Louise said, as we started up the mountain, passing a circle of dusty drivers who were not in the least surprised to see us. One of them was chewing on a piece of yak rib, which he generously thrust towards us. Instead, we paused to share an acrid cigarette, but we still didn't understand what was going on. These men from the high plateau had no

Chinese, and we not a word of Tibetan.

I recalled the job which Louise had mentioned. Not long before, at Louise's workplace, Liverpool Museum, we'd been at a new exhibition's private view. I'd been asked by the museum's director to take care of another guest. China's Consul-General was a man whom I knew from not infrequent visits to his official residence, a large Victorian mansion in parkland, south of Manchester. I was making reception small talk, glass in hand, when a tall besuited character with his back to me turned on his heels and greeted me with just two words: 'Hello, Kirkby'. Whoever it was addressing me in this quaint upper class, bygone manner then turned around again and resumed his conversation. It transpired some minutes later that this was someone I'd not set eyes on for over three decades. My old Ackworth Quaker School classmate John, even then a brilliant but eccentric botanist. Now, it transpired, he was a colleague of Louise's at the museum.

When he heard of our plans to be in the high mountains bordering eastern Tibet, John decided this was an opportunity not to be missed. Issuing us with several dozen empty, numbered envelopes, his instructions were to get ourselves on a Tibetan mountain and collect, at random, bits of moss and lichen, noting on each envelope altitude and aspect. This track near the summit of Mount Erlang provided the perfect opportunity to do our duty by John. As we laboured upward carrying our bags and plucking our samples from the banks, we laughed together at our little game of amateur botany.

Eventually the track began to level out, and ahead of us we could see the pile of *mani* stones and prayer flags which marked the pass. Just then Louise spotted three men shadowing our progress, walking partly out of sight just over the edge of the road. 'Farmers by day, bandits by night', we said to each other, as we hurried on towards the next line of stalled trucks. Curiously, someone had decorated the road with a pack of Western-style playing cards, and for good measure and missing my lucky jade I slipped the ten of hearts into my bag. Meanwhile, when they saw we'd caught up with some parked trucks, the shady-looking threesome disappeared from sight.

Once over the pass and starting our descent, we realised what the stoppage was all about. A group of drivers was peering into the ravine where five hundred feet below us was an overturned truck, its cargo falling away beyond it. A few hundred yards further on another had met the same fate.

'The Tibetans are refusing to move out of respect for the dead,' was Louise's take on the matter. Our adventure had taken on a sombre tone, and for the next hour we continued the descent in silence. Some peasant women had materialised out of nowhere to take advantage of a captive market, and we were fortified in our long descent by a bag of hard-boiled eggs.

After another two hours had passed, we began to wonder what had happened to our transport. Had it finally met the fate which Mr Nasty, and he alone, deserved? Just as we were pondering how we'd get back to distant Chengdu, down the road at breakneck speed came the IVECO. It squealed to a halt, and we swallowed our pride and hopped back in and resumed our seats, our fellow passengers greeting us as wayward and misguided old friends.

Soon we were back on the asphalt road, rolling past the semi-industrial valley-scape with the great Sichuan plain opening up before us. On a straight section which tempted speed, we came across another casualty of the convoy. A truck had careered a hundred yards into a field, overturned and shed its logs. A crowd of onlookers stood around the wreck, no-one apparently concerned about the trapped driver.

Once past the danger zone, I became too weary for further

backseat driving. We arrived in Chengdu late in the evening and without incident. Finding our way to the University *zhaodaisuo* and checking back in, the young woman on the desk produced my jade.

'It was taking care of us after all, just as godfather promised,' remarked Louise.

So I got my jade — and Liverpool Museum got its moss from the high Tibetan foothills. As for that ten-of-hearts playing card, it rests in my wallet to this day as a memento of our Kangding journey.

―――∽∞∽―――

The following morning, we sought out old Liu Changcheng, my mother's childhood friend from the 1920s. He and his wife had moved from the house of my grandparents in Green Dragon Street to a peaceful lane not far away. The old family home, which as related in *Chengdu by Coincidence* (in the first volume of my China memoir) I'd first visited under duress in 1979, was no longer. Now a skyscraper towered in place of the old Quaker compound, prime property within Chengdu's inner ring.

'I designed this new house myself,' Liu told us with pride, while his wife tinkled away in the background. The long-banned piano had made a come-back in China and wife Mary Shiao was teaching a young girl her scales. In contrast to the large bat-eaved and half-timbered mansion on Green Dragon Street, divided into eight makeshift apartments, their new home was an airy, *bijou* two-up, two-down, and all their very own.

We set about describing our eventful journey back from Kangding, and it was soon clear that Mr Liu knew the reason behind that Tibetan convoy. The summer before, the lower reaches of the great Yangtze had suffered terrible floods, the like of which are more normally associated with the Yellow River. I recalled seeing newsreels of soldiers desperately shoring up dykes and rescuing peasants from their flooded homes. China's headlong construction boom had an inexhaustible appetite for timber. The powers-that-be, with the new environmental awareness that was beginning to dawn in China, had understood that the disaster was caused by decades of deforestation in the eastern Himalayas. Literally on pain of death, throughout the vastness of Tibet a complete ban had been decreed on further felling of trees. It's always striking that despite the apparently chaotic capitalism of the post-Mao era, draconian powers could still be invoked.

One final, monster convoy of logs had been permitted, and trucks had foregathered from every corner of Tibet for an assault on the great Erlang pass. We only knew later that just a few weeks after our Erlang Pass ordeal, a road tunnel replaced the hazardous mountain pass. En route for Kangding, we'd noticed the construction machinery at the point where the road took an abrupt upward turn from the hitherto gentle valley. The tunnel was hacked straight through the mountain for 8.5k kilometers, straight into the bottom of the great Dadu River valley. To cite *Wikipedia*:

> It was built to reduce time and replaces one of the most dangerous parts of the highway, which had frequent accidents because of landslides, rain, and foggy weather.

Precisely! And not satisfied with a two-lane tunnel highway, incredibly, in 2018, China's indefatigable civil engineers completed a new tunnel over thirteen kilometers long and of six lanes— the crowning glory of the link between Ya'an and Kangding proudly dubbed the Yakang Highway. With the new airport at Kangding, and a superhighway penetrating territory which for centuries had been only accessible on the feet of men and beasts of burden, eastern Tibet is now not merely opened up big-time, but vulnerable to anything heartland China wishes to throw at its fragile cultures and environments.

As to our Kangding odyssey, Mr Nasty's words will always ring in my ears: 'You ain't seen nothing yet!'

X
THE TREASURES OF DR LUO
(2007)

I ONCE SHOCKED my upright brother—now three years in an untimely grave—by announcing that all antique dealers are liars and cheats. Craftiness without exception, epitomised by the scoundrel in Roald Dahl's *Parson's Pleasure*. Dahl's Mr Boggis, the fake reverend antique hunter, inveigles himself into the homes of the impoverished gentry, making them offers they can't refuse. The 'reverend' is of course a caricature, but he gives the flavour of the species. And for some years I had occasion to observe it at close quarters. The antique merchants who've crossed my path have been past masters of all the ruses, and a few of them have stooped to the lucrative sport of granny farming, the patient, snake-charmer-like grooming of some elderly soul, to be viciously robbed of family treasures. When I too was an unwilling member of the antiques brotherhood, it was merely the routine petty deceptions which I can confess to. You've all heard it: the dealer's stock reaction to a customer's offer. 'I couldn't possibly, it cost me more than that in the first place.' Rarely had it done so.

The lying and cheating is no means confined to the minnows of the antiques business. A couple of decades ago, when first wandering down London's New Bond Street with a few choice trinkets for the great and the good to peruse, I found a surprising situation. Closely observed by uniformed doormen, you entered the foyer of one of the august stalwarts of the global fine art trade. At the reception desk, plummy young women straight out of Cheltenham Ladies' College would put on their sweetest smiles and carelessly conceal their disdain for the latest hopeful from the provinces. Recalling it, I'm put in mind of a passage from Kate Atkinson's novel *Transcription*, which tells of the gatekeepers at Bush House, home of the BBC:

> She had a pruny sort of face, as if everyone who came through her door fell short of her standards. Did they breed these supercilious girls in a special hatchery somewhere?

'And what is it which you would like to show our specialists?' a pruny face would enquire. One's treasures would be laid bare, and if the damsel cared, a call would be made to the right person buried deep in the great Georgian labyrinth. Sooner but usually later he — always he it seemed — would deign to appear. More than likely the verdict would be: 'Sadly, not for us this time.' And sometimes: 'But it's possible the people up the road might help you.'

The 'people up the road', when you found them with hushed instructions, were through a dark entrance, from which you ascended a narrow staircase quite out of keeping with patrician New Bond Street. At the first floor the stairwell was blocked by a man seated at a deal table. Another public schoolboy, from his voice.

'Do show me what you've got,' the man would say, cheerily. 'Mmm — we might just be able to do something for you.' A paltry sum was then passed to the poor provincial who had come a hundred miles and more with his or her treasures. You can make of this what you wish. But I wasn't much surprised that Sotheby's was fined tens of millions for price fixing over a long period of the 1980s and 1990s. The former chairman of Sotheby's was placed in detention and personally fined millions too. Venality in high places.

One of these visits to London brought another unlikely scenario. I was seated, as described, in the reception area of one those august auctioneers, with my wares exposed on the table provided, awaiting the descent of the god-like specialist. A well-turned out, attractive woman in her forties addressed me. She was seated at the adjacent glass-topped table, and had unashamedly been listening in to an unrewarding exchange.

'What a pity! Do you mind if I have a look at what you've brought with you?' she went. 'Perhaps I can help.'

The outcome was a pleasant pulling back from the brink, from the waste of a day and a long train ride. On the spot, the woman was happily entrusted with my Chinese treasures, which she undertook to sell for a guaranteed sum at her perfectly respectable gallery on the perfectly respectable Kensington Church Street. Nothing went amiss with the plan, and in a few weeks I received the proceeds of the woman's (let's call her Heather) efforts.

Now, at the time my curator-partner had the huge responsibility of sorting through a vast and secret warehouse near Liverpool's old docks, an Aladdin's Cave stacked with riches from every land the British had penetrated in the colonial era. Included were a large number of artefacts resulting from a hundred and fifty years of the Liverpool China trade. In 1834, the East India Company had lost its charter, and thereafter ports other than London could trade with the Far East. Liverpool took the lead, and hence the cornucopia of precious objects, some of the most important which had arrived at the museum as donations from moneyed locals such as Port Sunlight's Lever Brothers. The great jumble of a warehouse came into being as, on the outbreak of Hitler's War, Liverpool Museum's important holdings were evacuated to remote places of safety in North Wales. They returned to the city in the 1950s in utter disarray and the creaking dockland warehouse was where they eventually landed. It was not so jokingly said that numbers of the Oriental cases were missing their contents, and that many a Bootle mantelpiece was graced by a Ming vase.

When my acquaintance from Kensington learned of this Liverpool trove, she begged a visit. Not an unreasonable request, and it was granted. Chinese antiques are a puzzlingly difficult area and the more one can see (and, if possible, handle), the more one can learn. Through the generosity of others, in this very way I myself had acquired much of my understanding of the intriguing, infuriating subject. So Heather made a trip to the city, and duly rooted through the vast store in that unmarked treasure house by the docks. Afterwards we went for lunch and on the way a bizarre happening on the main road just to the north of the University: she took it into her head to drive on the left-hand carriageway, as though her Volvo saloon was back in Sweden. This persisted for fifty metres, with vehicles hooting and flashing and coursing right at us. Cool as a cucumber, she then switched back to the correct, the right side and on we went. There was no flicker of concern, or any remark from Heather. I remember saying later to my partner, 'Something's not quite right about this woman.'

On the advice of my redoubtable antiques mentor, I'd recently acquired what looked to me to be an important jade, a dragon motif about 15cm. in length, flat in form and in the Warring States style. Jade, though one of the hardest minerals known, can easily shatter, and the magnificent piece came in two halves. Despite this, Heather took a shine to my jade, and with an innocence long since departed I accepted it as gospel when she announced that she knew a place in London which could fix it. I now know, as is obvious, that you can no more seamlessly fix broken pieces of jade together than you could two pieces of a broken glass mirror. But at the time I merely expressed gratitude to my new friend. The weeks passed, and nothing from Heather. But I took that in my stride.

The story now moves thousands of kilometers, to the west coast of North America. With my position as a specialist in the built environment of 'developing' countries (I was editor-in-chief of an international journal in the field), I was monitoring the work of the Centre for Human Settlements at the University of British Columbia. CHS had won a multi-million action-research fund from Canada's overseas aid agency. The object was to enhance the knowledge and skills of academic and practising urbanists in China, in Vietnam, Indonesia and Thailand. This required on-the-spot involvement in projects and conferences in each of these countries, where I had to assess whether objectives were being met and money well-spent. On one visit to Vancouver, Christmas, 1998, partner and I were duly ensconced in the University's campus accommodation and here we prepared our Christmas dinner (I recall being amazed that in oh-so-tame Vancouver it was impossible to find a Christmas Eve booze shop).

After my work was done, we took a coach south to Seattle to see my American sister and to visit the Seattle Art Museum, whose curator of Chinese collections had invited us on a private tour. During it we were accompanied by one of the museum trustees, a friendly and confident character of middle-age who invited us to ride in his flashy Mercedes to see his fine collection of Chinese jades. We arrived at a suburban middle-class villa and were ushered into the principal room, all set out with glass showcases.

'Let me show you my absolute prize jade,' the man said. In pride of place in the first glass case was — my Liverpool dragon.

'What, how, that's mine!' I gasped. 'How the hell did you come by it?'

'Look, I got it from my favourite dealer in London,' the man said. 'No way could it be yours. And I paid good money for it,' he added sharply.

'Bu…ut' I stuttered. I was reeling. But further protest would clearly get me nowhere.

Returning home, I wasted no time in confronting Heather. She dissembled. Nothing to do with her! After several months and finally mild threats of legal action, a cheque for £300 appeared in the post. I had a lot going on in my life and I left the matter at that. All antique dealers are liars and cheats....

We're inching nearer, I promise, to Dr Luo of Ningbo and his fabled collection of Chinese ceramics. And how was it that I was involved with a Chinese eye doctor and his cache of supposed treasures, let alone the wheeler-dealing which awaited me after I gave up the academic life? I've always lived with old stuff around, which comes of having an antiquarian father who in the end, after a turbulent career, surprised us all by ascending to the directorship of a national museum. The cobbler's child is never well shod, and the furniture and works of art which graced our home were sometimes magnificent but always worm-eaten and deficient. Then there was my mother's famous chest of Chinese treasures. In early 1927, she and her family had returned from deepest China with a packing case of pretty things. Amongst them were delicate embroideries stuck onto sheets of thin white paper, to be applied to silken robes, Most ended up in picture frames, adorning the walls of my siblings. The chest also contained a variety of unfamiliar handicrafts, like the little folding bamboo lectern now in front of me on my desk.

RICHARD KIRKBY

Mother's elder brother Henry got the lion's share of the ceramics brought back in 1927, and whether he added to them during his wartime service in China I can't say. But I doubt it. I recall the well-polished vitrine with its shiny vases and bowls in my Uncle Henry's and Aunt Hilda's Derby living room. As a child, though, I gave the pretty objects from China hardly a glance. But perhaps there was a subliminal registering, both of Henry's things and of my mother's. In his final years, Henry presented me with a small number of his trophies; some I bought from him to help him pay for his irregular trips in the 1980s to his beloved China. Henry had been a stalwart of the Friend's Ambulance Unit, sent to south-west China over the Burma Road by the British government to give token support to the Nationalist troops battling the Japanese. He used to regale me with stories about how to keep an old Ford truck puffing along hardly-existent roads, fuelled not by gasoline but by a charcoal burner. This cylindrical contraption wrapped around with pipework was stoked by a coolie who clung to the sides of the truck.

Other Chinese and Japanese things which knocked around our family home came from the paternal side of the family. In the mid-1850s, at the tender age of fourteen my great grandfather had left for the China coast. His father had a master's ticket and captained those greyhounds of the ocean, the clipper ships, sailing out of Liverpool to gold-rush Australia, and to the China coast for the tea. Great, great grandfather, also a Richard Jonathan, was briefly the master of the *Red Jacket*, a clipper renowned for its record runs on the long haul from the Far East, round the Cape.

But the sailor's life was not for his son. Great grandfather Richard Jonathan jumped ship in Shanghai and went to work for his brother, who ran an outfit indispensable to the newly opened Treaty Port—a steam-tug company which hauled the foreign ships up to their berths or lighter anchorages on the swirling Huangpu River. But the lad had other dreams. It was now 1868, and at the tender age of fourteen, Richard somehow fetched up across the sea in Japan, where the Meiji clan had just re-established itself against the last of the great samurai lords. He was to spend the rest of his life as a scholar-merchant in Japan, rising to eminence as a go-between with the industrial and financial backers in Britain of Japan's amazing modernisation drive. Richard Jonathan arranged many of the iron working and railway loans, was the first manager of the Kobe Iron Works (later Kobe Steel), amongst many other positions. Bizarrely, he also acted as consul for both Greece and Chile. Why Greece I have no idea. Chile, however, had become important not because of copper, which came later, but due to its rich deposits of nitrates, not forgetting the deep beds of guano which had accumulated on the offshore islands of Chile and neighbouring Peru. Guano was described in the late 19th century as the cause of a 'new gold-rush': fortunes were made. Before the age of more refined chemical fertilisers, raw mineral nitrates and bird droppings fed the modernising agriculture of Japan and elsewhere. I suppose that Richard J must have greased the wheels of this odd trade.

My great grandfather can rightly be described as a scholar-merchant as, unlike most British expatriates in China, he as many Westerners in 19th century Japan was respectful of the indigenous culture. In the pernicious, Social-Darwinian categorisations of peoples, the Japanese were never 'savages'. Often resident foreigners in the country following its forced opening by Admiral Perry became proficient in the language. Richard J himself wrote and published learned papers on obscure 18th century Japanese economists in the *Transactions of the Asiatic Society of Japan*, in which he was an officer and sometime treasurer and vice-president.

I was perhaps eight years old when, delivered to our York

home from heaven knows where, were four large tea chests. Within, bedded in wood shavings, were 'treasures' saved from the family's Japan days. Most of their possessions had been consigned to the Straits of Malacca by a Japanese torpedo, and this, I was told, was all that remained. My father permitted me to unpack the chests, a gigantic lucky dip. Out came strange Oriental vases, Waterford decanters, rolls of embroidered textiles, and most memorable to a little lad, Great Grandfather Richard's favourite double-barrelled 12-bore Purdey shotgun in a beautiful baize-lined fitted case. When all was done, I was allowed to put my own treasures into the magic chests, and fishing them out again my hands closed around a clutch of fine cut glass tumblers which had somehow been overlooked. If I can date my gambling delight in antiques to anything, it was to this magical moment.

If all that wasn't enough introduction to antiques from the East, from time to time when I visited her in her stockbroker-belt mansion in deepest Surrey, my paternal grandmother Nora pressed upon me intriguing and beautiful Chinese things. I never thought to ask where these had come from until years later when I learned about my great uncle Eric, her brother-in-law. It turned out that for nearly a decade from 1919 on, great uncle was the interpreter and private secretary for the British ambassador in Beijing. He was also known as a collector of what were then quaintly called 'curios', some of which, a century on, are now in my hands. From 1936 to 1945, Sir Eric, as he became, was assistant private secretary to King George, and later, Mountbatten's right-hand man during the dismantling of Britain's Indian empire. I'm told that when young the late Queen Elizabeth knew my great uncle as 'Uncle Eric'. As a confirmed republican I'm amused rather than in any way proud of this fortuitous connection.

SHIFTING GEARS IN CHINA

Back in my Nanjing days of the 1970s, I knew little of Chinese art and antiques and cared even less. Indeed, I openly disdained such matters, for wasn't I a confirmed politico, trying to cast off his father's bourgeois taint? The few cities in which foreigners were permitted sometimes had a 'Friendship Store', so friendly that they were out of bounds to the locals. The larger of such places on the foreigners' China circuit, our Nanjing one included, had an antiques section. Though the occasional Japanese tour group did take an interest in its offerings, very few foreigners passed through the city and very little shifted in the antiques part of the store, I mainly confined my Friendship Store shopping to the booze section—to bottles labelled 'Vermouth', *Xiangbinjiu* (a Chinese 'Champagne' concoction) and of course the famed Qingdao beer from the brewery that had, long ago, been set up by the German colonialists of Shandong. But occasionally I did browse the antiques under the glass counters and invested in a few trifling trinkets. I recall with non-buyer's remorse a particularly garish snuff bottle which the idle assistant assured me, with reference to her dictionary, was carved of emerald. It was marked up at 3,000 *yuan*, several years' salary for our university colleagues and a year's for us—doubtless worth a fortune in today's crazed market.

Once, in 1976, we were allowed to visit the gardens of Suzhou, and on a mean street I glimpsed into the dark cavern of a warehouse which was piled to the roof with antique hardwood furniture. All of it must either have been taken in the Red Guard rampages, or simply abandoned out of fear by Suzhou's old families. Today, Ming and Qing furniture can command a very high price. And on the few occasions when the cadres let us have travel passes to the wondrous Shanghai, we would make a point of visiting what others of the tiny foreign community knew as 'the prostitutes' shop'. Rumour had it that much of its stock had once been the property of the courtesans and playboys of old Shanghai. Whatever, on a quiet corner of the city's former French sector, not far from China's then-highest building, the 1929 Jinjiang Hotel, was the small store cluttered with the residue of high foreign living in the 1920s and '30s. Amongst the mouldering mink coats, the brocades, the silver tea services, the diamond rings and costume jewellery, was a clutch of antique pocket watches. Many of them were rather special 'repeaters'. You pressed a button and the sophisticated Swiss masterpieces would chime the time down to the minute. The stock of the place was different from the antiques displayed in the foreigners' Friendship Stores. In these, much of their exclusively Chinese offerings most likely came from the state repositories which had been replenished by the Red Guard raids of 1967-8, for not all of what they ferreted out in their terrifying searches was smashed on the spot.

Like the Friendship Stores, the French sector antiques den had no local customers at all. It wasn't as though there were guards on the gate: in the tense political days of the Cultural Revolution, its goods were as venomous serpents, to be shunned by all Chinese who valued their lives. I'm sure the assistants often went through whole days, a week or two even, without a single customer entering their eerie domain. In the 1970s the foreign residents of Shanghai, mostly 'experts', numbered hardly a score, and they were hardly the types to take an interest in antiques. If the occasional foreign dignitary accommodated in the nearby Jinjiang was able to escape the dawn-to-dusk attentions of their hosts and wander the streets, perhaps they might have stumbled across the little house of treasures. But that was about the size of the 'prostitutes' shop' customer base.

The Chinese, or at least urban Chinese of a certain economic stature, have a passion for clockwork. While this was expunged in China in revolution, living in Hong Kong in the late 1970s one couldn't help notice the prominence given to expensive Swiss timepieces. Whole mini-skyscrapers were emblazoned with neon displays for Tissot, for Omega, Tag Heuer, even the really costly brands such as Breitling. Every cheap magazine was kept afloat by full page displays for watches with price tags in their tens of thousands of Hong Kong dollars. I lived on the fisherfolk island of Cheung Chau; here, my neighbours would emerge from their squatter huts ostentatiously sporting every make of fancy Swiss timepiece. I took them to be fake: they were not. At work, I was actually told by my British Council students—all of them from modest backgrounds—that I lost face, for *them*, by wearing a watch which had cost just a few dollars and was far inferior to most of theirs. All this is deeply embedded. After the Jesuits arrived at the court of Beijing some four hundred years ago, China's elite classes acquired a fascination with the horological skills of the West. It's fair to say that for long periods in the Qing dynasty, the missionaries of the Vatican were tolerated largely because they were active in passing on to the Qing court their cartographical, astronomical and indeed, their horological knowledge. By the 18th century, the great Qianlong emperor was filling whole chambers of the Forbidden City with the most elaborate, showy and complex timepieces the English clockmakers could devise. Many of these gilded, bejewelled clocks and musical gee-gaws, as they were called, remain in the Forbidden City to this day. Those that leaked into the outside world after the collapse of the Qing dynasty occasionally come up at auction, going for fabulous sums.

 The much sought-after repeater watches I acquired in Shanghai later went to a well-heeled collector in Hong Kong, a Scottish expat lawyer. I put the proceeds towards my studies at an occluded research establishment in the colony, where I started on the work which was to lead me eventually into the rarefied world of Sinology. So on the personal level, the conspicuous consumption of Shanghai's wicked past was put to good purpose. My watch trading days weren't, however, over. Just as the 1970s had found me bringing foreign clockwork out of China, now, in the 1980s, I was going to be taking some in. Up the M6 motorway, less than an hour's drive from my Liverpool home was the Charnock Richard service station. On Sunday mornings, large sheds behind it served as a kind of clearing house for the region's antique dealing fraternity. You turned up in the middle of the night with a torch and a wad of cash, and could go away your trophies, most of dubious provenance. It was clockwork that drew me to the Charnock bazaar, for there was normally a good choice of silver and gold pocket watches, mostly 19th century but some earlier. Making friends with a regular trader, I could bring away from Charnock Richard as many as my wallet would allow.

By the mid-1980s, with the austere age of Mao now past, the sophisticates of Shanghai were once again indulging their passion for clockwork. Mr Chen was a tall and good-looking lad in his twenties. I came across his booth during one of my regular visits to the city's main antiques street — long since erased in China's 21st century skyscraper metropolis. I learned some good lessons from my dealings with Mr Chen: first, in China, always ask twice as much as you really want for something. Second, never delude yourself into imagining that there's such a thing as friendship in business. Buying and selling is a game, and in the Chinese entrepreneurial mind, if you're foolish or ignorant enough not to know how to play it, you lose. You have no-one to blame but yourself.

The enterprising Chen's wares looked pretty miserable: dented Soviet nickel-cased pocket watches with a few broken silver 'Chinese market' pocket watches from the late 19th century with Chinese numerals on their enamelled dials. I was to change all that, to upgrade Chen's tastes and supply him with some novelties from Olde England. In my frequent trips to China at the time, whenever Shanghai was on the itinerary I'd pack a little pouch with a few antique watches, and come away from my rendezvous with young Mr Chen a happy man. This then was how I would finance a growing but modest interest in the mysteries of Chinese antiques. And along a twisting road, this one day was also to lead to the treasures of Ningbo's Dr Luo.

So now, finally, to Ningbo's Dr Luo. I had an academic acquaintance in Liverpool from China called Wang. *Dr* Wang in fact, and an interesting person too. I first came across him in the early 1990s, when my comrade, the renowned Japanologist Michael W, was called to Liverpool's John Moores University to appraise a candidate for a new post in Japanese language. Rather bizarrely, the candidate in question was a Zhejiang native with a Sheffield doctorate in Japanese studies. This is how our Chinese Dr Wang improbably ended up teaching Japanese to the wide-eyed youth of Liverpool's 'other' university.

It was some years later and after I'd left the city that I was briefly courted by Nottingham University, the first British educational establishment to develop a campus in China. The pro-vice chancellor, an old adversary from Sheffield days, wanted me to join the staff and teach Chinese undergraduates about China, a task even stranger than Dr Wang's in Liverpool. Politely declined, but Nottingham's invitation to Dr Wang he gladly accepted. He was now the University's general fixer in their project for a branch campus on the fringes of Ningbo, the large port city of Zhejiang province. Dr Wang was undoubtedly the ideal man for the job. He hailed from the province, could speak its dialects, understood U.K. and Chinese higher education, and so would be in prime position to smooth the way for Nottingham. For a couple of years I heard nothing from him. One day, out of the blue, I took a phone call and it was Dr Wang, back in England and wanting to discuss a certain matter.

Dr Wang's time in Ningbo had come to an end — mission accomplished. He explained that one of his close Chinese colleagues in the Nottingham/Ningbo project was a woman who was friends with a retired eye doctor, Dr Luo. Wang had been led to Dr Luo's home, where, according to his untutored but intrigued eyes, he found a standard drab urban apartment brimming with antique Chinese ceramics. Old Dr Luo had begged Wang to find a foreigner to buy his entire collection. Wang immediately thought of me, but not, of course, of the obstacles to Dr Luo's naive request.

By sheer coincidence, that very summer I was planning to pass through Ningbo with my partner, Louise, on the trail of an elusive Victorian army officer, one William Edie, Captain of the Grenadier Guards during the First Opium War. My partner had made the chance discovery that in a temple on the nearby island of Putuo, Edie had come by some supremely important Buddhist bronzes, amongst them an impressive 'thousand arm' Guanyin. Putuo is one of China's major Buddhist pilgrimage sites and the whole island brims with shrines and temples devoted to the deity Guanyin, Goddess (and sometime God) of Compassion. Those Buddhist bronzes had, extraordinarily, ended up in my partner's very own care, at Liverpool Museum. But that's another story, which she tells in her own words.[15]

We arrived in Ningbo on a sticky summer afternoon, Louise

---

15   Tythacott, Louise, *The Lives of Chinese Objects: Buddhism, Imperialism and Display*, New York & Oxford: Berghahn, 2011.

and our infant daughter heading off for the ferry port and Putuo, and I remaining in the city to fulfil my mission with Dr Wang. We met up at the Nottingham Ningbo campus, newly built on the outskirts, and took a taxi to a typical 1980s workers' residential estate, made up of five-storey blocks set along wide tree-lined concrete pathways. Not an unpleasing environment by any means. At one of the many entrances stood an elderly soul with grey straggly hair to his shoulders, a half-smile on his lips. Alongside him was a man in his forties, pulling anxiously on a cigarette. The old man remained silent; beckoning us into the building, we found ourselves climbing the dirty concrete stairwell, its flaking distempered walls scuffed by the bicycles and other things carried aloft to be parked outside front doors. We rose to the fourth floor, the old fellow going ahead surprisingly nimbly. At one of the purple-brown lacquered doors he rasped something and a key was thrust through a gap and into his hand. The younger man then unlocked a sturdy steel security grill and we found ourselves in a narrow passage lined with cardboard boxes where an elderly woman nervously smiled a greeting. Behind her hovered a younger female, but not bothering with introductions, Dr Luo hustled us into a small living room with too many chairs, more boxes stacked around it, and a tall glass-fronted cabinet. The younger woman delivered us the familiar lidded mugs of tea; our remarks addressed to Dr Luo were fielded by the chain-smoking son of the house, so it was evident that he was going to be in charge.

A nod from Dr Luo and the son opened the door of the adjoining room, a bedroom in all but function. The floor and bed were piled high with those blue padded boxes with lids fastened by bone tags which are instantly recognisable as Chinese 'treasure' caskets. Into the room he brought a pile of these, dumping them precariously on a spare chair. Dr Luo leant over and grabbed the top box. From it he drew a magnificent famille rose vase, and if truly an authentic mid-18th century creation from the reign of the Qianlong emperor, it had to be worth a six-figure sum. The doctor thrust the vase at me, watching carefully as I turned it to its base and examined the imperial reign mark and the material of the foot ring. Unexpectedly, Dr Luo carelessly grabbed it back and returned it to its box. 'There was another one like this but I smashed it,' he remarked casually and without a hint of remorse.

Whatever this was all about, I could see that given the stack of boxes all around it was going to be a long day, and one which I should make sure I made the best of. I got out my camera and adjusted the settings for good close-ups. But after an hour of opening boxes one after the other, and musing at their seemingly amazing contents, I was bursting to delve deeper. I knew that in the 1950s, shortly after the Communist Party had come to power, those families known to possess significant collections were leant upon by the government to 'donate' them to public museums. In some cases, compensation was paid, but for most their 'patriotic' generosity was seen as something of a political insurance policy against turbulent times ahead. By the time the Cultural Revolution broke upon China, the rapacious activities of the Red Guards in seeking out the 'Five Olds' meant that anyone still harbouring antiques was likely to have lost them. In countless distressing confrontations, vases, bronzes, ancient scroll paintings, jades were removed from their owners. In an orgy of vandalism, many of the antiques taken from the homes of 'bourgeois elements' were smashed on the spot, while the residue usually ended up in those state warehouses. Some say that the government saw China's heritage as a means of raising foreign exchange, and while a part of the stolen treasures went to the 'Friendship Stores', many were secretly consigned to overseas collectors or auction houses. What is clear is that after the rampages of the Cultural Revolution very little confiscated property, other than some urban buildings, was restored to former owners.

In the boxes which kept being opened and thrust onto my lap were delicate Ming bowls with Chenghua marks, robust Qingbai vases from Yuan times, and plenty of Qing vases of all shapes and styles. I had a few years of looking at Chinese ceramics under my belt, and certainly the things weren't obvious replicas. But all Chinese antiques are guilty until proven innocent, and I had to assume that it was just a vast assemblage of fakes. Since the dawn of the new era of strident Chinese capitalism, the ceramics faking industry of Jingdezhen had proved capable of fooling the world's leading auction houses with its products. There was a time in the mid-1990s when a goodly part of the highly priced Chinese porcelain passing through the hands of the major global auction houses was said to be suspect. So what was I looking at here in this unlikely apartment in a nondescript workers' estate of East China? If all these weren't merely good modern copies, how had Dr Luo managed to hang on to such a large collection through the vicissitudes of recent Chinese history? And just as interesting, how were the delicate vases and bowls being carelessly thrust onto my knees in an unlikely corner of Ningbo get into the Luo family's hands in the first place?

As Dr Luo's wife topped up my tea and thrust at me a bowl of White Rabbit toffees, I turned to her son with the big questions. He was ready with his story: Zhejiang province, he reminded me, was the heartland of the Nationalists, Chiang Kai-shek himself hailing from nearby Shaoxing. And in 1948 and 1949, with the Communist forces advancing quickly behind them, his defeated armies fled in disarray to Taiwan. Around one million 'Mainlanders' took to the Taiwan Straits, many from Ningbo port; those in flight for their lives were limited in what they could take with them.

'My grandfather was a bank manager in the city, and he agreed to guard many treasures of the rich families,' the son explained. The Nationalists, after all, believed that the U.S. would ride to their rescue and soon restore them to power on the Mainland. And their temporarily abandoned property would be redeemed. That part of the Luo Junior's explanation seemed plausible. Of course, despite every effort of the U.S.-backed regime to effect a return, their goose was well and truly cooked. On Taiwan the Mainlanders stayed, much to the disdain of the existing population of the island, the original non-Han peoples of the mountains, and the millions of descendants of early settlers who'd come over from Fujian province.

By the mid-1950s, in common with all other private enterprises, the Ningbo bank where the treasures had supposedly been hidden was taken over by the state. If there was truth to the story, before this happened Dr Luo's family must have somehow spirited them out of the bank's strong room.

'But what about the government and the Red Guards during the Cultural Revolution?' I enquired, still mystified. 'Surely everyone would have known that your family had got these treasures.'

'Ah — we'd thought of that,' the son responded. 'Long before the Cultural Revolution we managed to cart everything to a village and at night we buried it all in straw, in a large pit which our relatives had prepared. They'd told people they were digging a pond, even though the site was on a bit of waste land which was quite high up.'

The Red Guards largely confined their smash and grab raids to the cities, and apart from attacks on dispossessed landlord families, the villages escaped the worst ravages. But did it all add up? Nowadays there were many fine new collections in the hands of the new class of rich Chinese. Provided they had the money or influence, in post-Mao China citizens were once again free to collect whatever took their fancy, from porcelain vases to Rolls Royces, and millions of the newly affluent were doing just that. I'd recently come across a guesstimate of the size of China's diverse community of collectors: eighty million, no less. If all that was being told to me was true, the Luo family ceramics collection had surely to be one of the greatest pre-1949 caches in still private hands.

'What do you want to do with these things?' I asked the doctor.

'You're a foreigner and you can buy them,' the son responded with complete but entirely unwarranted confidence. Firstly, contrary to what many Chinese still believed, not all Westerners were millionaires. Secondly, even if I had been in the money, the Chinese government had strict rules about the export of the nation's cultural heritage. Recent adjustment to the law meant that nothing older than 1795 could be removed from the country, while in practice most artefacts pre-dating the fall of the Qing dynasty (1911) were banned from export. If they weren't actually modern replicas, and that remained a big 'if', absolutely nothing laid on my lap by Dr Luo's son could be removed from China legally. Were they simply trying to fool a gullible Big Nose? Whatever, I was enjoying the unparalleled opportunity of playing the connoisseur, though I knew that fake or authentic, this wasn't going to lead anywhere. I wasn't going to stop until the contents of every one of those blue boxes had been revealed.

Tea was replenished and cigarettes distributed so I called a temporary halt to the dazzling parade. 'Why not sell the collection here in China?' I put to Dr Luo, thinking this might get me nearer the truth. The Chinese government had recently licensed several auction houses of their own, mainly in Beijing but also in nearby Shanghai.

'We tried that out,' the son explained, 'but we don't trust them—they make trouble.' He went on to relate how they'd tested the best known of the Beijing auction houses by consigning a few objects. On the day, their lots remained unsold, as is the case for a good percentage of items in any antiques auction. In most cases in the West, no or minimal charges are imposed when one retrieves one's unsold property.

'They are very tricky, the Chinese auction houses,' Dr Luo's son said. 'They deliberately ignore bids and tell people their lots are unsold because they want to get hold of them themselves, for little money.' He went on to explain that when they'd tried to retrieve their property a small fortune in 'unsold' fees was demanded and in one case a potentially valuable vase simply went missing. This tale did at least suggest to me that the items consigned for auction might have been genuine, but then again.....

As if to answer my doubts about the entire scenario Dr Luo said something to his son, who went into the next room for a large manila envelope.

'Last year, the city officials here in Ningbo organised an exhibition of fine antiques and we were asked to put in some of our porcelain,' the son said. He drew from the envelope a sheaf of official-looking certificates, each with a photo of a ceramic, with a brief description alongside. I had a close look at one of them: they each appeared to bear the signature of a specialist from the State Bureau of Cultural Relics. In the decades since Mao Zedong's rule, the robbery of ancient graves had continued apace and a crucial purpose of the State Cultural Relics Bureau was the regulation of the illicit trade in antiquities.

Why a Beijing bureaucrat from the central ministry concerned with antiquarian issues should be involved with this kind of venture in Ningbo wasn't clear, but then nowadays there was a great deal of blurring between public and private. This was 2007, and long before President Xi Jinping launched his anti-corruption campaigns, which caused the illicit antiques trade to go further underground. I decided that this person lending his name to the Ningbo exhibition was most likely just moonlighting. But a further obvious question turned on his declarations of authenticity. There have been numerous examples of officials and other experts, real and ersatz, selling 'authenticity' as a lucrative sideline.

Sent on our way with a lavish banquet in a Ningbo restaurant, Wang and I left Dr Luo after that first visit with some non-committal noises on both sides. But the glitter of fool's gold (or not?) had seduced me and I couldn't bring myself to confess my irrelevance to Dr Luo's hopes. A whole year later there was a chance to return to the port city in the company of Dr Wang, who was intent on some unusual research for a man back in Merseyside by name of Mr Body, an appropriate name if ever there was one. Despite the growing number of Chinese in Northwest England, especially Manchester, Buddhist and Daoist temples were conspicuous by their absence. Equally, there was no dedicated graveyard with all the attributes of *fengshui* necessary for a good Chinese send-off and a peaceful afterlife. This is where Mr Body came in. He'd leased a large, undulating few hectares on the Wirral bank of the River Mersey and was busy marking out burial plots and walkways and sites for little pavilions in the hope that Dr Wang, through his connections with Chinese community organisations, could drum up the customers. I was intrigued by this entrepreneurship and spent an afternoon at the site, noticing that quite a few plots had already been occupied and the landscaping was coming on. In China, the industry of death had developed apace since Mao's time, when urban citizens were obliged to choose cremation as the only option. Now things were loosening up and money was to be made with everything from sea-burial to the traditional grave on a *fengshui* hillside. So Dr Wang was in China again, this time to meet funeral bureaucrats and get ideas. But he saw Dr Luo as unfinished business, as I very much did too. (Not long after the personable Mr Body did a runner with all down-payment cash; he was last heard of in Kenya where he'd set up a company to add novelty to the African way of death.)

Returning to Dr Luo's building, this time instead of rising to the fourth floor the sprightly doctor continued to the top, the fifth. So, concealed from us the first time round, the Luo family actually had two apartments on the stairwell. We were shown into mirror-image premises stacked to the gunnels with those blue treasure boxes. It occurred to me that we were getting the treatment I'd met in the more upmarket antique shops in Shanghai, where the proprietor only shows you the outer chamber until you've demonstrated a little knowledge. Then you're led into the inner sanctum where the real stuff is kept. On our earlier visit we'd been served the hors d'ouevre, which doubtless included quite a few indigestible fakes. With no avowal of their authenticity, we'd actually each been presented with a couple of tiny bowls with 15th century Ming marks of the Chenghua emperor, which had they been the real McCoy would have been worth a small fortune. Was Dr Luo trying to tell us something, or test us by revealing obvious fakes amongst his collection? Were we to assume in this game of smoke and mirrors that the inner chamber to which we'd graduated was filled with items in which the family had complete confidence? We spent a day there photographing the secret cache, imagining that now we might be able to take the whole thing further by finding, perhaps, a buyer within China.

This second visit over, Dr Wang and I headed off in his family's saloon towards the great eastern metropolis of Shanghai. Dr Luo had set us a test: he had a number of landscape paintings, and one which was by a B-list artist of the 20th century whose works commanded anything up to $100K. Our job was to find a client for the painting in the big city, or anywhere else for that matter. There were two things that remained seared in my mind about the road trip to Shanghai. Firstly, the terrifying velocity of the mild Dr Wang's driving. Why is that so often the most retiring, polite people are the worst devils on the road? The second thing was that as we whizzed through most of Zhejiang province and Shanghai's attached counties at 150kph, overtaking, undertaking, hooting our horn, by the side of this one six-lane highway alone there were surely more factories than in the whole of our denuded, hollowed-out United Kingdom.

We had no idea how we'd go about disposing of Dr Luo's painting, so the following day I headed for my umpteenth visit to the magnificent Shanghai Museum. I wanted to have a good look at the gallery housing the ancient bronze vessels, a particular interest of mine. Later, I was in the museum bookshop leafing through a tome on Shang dynasty metalwork when John Li entered my life. I was used to being ignored by the locals in this the most cosmopolitan of cities, and was surprised when a suavely dressed character of late middle-age sidled up to me. I couldn't help noticing his splendid navy-blue mohair jacket and his well-groomed, pomaded hair. 'One of Shanghai Museum's circle of millionaire Friends with a capital 'F',' I thought to myself.

'You are interested in Chinese bronzes, and how is it you're looking at a book in Chinese?' he addressed me in Chinese-American English. I explained that I had a long-established interest in Chinese antiquities and back in England I had a few bits and pieces.

'I'm a collector too and I'm originally from Taiwan but my home's now in Silicon Valley. For the moment I'm a Shanghai resident though,' he explained. 'What are you doing this evening? If you'd like, you're welcome to visit my home and see some of my collection.'

It wasn't at all usual for such an invitation to come one's way in China. Without a second's thought I was expressing my thanks, and asking if my travelling companion could come along too.

'By the way, please call me John — John Li,' he said. Wang and I had booked into the Shanghai Daxia, the great King Kong Art Deco building just over the Suzhou Creek's Garden Bridge from the Bund. In this modern capitalistic world, along with many other institutions with roots in the bad old days, the Daxia had reverted to its original name of Broadway Mansions. In the 1960s and '70s, this was the building, on the padlocked fourteenth floor, where the few foreign teachers in Shanghai were obliged to live I had fond memories of gazing down on ocean-going junks with their bat-wing ochre sails as they tacked up the brown, swirling Huangpu. Though the Daxia had been gutted of its maple panelling and matching furnishings in a mad fling of 'modernisation', it still felt something of a home-from-home.

I told John where I was staying and asked him where we should come that evening.

'Don't worry — just give me your room number at the Daxia and someone will come by and collect you,' he said. I scribbled down the details and at seven o'clock, reception called and Dr Wang and I descended to find a black Mercedes limousine and uniformed chauffeur. We were whisked in silence and at some pace through unfamiliar lanes of downtown Shanghai until the car halted at a high steel gate which parted before us, admitting us to a small paved yard. The driver motioned us into a lobby and pressed a lift button. In a matter of seconds, we were stepping out directly into a huge penthouse space set about with banks of black leather couches. On a long shelf under a picture window were half-a-dozen framed photos of our host, alongside the current Chairman of the Communist Party, the premier of the State Council, as well as a couple of former premiers of the People's Republic. Around the huge room, on side tables and in elaborate cabinets were what appeared to be important Qing dynasty ceramics — imperial pieces without exception.

'Come and see my latest buys' John said as he ushered us up a couple of steps to an ante-chamber, where we admired a vitrine with an early 18th century Yongzheng emperor 'One Hundred Deer' vase, and a huge carved armoire of the rare *zitan* wood. He then motioned us back to one of the long black leather settees where gin and tonic was served by a white-jacketed flunky.

Lounging on the settee was a plumpish, thickset man in his thirties with bad acne. Apparently, our fellow guest, though there were no introductions. John and the man fell into conversation, and as Sotheby's and Christie's sales in Hong Kong and New York were mentioned I guessed that the man was one of those scions of the new billionaire class who globe-trots around the great auction houses. If you ever receive one of those fancy invitation cards to a private view in London's New Bond Street on the eve of one of the yearly Asia Week auctions you would find a whole gaggle of such folk. Here are the companionable adversaries from China and its super-rich diaspora on their endless quest for prizes in the great casino of the Chinese art market.

Without warning and almost magically, Chinese flute music sounded softly, and in front of the window a huge screen descended from the ceiling. For the next half an hour we were on a virtual tour of John's collection of ceramics and objet-d'art. The film concluded with computer-aided imagery of the private museum which John planned for his California villa complex. I just had to discover more about our unusual host with his unusual friends in high places. John had anticipated my questioning:

'I have no love for the Chinese Communists, but I couldn't resist their offer,' John volunteered. 'Over in California, I was a well-known electronics scientist and I think I can say that I played a big part in the development of the silicon chip.' More American than Chinese in his uncharacteristic immodesty. Until the mid-1990s, John explained, China's burgeoning electronics industry had had to rely on imported chips. This surprised me, given the country's already massive volume of exports of products incorporating electronics.

When a spanking new semiconductor factory was planned for Pudong, the scientist from Taiwan (and, I guessed, senior Nationalist Party member) was persuaded to take on the management of the new plant. 'But they had to promise me a big enough salary and if I had problems, I wanted to be able to contact the right people,' he said with a chuckle while gesturing towards the photographs under the long window.

Naive as ever, my first thought was the obvious, practical one: 'But how can you get all your antiques out of China?' John's reply was disarmingly candid: 'When I want to ship something I just get in touch with one of these,' he said, pointing again towards the array of photos of Chinese leaders. '*Meiyou wenti*,' No problem!

Back in the hotel, it didn't take long to come up with the perfect plan. 'We'll offer John Dr Luo's painting at a come-and-get me price as a taster and then introduce him to the main course,' I said. Wang seemed to think this a fine strategy, and the following morning he called John. But far from being an offer which the man couldn't refuse, disregarding what we'd agreed, Wang laid the price on so thickly that John demurred. In no uncertain terms. With my own experience of this way of doing things in China, it came to me later that Wang's was just the standard opening gambit: ask double what you intend to accept. But John Li was used to doing his deals the Western way. After his generous hospitality of the night before, he was furious. I let things rest for an hour or so and then gave him a call to mollify him. He seemed to have calmed down so I mentioned the amazing collection of ceramics in Ningbo.

'They'll all be fakes,' was his first and not unreasonable reaction.

———∞———

In the event, a week later we did persuade John to take a look at Dr Luo's treasures, or at least a small selection of them. Dr Luo's son agreed to deliver ten of the best ceramics to a hotel in a small town in northern Zhejiang where Wang, whose family home was nearby, had a certain *guanxi* with the owner. All our plutocrat had to do was hop in his Mercedes and within an hour he'd be there. The hotel was an outlandish over-the-top building, the kind you'll find in many county towns of East China. Courtesy of Wang's friend, we were provided with a chamber hung with enormous chandeliers. We'd laid out Dr Luo's ten finest Qing dynasty ceramics in a tasteful manner, and waited nervously for John's limousine, which soon turned into the hotel's canopied entrance. He stepped out with another man in tow to whom we were given a very cursory introduction. 'My friend here is my antiques adviser,' John said. To me, the tightly-besuited and rather muscular 'adviser' looked rather more like John's bodyguard. A waiter stood in the corner over a table laden with Western style cupcakes and bottles of red wine. But John Li clearly wasn't there for polite refreshments.

Fake, fake, fake, fake...' rasped John's 'expert' as the two of them passed down the long display table. I was awfully conscious that we'd angered John over the painting. Even worse, I'd called in a big favour from one of Taiwan's most heavyweight Nationalist Party members and got him to lean on John, just enough to persuade him it was not worth his while not to turn up to our 'exhibition'. John said nothing at all; his man's damning assessment, not based on a thing as he didn't even get near the table, was just a contrivance. John and his companion were already heading for their car and Shanghai, never to be seen again, while Dr Luo's son stood quietly cursing. So ended the saga of Ningbo and our money-making jaunt. But it had all been worth it, for the intrigue, the handling of beautiful objects real or fake, and of course, 'the crack'.

XI
CHASING THE CHICKEN CUP
(2017)

'LET SOME OF the people advance to riches first', declared China's supreme leader Deng Xiaoping in 1992. The bright green light to entrepreneurship proved that the late Mao Zedong's suspicions about Deng's 'capitalist roader' tendencies were right on the mark; within just a few years, the world began to wake to the fact that China was now a country which could do a hybrid capitalism better than its Western competitors. By the late 1990s, those who had 'advanced to riches' had already begun to outgrow foreign limousines or $1,000 bottles of brandy as status-confirmers. Rather, they were now intent on burying their *nouveau riche*-ness by becoming instant art connoisseurs. For the new *yuan* billionaire class, 'cultural heritage' as we can sedately call it also held out the excitement of the chase and the kudos of possession. Not to mention the staggering profits to be made in a market which only went one way—upwards. With the arrival in the 2000s, in Beijing and Shanghai of antique auction houses such as Poly and Guardian, with Chinese publishing houses pushing out weighty volumes on antiques and collecting, with TV stations hosting wildly popular antiques programmes, cultural artefacts were fast becoming the chips in a frenzied casino.

For years, the Chinese government had restricted the export of anything made before the abdication of the Qianlong Emperor (1795), though in practice most exportable items were modest in age and value, dating from the late 19th century. Now, in the third decade of the 21st century, nothing earlier than the Republican Revolution of 1911 could be removed from Chinese shores. The severity of this ruling reflected both new nationalist sentiments, and a huge domestic demand which goes far beyond the new billionaire class. Collecting antiques is now a major pastime of the new Chinese upper middle class, numbering today in the low hundreds of millions. The huge pressures on a limited supply of genuine artefacts have been added to by the new craze of museum building which has hit every self-respecting municipality and town.

In the West, of course, there had long been a lively market for Chinese export porcelain, especially the popular 'blue-and-white', tens of millions of pieces of which were transported to Europe from the 17th century onwards. Indeed, by 1800 it was *de rigeur* for the gentry of the British Isles to possess a Chinese porcelain dinner service, often bearing their supposed family crest. Here was a marketing exercise of Fordist complexity, its production system located in the porcelain capital of Jingdezhen and the decoration and consignment to foreign vessels at the port of Guangzhou hundreds of miles to the south. Back in Britain, the order of a dinner service of dozens of pieces would arrive at their customers' doors a year or more later, through an elaborate network of agents, supercargoes and a journey half-way around the world on tiny fragile sailing ships, ending with a horse-drawn cart.

Other more valuable items, all of them of 'Chinese taste' rather than export items, came to Europe's shores as trophies of war. The British military in particular were accomplished looters, and when marching out on a campaign even had well-developed regulations governing this rewarding activity. Inheritance and ignorance meant that often highly valuable items were later disregarded by their European owners. One

SHIFTING GEARS IN CHINA

dark winter morning in 1992, I drove up the M6 from Liverpool to what I used to call the 'thieves market', at Charnock Richard. On an otherwise undistinguished stall was a fine inlaid wooden box, and inside it a Chinese inkstone. On the underside of the 15cm-long slab of prized Duan rock-carving was pasted a strip of paper. 'Taken from the palace of Lee Hongchang, Tientsin, 1900' it read in a faded Edwardian hand. In the twilight of the Qing dynasty, Li Hongzhang was China's leading statesman. His Tianjin palace was thoroughly gone over by the British troops as they made their way to Beijing to fight the Boxers, and an officer thought it worth grabbing a mysterious lump of stone from the Mandarin's desk.

In their Second Opium War (1858-60), the major assault on the Qing empire by Britain and France culminated in the sacking and burning of the complex of palaces in Beijing known as the old Summer Palace, the Yuanmingyuan to the Chinese. Of the 'century of humiliation' following the First Opium War nothing has spurred today's resurgent Chinese nationalism more than the wanton destruction of the Yuanmingyuan. The British and French armies trashed or stole perhaps three million imperial treasures, and in a remarkably short space of time many were being sold off in faraway European auction houses. Queen Victoria was delivered, amongst many other items, a palace dog which she unashamedly named 'Looty'. The Empress Eugénie, wife of Napoleon III, certainly got her share, and at Fontainebleau she remodelled a suite of chambers to exhibit the cream of the Yuanmingyuan war booty. Across the channel, where the custom is to display special trophies of war in the army officers' mess, the various surviving regiments hung on to some notable Yuanmingyuan objects. Not long since I was able to feast my eyes on some of them. Numerous Imperial treasures from the sacking of the Chinese palace eventually made their way into the holdings of major museums, notably the British Museum and the Victoria and Albert. Wary of the growing clamour for restitution, today these places remain coy about the provenance of some of their prime Chinese exhibits. A few years ago, Beijing sent out a large posse of art experts to scour the world for the Yuanmingyuan treasures, but at most museums including the London ones they drew a blank — official obfuscation reigned.

The East India companies of several nations had, over centuries, saturated Europe with the Chinese porcelains designed only for export. But in the late 19th and early 20th centuries, Western incursions into China and the crumbling of the Qing court and its elite families meant a new audience for the types of ceramics which had long been highly valued by the Chinese. Very rapidly a new connoisseurship for the higher arts of China took root amongst certain refined sections of the European elite. A more exclusive trade in domestic Chinese wares from the Song and Ming dynasties became the focus, as did some of the less gaudy creations of the Qing.

Dominating this new fashion was a number of European and American dealers, many of them unsavoury and unscrupulous, whose tentacles stretched back to the right places in China. With the downfall of the final dynasty in 1911, the eunuch courtiers had turned their energies towards theft of the Forbidden City's incomparable trove. It was canny Beijing dealers, in turn, who got their hands on much of it, and from there a significant amount passed overseas. Much went into the hands of private collectors, who in London identified themselves with a new connoisseurs' club, the Oriental Ceramics Society. London's major museums as we have seen also acquired rich caches of Chinese artefacts, the Percival David collection now housed at the British Museum being the prime example. This fabulous array of Imperial porcelains which had 'escaped' in the 1920s from a massively weakened China, did so not through naked robbery, but rather by purchase from those highly dubious Chinese middle-men. Only in the strictest juridical sense could it be argued that the peerless ceramics were legitimately acquired.

In the main, Chinese collectors are not in the least interested in the ceramics they produced exclusively for export to the ignorant barbarians. Rather, wherever Chinese works of domestic taste have accumulated outside China, the new class of buyers have sought them out. Both London and New York have cashed in by organising twice-yearly 'Asia Weeks', which are really in the main China Weeks. The super-rich from the East, and the Chinese diaspora of every continent converge, to be seen at the many private views, to party, and vie for the best items; the auction houses and dealerships rack up sales in the tens and hundreds of millions of dollars. Hong Kong and the new auction houses in Beijing and Shanghai soon came into their own in this glittering market. Sotheby's and Christie's beefed up their operations in the ex-British colony and were soon joined by the third of the 'big three' — Bonhams. At the same time, the Chinese government itself wanted a larger bite of the action, licensing a dozen or so quasi-state auction outfits in the capital and elsewhere.

In another mode of re-acquisition, all over Europe, wherever there were museums with rich Chinese pickings, smash and grab raids took place and the thefts went on their way to private collections, probably mostly in China. That peerless collection of the Empress Eugénie at Fontainebleau wasn't overlooked by the raiders, highly important artefacts disappearing into the Oriental ether. Another victim was the Museum of East Asian Art in Bath. The thieves simply drove a high van onto the pavement, climbed on its roof, and hopped into a first-floor gallery of the Georgian terrace, to make off in a matter of seconds with a small fortune in jades and porcelains. Perhaps, I suppose, that in view of how most of such museum objects were acquired in the first place, the morality judgment is moot.

———~~~———

Of the theft of China's imperial legacy by invading armies, there's no more celebrated case than that of the Yuanmingyuan's *Rat* and *Rabbit*. One amongst the hundreds of buildings of the Yuanmingyuan is more famous than others, as its ruins have survived until this day. That's because unlike nearly all the other palace structures, the edifice known as the Haiyantang was built of stone rather than timber. And that's not its only distinguishing feature. The 18th century Qing court decided to specify some exotica: they commissioned foreign Jesuits — said to be led by the great Giuseppe Castiglione himself — to design a 'European' building in more or less rococo style. In front of this elaborate creation was a fountain with a complex hydraulic mechanism of European invention, flanked by the twelve bronze animal heads of the Chinese Zodiac which acted as water spouts. These, too, weren't really in any style which drew on tradition, but they were a celebrated addition which flatteringly Sinified the Haiyantang.

In the course of trashing the Yuanmingyuan complex of palaces during the Second Opium War, these fanciful bronze embellishments, each less than half a metre high, were carried off by the French and the British. One hundred and fifty years later the Chinese government, principally through its People's Liberation Army-owned Poly Group (armaments manufacturers) oddly set up a special museum for important objects taken by China's 19th century humiliators. The Poly Museum set itself the task of retrieving each of twelve bronze heads from wherever they were scattered throughout the globe. Not short of hard cash, the Poly Museum has achieved a good degree of success, and visitors to Beijing can now marvel at a total of seven of the interesting creations. But it's the most recently added two bronzes which tell a tale which is illustrative of Western greed, the fervour of patriotism in today's China, and the wiles of deal-making. When the fashion mogul Yves Saint-Laurent died, in his estate were discovered two of the said Zodiac heads, namely the Rat and the Rabbit. Pierre Bergé, partner to the deceased, decided to sell, and the two heads were listed in a Christie's auction to take place in Paris. A highly displeased Beijing made strong representations to the French government, and even to the French courts, all to no avail. So in 2008 the sale went ahead, and the bronzes were bought for almost $20 million by a well-known and eccentric Chinese collector. Chaos! In the spirit of the new nationalism, cheered by millions in China, he then refused to pay. The poor Rat and Rabbit were dead in their burrows. Unsalable and the diplomatic impasse remained at impasse.

Onto the scene arrived a deal-maker in the person of François-Henri Pinault, the chief of the luxury products group which includes in its stable Gucci, St Laurent Paris, Stella McCartney and yes, Christie's. In June 2013 this business magnate (his fortune said to be in the tens of billions of dollars) was in the entourage of French President Hollande on a state visit to China. At a well-publicised ceremony attended by a Chinese Vice-Premier, Rat and Rabbit were returned to Beijing gratis. Christie's, or more likely Pinault himself, had taken the slight pain and for an undisclosed sum had 'bought in' the bronzes. Hitherto, foreign auction houses had been banned from operating in China proper. They had to confine themselves to exhibiting, usually in Shanghai, the juicier objects to be auctioned off in Hong Kong or London. But guess which of the big three, Christie's, Sotheby's, Bonhams, was the first to be granted a licence to hold sales in China? You've got it. Furthermore, Pinault's Kering Group then went on an acquisitions spree for a number of China's own luxury goods labels.

The sacking of the Yuanmingyuan was the most egregious but not the last of the depredations of foreign invaders; on the cusp of the 20th century things came to a nasty head when eight foreign armies arrived on China's shores to deal with the Boxer forces besieging the Beijing foreigners. With the Boxers' defeat, the Northern provinces witnessed an orgy of looting. This was mainly a British affair, and the raiding and razing of villages far and wide went on for months, sometimes even led by missionaries. The shamelessness of this thieving with menaces was astonishing: none other than the wife of the British Minister (as we quaintly called ambassadors back in the day) was observed packing off over ninety large cases of loot to the port of Tianjin. Her comment was 'and that's not all of it by any means'.

———∽∽———

As the collecting craze took off in the early 1990s, fuelled mainly by the new class of Chinese super-affluent, a tiny cup dating from the 15th century became emblematic of the fabulous riches attaching to Chinese porcelain. This is the 'chicken cup', a creation of the supreme but short-lived phase of porcelain manufacture under the reign of the Ming dynasty's Chenghua emperor. Back in the late 1990s, the world of collecting was astounded by a new auction record for a Chinese artefact. A Swiss buyer paid nearly £3m for one of the few Ming chicken cups ever to come to market. In 2016, the self-same cup was again put up for auction, its hammer price (excluding buyer's premium) now £21.5m. The purchaser was a former Shanghai taxi driver said to be worth £1bn, a matter emblematic in itself of the fabulous riches (not to mention the crying income inequality) of a country still calling itself 'socialist' and tightly run by a 'Communist' Party.

The media fanfare about Chinese treasures has brought many

things out of their hiding places. Reaching British shores at some point in the past four hundred years and often unremarked by their unwitting owners, Ming vases carelessly used as a stick-stands, precious porcelain bowls long used for breakfast cereal have netted fabulous sums. Iconic chicken cups apart, the most astonishing such find happened in 2010 at an obscure auction house called Bainbridge's in the Western suburbs of London. A couple had brought in a vase which had been valued for insurance purposes at £800. Years earlier, the gaudy ceramic had been dismissed by an antiques expert as a not-too-clever reproduction. It so happened that the Bainbridge sale, dominated as ever by almost worthless bric-a-brac as well as the usual beaten-up washing machines, happened to be scheduled during London's Asia Week. Someone in the trade must have got to hear about an interesting vase, and lemming like, the dealers and the Chinese purchasing agents rushed off to West London and crowded into Bainbridge's modest premises.

You can easily find a YouTube recording of the event. The vase is bid up from one crazy figure to the next, and finally the astounded Peter Bainbridge brings down his gavel at £42 million, bashing it so hard that it breaks. Ragged cheers go through the room. The vase is then removed from its display table by an assistant, who almost smashes it as he squeezes through the crowd. With commission, the buyer—rumoured to be a property tycoon from Northeast China—is presented with an invoice, including buyer's commission, totalling £51 millions. The Chinese antiques world would never be quite the same again, for all sense of reality had in one great swoop been left far, far behind.

Chinese buyers, however, have a particular view of auctions and it isn't one which finds favour in the West. You may have won the bidding, but thereafter all should be negotiable. That's how they tend to see things. Consequently, most Western auction houses soon took to demanding a cash deposit as a condition of bidding on a particular lot—of Chinese bidders at least—which in the U.K. probably contravenes race discrimination laws. Anyway, it's said that the purchaser of this elaborate vase purportedly dating from the 18th century balked at Mr Bainbridge's stiff commission, failing to have it reduced to his satisfaction. For some months the antiques world was abuzz with the intriguing story. Did Bonhams step in and negotiate a new sale with another buyer for a derisory £25 million? That's what's rumoured, but who knows?

As well as rare ceramics from the most accomplished periods of Jingdezhen, the headquarters of Chinese porcelain, other objects of desire have long been on the wish-list of the Chinese elite. Take, for instance, the obsession with rhino horn as a male potency booster, for centuries creating an insatiable demand for the poor rhino's phallic-like proboscis. It was the (English) East India Company, along with Arab traders, which came to feed this obsession. By the early 17th century, Canton carvers were already hard at it, embellishing rhino horns with delicate scenes taken from Chinese literary tales such as the *Red Cliff*. From the off-cuts, they fashioned ferrules and handles for walking sticks and canes to be sent to Europe. China's pharmacopeia is sophisticated, tested through millennia; in this age of conservation of nature, however, rhino horn gives it a bad name. But the 21st century frenzy in the market for Chinese antiques in the West has by no means eschewed rhino horn carvings, and in particular the little ceremonial vessels known as libation cups. They began to reach stupendous figures at auction: catalogue estimates of, say, £50,000, might be exceeded ten-fold. But finally the internationally-binding CITES regulations, aimed at preventing the illegal trade in endangered species, began to catch up with both rhino carvings as well as those of ivory. National governments, and that of the U.S. in particular (its sensibilities extending to African beasts while it was happily bombing the hell out of Middle East communities), started to impose draconian regulations on cross-border movements. China's antiques agents in Europe began to think better of trying to smuggle their now-illicit buys back home, but not before a few of them had been caught at borders and punished. One known to me languished in a New York jail for months and was only released after paying a princely ransom. As a consequence of the general clampdown, rhino horn auction prices began slowly to retreat from what had been an extraordinary bubble.

By my reckoning, based in the England alone there are perhaps one hundred of those Chinese nationals who daily scour Western Europe for their country's precious heritage. From one end of Britain to the other, at auction houses where I've happened to be for my own purposes, I've quietly observed them in action. Indeed, I've come to recognise a great many of these enterprising magpies; sometimes, just for fun, I might surprise them by sidling up and offering an opinion or two on whatever they happen to be examining before the auction begins (maybe they take me for some kind of Chinese-speaking police spy). It seems that most of the agents operate on behalf of moneyed principals back in China, individuals and syndicates who can put up the substantial sums involved. Some, though, are also dealers in their own right, taking commissions from their bosses' purchases while creaming off some juicy items for themselves.

All auctions these days have their catalogues online, so it's easy to be well informed about what's going on. Say there's a fine art auction at Tennants of Leyburn in the far north of Yorkshire, and some interesting Chinese items have featured in the catalogue. Said auction commences at 10:00am. If you were standing in Tennants' substantial car park at 9:00am you would see a smart Mercedes minibus swoosh in through the gates, hot from London (departure 4:00am?). It disgorges a dozen Chinese males and one or two females, all dishevelled, and some appearing no more than teenagers. Now they'd be seen racing to the reception lobby and queuing to register as bidders, those with dubious records being asked to pay deposits on prospective purchases. I was curious when I first observed this invasion and decided to engage the minibus' owner-driver in conversation. He was a tall, open-faced man from my former home in Jiangsu province, this giving me a conversation opener. The driver readily spoke with me over a coffee.

'Almost every day,' he told me between deep draws on his cigarette, 'I take these people somewhere.' If you were to browse the auction listings in the weekly *Antiques Trade Gazette* you would find that Christmas and New Year's Day apart, on any given day of the year you could bid at perhaps as many as a dozen auctions in the United Kingdom. The minibus driver's daily business was the auction business, anywhere and everywhere. Once the Chinese contingent has each seen to his or her registration, just a matter of minutes remains before the auctioneer mounts his podium and bidding begins. Special items at an auction viewing are always sealed behind glass counters, and here the agents now form a jumbled queue, hoping to get a closer look at what they'd spotted in the catalogue. The counter staff bring forward the target items slowly, one by one, for examination, on velvet cushions. Out comes the Smartphone, snapshots taken and transmitted to principals in China. Shouted queries can be heard coming down the line, and instructions taken. The catalogue is worked through by the tireless auctioneer, and the items of interest finally arrive. Now the bidding becomes frenzied, thousands of pounds being expended within seconds.

A mixture of rivalry, double dealing and temporary alliance pervades this band of highly individualistic characters, and soon the agents can be observed outside the auction, in earnest knots, doing deals between themselves on what they've landed. This is 'the ring' busily at work, the illicit but not uncommon way of restricting bidding by roughly agreed formulae between the buyer and his gang, allowing all to benefit, excepting, that is, the vendor and the auctioneer. Nothing new here. Unlike the native ring-operators, here the mask of language allows those involved to argue their corners in the open, for all to see.

Beyond rhino horn, from time to time there are bubbles in the market akin to the much-hyped 'tulip fever' which hit 17th century Europe. One such example, not long since, concerned porcelain wall plaques painted with landscape scenes, these produced in the 1920s and 1930s by a group of supreme Jiangxi-based painters known as the 'Eight Friends of Zhushan'. I noticed that the fakers of Jingdezhen were off the starting blocks immediately, and in a short space of time their convincing copies often in genuine old frames were turning up in auctions all over Europe. For reasons more social rather than commercial, I used to visit Scandinavia's premier auction house when they staged their fine art sales which often included a smattering of worthwhile Chinese lots. There I would meet a regular buyer, a friend of a friend, a young man, late twenties, whom we shall call Mr Wu. With his slim good looks and his science degree from elite Jiaotong University, Mr Wu had somehow become a big cheese in the antiques game. Perhaps when you tried to contact him he'd be viewing an auction in New York, or Sydney, or Tokyo. But now the well-dressed Mr Wu was seated in front of me at an auction in Copenhagen, and conferring with a scruffy, shaggy-haired person wearing dirty jeans, their frayed cuffs catching under his trainers. In the regal surroundings of the rich man's auction house, an unexpected sight. A pair of 'Friends of Zhushan' plaques were coming up, and I observed Wu with complete amazement as he bagged them for a cool £400,000. He was clearly in no doubt that they weren't modern fakes. After the auction, Mr Wu invited a close friend and me to a late lunch in a smart *nouvelle cuisine* Chinese restaurant. After the usual courtesies, during which I was introduced to Wu's companion, I rather directly enquired of the latter person what his interests were. Wu answered for him: his friend owned a pottery in the famed Jingdezhen and he specialised in replica porcelains — aka fakes. The $64,000 question with all Chinese ceramics is 'Is it right?'. As an insider and cognizant of all the tricks of the trade, Mr Wu's colleague was the perfect person to confront this question as the pair of them trawled the world's auction houses. A partnership made in Chinese heaven.

In recent years, with the very hands-on Chinese President Xi Jinping and his anti-corruption drive, there's been a lull in the trade. But only for the middling rank of Chinese artefacts — the top-rated items can always be certain to zoom into the stratosphere. One of the Chinese agents explained it to me: antiques had become the currency of illicit gifts to corrupt officials, and with not a few heads being removed from shoulders, this part of the business had quietened. And then there was the question of import duties. There was no let-out clause for China's very own heritage that had ended up overseas. These import duties are, it was explained to me by one of them, the reason why the Chinese agents had suddenly taken a particular interest in small items like jades or scholars' desk items, things you could pop into an inside pocket as you arrived at the airport in Shanghai or Beijing. I said it earlier and I'll say it again: all antique dealers are liars and cheats.....

SHIFTING GEARS IN CHINA

There's a popular but upmarket British TV programme about authenticity called 'Fake or Fortune', an investigatory series in which the *hoch* art establishment trio embark on undercover work in an effort to return an orphan painting to its artist, or otherwise pronounce it fake. It's a professional act, and unlike that other BBC production, the *Antiques Roadshow*, the lucre potential is, as they say, filthy. The trio's sleuthing, alongside that of their expert witnesses, can result in a work of art being valued in the hundreds of thousands, if not millions. The labyrinth of history and provenance with its dead ends and disappointments, the science of pigments, the high-tech forensics brought to play, the arty-farty world writ large — all these aspects fascinate. But as with the BBC'S Antiques Roadshow, perhaps, just perhaps, the bottom line, the viewer's suspense, rests on the verdict. Is it or is it not?

Long experience of Chinese material culture, aka antiques and antiquities, has routinely brought me up against the essential 'is it or is it not?' question, But what we might flippantly call faking is not always that. As a tribute to the skills of the ancestors, down the ages desirable objects, whether they be of metal, ceramic materials (earthenware to porcelain), jade, or any number of organic materials (tree-sap lacquer, ivory, wood) have always been copied. You can find Shang bronzes recreated 3,000 years on, in the Song dynasty, and later on again too. By the time we get to the last of the dynasties, the Qing, their emperors were given to paying obeisance to the ancient ancestors by re-creating their bronzes, as well as a host of other artefacts.

There are expensive, faithful copies of bronze censers or porcelain teacups which you can buy in China's museum shops. But over the past decades, the black arts of antiques deception have been very much to the fore. In modern times, this faking-to-deceive began in earnest in the mid-19th century, to bolster the export market to the West. When Liberty opened the Regent Street store in London in 1885, a whole section was filled with brand new blue-and-white porcelain from China bearing four-character marks of the long departed Kangxi emperor. A century-and-a-half on, faking is endemic to the point that, outside the plethora of China's new quasi-state and private auction houses (where many of the lots should fail the authenticity test too) there are practically no genuine items available to foreign buyers. Certainly not at in the street markets or the private 'antiques' stores. The only genuine caches seem to be hidden in the state-owned stores, though the last one I went into in Nanjing was probably already half-privatised; mysteriously, there was no effort to sell me anything. The stock was uninteresting and prices were outrageously high. They seemed to be aimed at retention rather than sale, a rational strategy considering the ever-upward price trajectory.

If you were to stay at home and simply go online, you might trawl through international eBay's 'Chinese antiques' pages which list daily perhaps 200,000 items, nearly all from China. I can definitively reassure you that there is NOTHING with a China address against it which is authentic. The trick even extends to some of the eBay listings with, say an EU or U.S. location. These are actually dealers with the very same fake stock who are trying to fool you with their non-China eBay registrations. Copies-to-deceive seep unstoppably into general circulation; throughout the Western world the contagion affects most collectors and dealers in Chinese art.

———∞———

It was around the year 2000 that the market for Chinese antiques started to take on its freneticism; of the Chinese 'antiques' in any major auction a proportion were undoubtedly modern copies.

SHIFTING GEARS IN CHINA

In 2002, for example, I was ushered into the inner sanctum of a Shanghai jade carving factory; here was a single large green jadeite water buffalo. Next to it was a New York catalogue of either Christie's or Sotheby's, I don't recall which. The catalogue was opened at an illustration of a prize lot, identical to the lump of rock in front of me and sold for a low $million sum.

'That was one of ours too,' the owner told me with a shameless smirk. The top auction houses are meant to be staffed by teams of high experts, so what hope for the general antique dealer and collector whose knowledge is acquired on the hoof, often from images rather than from handling? As for the Chinese middlemen, those agents rushing from one European or U.S. auction to the next, sometimes convince their moneybags back home that an artefact is genuine merely because it's just been purchased from a well-known Western auction house. A thin provenance works with the rich but credulous, or those happy to be deceived for the benefits of ownership. For example, once in the possession of a wealthy Chinese collector, an object has acquired its magical provenance—and can be 'flipped' profitably back into the trade, if not internationally then certainly within China itself.

For most Chinese artefacts wishing to pass themselves off as genuine antiques there are few tests of science which definitively assert authenticity. Take for example jadeite, the more valuable type of jade. It has long been possible to 'improve' the stone's appearance by inserting apple-green dyes, but this is usually obvious to the experienced naked eye. Occasionally, though, science can usefully be brought to bear: where a large enough piece in all respects resembles jade, an incontrovertible specific gravity test can be applied. As far as metalwork such as ancient bronzes is concerned, once or twice I've resorted to the expertise of one of England's most illustrious universities in order to sort out whether a particular Chinese bronze is indeed as ancient as it looks. But the experience hasn't always been happy. The exercise hinges on various advanced techniques of microscopy and spectroscopy to determine age, and a database of scientific wizardry which has been built from the examination of a number of genuine bronzes. Big-time dealers in Chinese bronzes with whom I've discussed this metallurgical analysis are mostly sceptical: they choose to depend, as ever, upon the well-practised eye, sharpened by decades of handling experience.

The application of science to the dating of ceramics is a more straightforward story. At Oxford University, from the 1980s on, materials scientists began to apply thermoluminescence (TL) tests to the dating of pottery. The fundamentals of TL are that over the years, radiation is absorbed by pottery, and the more years — centuries indeed — the brighter a sample will glow when heated. There then follows some complicated high-tech manipulations employing highly specialised equipment. At the end of it the TL process can tell you when, within a broad time range, your ceramic was fired. After the current Chinese art boom began a couple of decades ago, the fakers gradually got onto the TL test and outright fraud raised its head. Fake TL laboratories (or sometimes even real ones) have done excellent business by simply selling certificates. Composite items have had modern bits added; for example, the famous and ubiquitous Tang dynasty pottery horse may have emerged from its ancient burial site with a leg or two missing. With the common clay of the Yellow River basin identical to that used through the ages, adding a brand-new kiln-fired leg is child's play for any half-competent potter. This trick means that all four legs have to be drilled to procure the tiny samples used in the TL test (and maybe other bits too — the mane, the tail). One step ahead of the game, fakers in China have found artificial ways to irradiate ceramics, to confer that all-important antiquity. As in computer hacking of bank accounts, where there's piles of dosh to be made the crooks are tirelessly inventive.

When you show your hoped-for Chinese treasure to an expert member of a top auctioneer's team, the first (and annoying and revealing) question you might expect is 'how long have you had it and where did it come from.' This in itself demonstrates the difficulty so-called experts have in authenticating Chinese objects. They're simply invoking the magical concept 'provenance' as a cover for their deficient intellectual toolkit. That's why paperwork can be so important. Take the hoard of Chinese treasures I came across by chance, an event to be shortly described. The fabulous sum achieved by the owners was entirely due to the fact that they had fortuitously hung onto ancient receipts dating back more than half-a-century. These had been scribed by the most illustrious of London's Oriental dealers. At the grand auction of the collection, the bits of paper were on offer alongside each item: only a fraction of the proceeds would have been seen without the flimsy, and actually essentially meaningless, documentation. Meaningless not merely because the prizes are so great that all kinds of forgery is now rampant, including the photo-shopping of a fake artefact into a genuine old photograph of an Edwardian mantelpiece, or the simple forging of those famous dealers' labels found on the bases of various treasures. Meaningless too because fine provenance is so easily 'acquired'. Decades ago — let's say in 1973 when such things were more easily done — a thief or fence dons his suit and tie and slips into one of London's St James's 'utterly respectable' Oriental galleries. Few questions are asked, and the object freshly stolen changes hands. It's later sold by the gallery, at a handsome profit. Bingo — an incontrovertible provenance, and with the original receipt and fading gallery label a half century on it can achieve at auction one hundred, one thousand times the 1973 price.

On another level, how about the 'excellent background' of treasures snatched by British and French soldiers from the ashes of the world's greatest-ever palace, the Yuanmingyuan, vandalised to destruction in the Second Opium War? In recent years, with the boom in values, many of these things have been brought to auction, sometimes by the descendants of military officers from the 1860 campaign. Sellers and buyers alike have then been able to announce their fine background based on nothing other than shameless and murderous theft. 'Yes, our ancestor took them from the Beijing palace, so they obviously have an incontrovertible provenance.'

Should you walk through the portals of a great auction house, flashing a gold-fringed card announcing your peerage, your artefact is likely to be delivered of a much more sympathetic hearing and positioning on the spectrum of authenticity than if you are Mr Joe Bloggs. Another issue is that, quite unlike the situation with, say, an unaltered 18th century Chippendale-style mirror, as Mr Bloggs (or Lord Bloggs for that matter) you can take the same *Chinese* object to all three opulent London domains of the 'Big Three' on the same day and get three quite differing verdicts.

There is yet another intriguing angle on the provenance question. I became involved not long since with a bunch of Oxford University Sinologists who wished to explore, generally, the concept of 'authenticity' in Chinese culture. At one of our discussions, a scion of one of the great auction houses commented that perhaps in Chinese terms, authenticity of antiques is on a spectrum, a continuum. There's no absolute 'right' or 'wrong'. It all depends whom you're engaging with, as well as other intervening factors which may be broadly called 'interpersonal'.

That certainly chimes with my own experience of the judgments of Chinese antique experts, and in particular those who are specialised in the authentication of paintings.

Mainly I've been a mere observer of the crazed Chinese art scene, but a few years ago I became something of a participant. *Chengdu by coincidence* is what I named Chapter XIX in the first volume of these, my China tales. At vital junctures in my life, serendipity has raised its smiling face, and I shall now relate one such instance in which my knowledge of Chinese antiques unexpectedly came into play. It was a routine day in the Cumbrian town which I call home, and I was at the local supermarket replenishing my old Volvo with diesel. Into the pay-shop I went, holding the door for a woman, elderly, somewhat lame and appearing somewhat discombobulated.

'My car's somehow locked itself with my keys and my handbag is in it so I'm not able to pay for the fuel I've taken,' the woman announced. A naughty thought came to mind: I once lived in Liverpool where there's long been a certain relationship with other people's motor cars, and particularly their alloy wheels. A joke went the rounds when the city was awarded the title of European Capital of Culture. One man to the other: 'What's all this capital of culture stuff, then?' His friend replies: 'The only difference it'll make to us is when we come out of the pub we'll find our wheels gone and the car up on a pile of books rather than bricks'.

A helpful man from the Automobile Association once showed me how it's done when you lock your keys in the car. Insert a stiff wire, a coat hanger for example, into the door jamb and depress the door-lock button, and hey presto! The problem was, this wasn't one of my ancient SAABs or Volvos. What I was looking at here was a newish Mercedes, a small saloon but doubtless with inviolable German locks.

'Ok,' I said to the woman, 'If you don't mind getting into my old car I'd be glad to take you home and get a spare car key, but have you got one?' Yes, she replied, she had one. 'Where are your house keys?' I thought to ask. They were in her handbag, in the car.

'But my cleaner comes every two weeks and she's there this morning, so all's well.'

The Volvo V40 is a low-strung beast, and the woman lowered herself cautiously into the passenger seat by grasping the door surround. We were then off in the direction of town, and mysteriously to an undeclared destination. But I didn't want to pry. For the next ten minutes it was 'straight on', and 'turn left', and 'turn right'. Finally, climbing the steepest hill in town, she said, 'There! Turn sharp left down that alley.'

We squeezed between two buildings and came out onto a long drive crossing a piece of parkland, at the end of which stood that mysterious villa which with its steep slated turrets was in silhouette something straight out of The Hammer House of Horror. This thought had often crossed my mind when I'd gazed up from the bottom of the hill, the villa silhouetted against the angry Cumbrian sky, the great trees shuddering in an Atlantic gale. The woman disentangled herself from her seatbelt and heaved herself out and disappeared for a few minutes, remerging dangling a set of keys. All then was well, and she was back in my vehicle.

'I'm so glad I've solved that one,' she said, smiling. 'Tomorrow I'm off to Shropshire for a reunion of my university friends.' My immediate thought was that though both my mother and her mother before her (born in the 1880s) were university graduates; it was still unusual to find a woman of advanced age who'd had a higher education.

'That's interesting. Where did you study?' I enquired. The woman, now identifying herself as Andrea, answered that she'd graduated in history from Bedford College, a women's institution which was part of London University, but no longer extant in its original form.

'Oh, *that's* a coincidence,' I responded. 'My mother also graduated from a women's college of London University which no longer exists. Westfield College, and she studied history too.'

'My late husband was also a historian,' Andrea volunteered, 'but he studied at Oxford.'

'Oh — my late father studied history too, and was at Oxford too. Queen's College,' I added, just in case the woman thought I was making it all up. I then put that silly question of bourgeois convention: 'And what did your husband do?' I'm not sure if I got a clear reply. Anyway, Andrea threw the question back at me. I decided on vagueness.

'I'm a Sinologist and amongst other things I'm interested in Chinese material culture,' I said. A less venal-sounding way of saying 'Chinese antiques' and all that it might imply.

She got the message. 'Oh, my husband collected Chinese antiques all his life,' she said wistfully, 'and now I'm not sure what to do with them.' I was beginning to reel from this improbable encounter. I should explain that after three decades of involvement in issues of China's economic and urban development, a gulf had opened in my life. I disposed of my unique academic library on China's urbanism to Nottingham University, and soon my bookshelves were laden with reference works on Chinese porcelain, jade, paintings, bronzes. It was no exaggeration to claim that Andrea's apparent knight in a rusty Volvo was one of the few people in the entire North of England who was equipped with a measure of all-round expertise on

Chinese antiques and antiquities. Conscious of the grannyfarming habits of some antique dealers, whereby a relationship of trust with a vulnerable oldie is slowly cultivated, the object being to part them from their possessions in return for a pittance, I forbore from suggesting an inspection of Andrea's Chinese treasures. It was several weeks later that she called me and suggested that my wife and I come for coffee. On the first of what was to be many occasions I found myself seated at Andrea's kitchen table nibbling her Marks and Spencer biscuits.

'Would you like to come and have a look at the antiques?' Andrea said as we rose to leave. 'They're hard to find sometimes so I hope you're good at creeping into roof spaces,' she added mysteriously. The following week I returned; the coffee-and-biscuits ritual done, a slightly embarrassed Andrea confessed that I wouldn't see more than the odd Chinese antique on display in the house.

'I'm not able to help you much,' she said, pointing to her stick. 'But you're a young man and you'll manage. It'll be something of a treasure hunt, I think.' I was beginning to feel that there was something a little odd going on. Was it that Andrea just had a rather fertile imagination? I put the obvious question. 'Have you any invoices or shop receipts for these things.' Andrea rose slowly from her favourite kitchen armchair and hobbled off down a passage which led to a much older part of the house, a hexagonal two-storey late-18th century summer house artfully attached to her late Victorian mansion. Minutes later she returned with a stained and curled file of bruised card and set it down before me. Glancing at the first few pieces of paper, my eyes almost popped out of my head. The receipts from the mid-1950s and 1960s were mainly handwritten on small notepaper bearing those quaint London pre-postcode and pre-direct dialling addresses and phone numbers. And they'd been issued by the most exclusive of

London's Oriental dealers. When for example in the early 1970s, a very good weekly wage was £20, the sums mentioned were generally in the high tens or low hundreds of pounds. Those from the smartest galleries such as Sparks, Bluett and Spink were, I noticed, made out not in pounds but in guineas. If that puzzles the 21st century reader, rather than the simple twenty shillings of the commoner's pound, a couple of generations ago ladies and gentlemen of a certain standing expected their bills to be issued in the arcane twenty-one shillings, the guinea. When I got to the more recent A4-sized receipts dated almost to the year when Andrea's husband had expired, I saw that they'd mostly come from a well-known foursome who'd set up a joint business in London's Mayfair. Andrea's late husband had been collecting non-stop for over half-a-century.

But where were the dozens of objects for which at least now I had proof of purchase? Had they been sold off in subsequent years or were they somewhere in the house? And what exactly was I doing there, what would be my role if the treasures were no chimera, and Andrea wanted rid of them? Though I had a knowledge of the market, my involvement with Chinese art and antiques tended towards the academic. My encounter with this woman initially was as a Boy Scout, doing his good turn. Had I now transmogrified into a potential dealer, putting pecuniary values on Andrea's property? I left the question hanging. I was intent first and foremost on discovering whether the many purchases listed in the paperwork actually still resided in this strange house.

'I'd like you to come here a couple of times each week', Andrea announced, 'until all the Chinese things have been brought out into the light.' I couldn't wait. The following week I embarked on the hunt, and it was one which was going to last for the best part of three months. We soon fell into a routine:

on arrival I'd spend half-an-hour in the kitchen with Andrea, sipping coffee, raiding the biscuit tin, and putting the world to rights. Then she would shift across the corridor to the dining room, where she'd take her place at the head of an Edwardian mahogany dining table. I would then go off into the depths of the house, rummaging through countless cupboards and cabinets and chests-of-drawers in that labyrinthine place. Under the eaves in the attic, in the damp cellar in old chests alongside broken garden furniture, in bedroom cupboards — the trove little by little revealed itself. The odd thing about it was that each item was a carefully contrived parcel, the outer covering thick opaque plastic, which once removed showed a layer of paper and under that something wrapped in a bit of old cotton torn from who knows what garment? Finally, under more wrapping paper or newspaper came the object. It was all a bit Russian doll-like, the parcel finally delivering something dramatically smaller than its dimensions promised.

An air of expectation hung over the dining room as I entered with the latest finds. One by one wrappers would be shed, and soon under the great bay window were several piles of discarded plastic sheeting, paper, rags, and great tangles of brown hairy twine. The object — a dish, a vase, a bronze, a jade — would be placed on the table and then a little guessing game would ensue as Andrea leafed through the file. I would keep quiet, though if we got stuck it helped that I was *au fait* with almost everything which turned up, assisted by the handwritten descriptions of the earlier receipts, scant and often misleading as they were. It dawned on me that the minute her husband's lavish purchases had arrived at the house they'd been squirrelled away: Andrea was setting eyes on all but a few for the first time.

Without much thought of what was to come next, I was merely enjoying the privilege of connoisseurship bestowed by the handling of genuine Song, Yuan, Ming and Qing dynasty artefacts of rare and high quality. In a final search I stumbled on an early Qing jade carving which had half-rolled under the piano stool. A few important items listed in the many receipts hadn't turned up, and that was worrying. I also came across quite a few supernumeraries, worthy objects not figuring in any of the paperwork. The missing items did eventually show: the son of the house remembered a space under a false floor in a compartment of a large wardrobe where they'd been secreted. I could sleep peacefully.

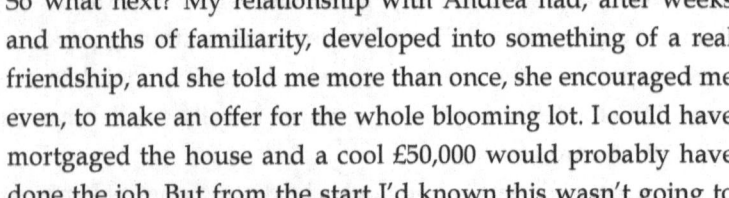

So what next? My relationship with Andrea had, after weeks and months of familiarity, developed into something of a real friendship, and she told me more than once, she encouraged me even, to make an offer for the whole blooming lot. I could have mortgaged the house and a cool £50,000 would probably have done the job. But from the start I'd known this wasn't going to be my game. Only exposure at a good auction could really give Andrea and her family a just return on the departed patriarch's lifetime of collecting.

I'd come across old Christmas cards addressed to Andrea's family from some of the very dealers who'd been supplying her husband's surreptitious habit. Life only has two certainties, as Daniel Defoe once quipped: taxes and death. In the obvious expectation that certain things, now far more valuable, were to be disposed of when time had taken its toll, it was evident that the dealers were intent on keeping in with the family. In a cabinet drawer I also found warm letters from one of the North's leading auctioneers, who not-too-subtly was angling to get his hands on the collection. I found too his dubious valuation lists of the pieces, which he'd been invited to compile some years earlier.

When Andrea suggested getting in touch with this company, I felt I had to steer her gently in another direction. Over a number of years, I'd observed their modus operandi; it would be folly to use a selling agent who conspicuously lacked the specialist expertise demanded by Ming jades, Song dynasty Ding-ware saucer dishes or fine Qing cloisonné. But I was anxious about the huge responsibility of the whole enterprise: finding the right way to dispose of it, my glaring lack of third-party insurance in case I dropped a valuable piece, not to mention the keen sense of people hovering, vulture-like. I was quite determined to deny the hoverers their kill.

On more than one occasion in this book I've made the bold declaration that all antique dealers are liars and cheats. I could really only think of a couple of honourable exceptions, and one in particular: Alan Winchester was the Asian art specialist at a South Coast auctioneers which was trying to get amongst the handful of provincial auction houses staging specialist Chinese sales alongside the well-established London rooms. After all, why not? Ming and Qing vases and the like were coming out of the closet all over the country, and especially in the natural habitat of the upper-middle classes, the Home Counties. As for the county of Wiltshire, it was the stomping ground of the old military families, some with regimental connections which placed them in China's 19th century looting hotspots. That accounts for how the Salisbury auctioneers Woolley & Wallis had initially stepped into the limelight. Once the Chinese market had started to boil, it was Salisbury rather than London or New York which took world records for Chinese antiques such as jade carvings and Yixing teapots.

I called Alan W, explained the issue, and soon enough he'd brought his well-honed bedside manner to the town and had gained Andrea's trust. To cut a long story short, I was engaged to authenticate and make an inventory of the dazzling array of artefacts, Alan created a stunning hardback auction catalogue, and when it came to the sale, the once occluded, trussed up medley of treasures was to the global super-collectors of Chinese art an irresistible beacon. On the day of the auction, with great excitement and a little trepidation, Andrea's eldest son and I seated ourselves in the gallery saleroom of the Dorset auction house. No worry! Lot after lot sailed past their estimate, the internet bidding was buzzing, and the hundred or so hopefuls in the room, including the usual contingent of Chinese agents, added to the buzz. It was the original receipts from the illustrious Oriental dealers of London which did it: that confidence trick called 'provenance'. So it was Andrea's careful bookkeeping over many decades which made a fine sale a spectacular one.

Andrea made use of some of the munificent proceeds to move from her forbidding but familiar villa to a swish old persons' settlement. Sadly, the move disrupted her well-tuned routines and she didn't live long enough to enjoy the bounty which was rightfully hers.

Way beyond that little chicken cup, the crazed world of Chinese collecting encompasses many such stories of revelations and riches. For me, none will ever come closer than the saga which began so opportunely on a petrol station forecourt.

XII
EMEISHAN (2019)

FEBRUARY 2019 and I was in Nanjing, where the city's renowned university, my *danwei* of the 1970s, had lured me to a seminar about global urbanisation policy. As well as a sprinkling of hangers-on, myself included, the main movers and shakers at the seminar were UN chiefs from Nairobi, Bangkok and Tokyo. I've a jaundiced view of international talking shops and I only agreed to take part because Wang, my former PhD student, was orchestrating this one; it would also be an opportunity to catch up with daughter Sophie who was enrolled at Nanjing University. As for Wang, two decades earlier, I'd stumbled across a Hong Kong society queen and property developer who wanted to ingratiate herself to the People's Republic, for that was where the big money was going to be made. She agreed to finance a 'Mainlander' at Liverpool University, to the tune of £50,000. Even in the late 1990s, that's what an overseas student had to fork out for the privilege of a foreign doctorate. So I'd made contact with old friends in Nanjing's renowned Geography Department, and told them to send me, Jesuit style, one of their brightest and best. Now all these years on, Wang was a fully-fledged professor – a bit of an obscurantist in his field, but nonetheless a leading light amongst China's burgeoning community of urbanists.

———∾∾∾———

Soon, and with a very different purpose, I would be a thousand miles to the west in my mother's birthplace, now home to my younger son. There I would be slumming it in the cubicled tower of an Ibis hotel chain. But for now, with fellow conferees I was directed to the extravagantly named Golden Summit Eagle Hotel, slap bang in the centre of the city with its huge rooms, breakfast buffet fit for an emperor, swimming pool and every luxury. Wherever you are in any major city's downtown boulevards, your eye is bound to light on one of these glittering skyscrapers. They might have been created with the coming foreign tourist boom in mind, but the reality is that their clientele is overwhelmingly domestic, taking entirely for granted the supreme comforts. Yet it was only a generation earlier that only the politically privileged few could move around the country. Their usual lot was common dormitories and stinking public latrines. Still with images of China in the mid-1970s floating across my mind, I have to remind myself that over the past three decades, a hundred million Chinese have transitioned to affluence. But many a conversation has taught me that there's little reflection on the past. To anyone under forty years of age, the era before Deng Xiaoping is alien territory; to someone born since the 1970s the strife of the decade-long Cultural Revolution is a closed book.

As for foreign visitors to any Chinese city, few would not be drawn to these luxurious towers. With an exchange rate designed to boost exports, these five-star havens are a gift to the average foreign traveller. Though what may give pause — it certainly does to me — is the cost of a couple of drinks at the bar. But I was tiring of China's standardised international-style hotels and intrigued by a website of a place calling itself the Jinjiang Nanjing Hotel. The images were slightly out of focus, like a familiar face after the plastic surgeon's scalpel. But it surely had to be the same place. Nanjing Hotel was where our alien selves had landed on a bright December day in 1974.

Long before our time, back in the 1950s the technicians sent by the Soviet bloc to catalyse China's ambitious First Five Year Plan had their Chinese hosts build them lavish accommodation. Excessive in that time of post-Liberation make-do-and-mend, though the huge Soviet contribution to China's first industrial revolution merits fulsome acknowledgment. It rarely gets it, either in Western accounts or in the Chinese story about how industry took root in the 1950s. Supreme amongst the accommodations created exclusively for the Soviet 'Elder Brother' was the rambling walled complex in Beijing's northwest suburbs, the *Youyi Binguan*, the Friendship Hotel. This particular monster (and a very pleasant one at that — it was sometimes our temporary abode) has long since been converted into one of Beijing's more distinctive tourist hotels. As for Nanjing Hotel, I remembered it as a symmetrical four-storey structure with typical Soviet-era central section and two wings to the sides, within a compound which in pre-1949 times had been the preserve of the United States military.

Arriving at the hotel as in a time warp, I thought I'd better orient myself, and took off for a wander around the grounds. Improbably, in the planned chaos of a Chinese cityscape ceaselessly metamorphosing, the hotel compound itself just off North Zhongshan Road remained largely unchanged. It took me a little time to get my bearings, as the old entrance was no longer — it had shifted to a wide dual carriageway which certainly didn't exist in our time. Near the former gatehouse, then guarded by PLA teenagers with Kalashnikovs at the ready, I found myself in front of the Art Deco building with a frontage curved like an old ship's stern. After 1927, when Nanjing became China's *de jure* capital and a major recipient of Washington's military dollars, the building had served as the American Officers' Club. Now a sign proclaimed it as the *Guoji julebu* – 'International Club' – though the sealed steel doors suggested an idea more in hope than reality. Outside the entrance of the main hotel building, the same great spreading firs loomed, but the massive concrete slab with an oversize depiction of that Cultural Revolution icon, the Great Yangtze River Bridge, had been excised. Behind this structure straw-hatted gardeners had squatted over flowerpots, nurturing their bonsai trees, an age-old one of which was placed in our lounge. Unhappily it expired, something about which I still feel a tinge of guilt. I poked my way round the back of the new annex, and what did I find? Glass houses, giant potted ferns and a new generation of straw-hatted horticulturists.

The main Soviet-era building of the hotel appeared unchanged, though did it have six storeys back then, and were there wings to the wings in those days, or were these additions? Stepping in from the covered portico, I found myself in a luxuriously appointed lobby which bore no relation to what was there before. On the right of the entrance had been the nerve centre of the building, an office with chattering telex machine and a telephone operator hidden in a little annex. To the left there had been a dark enclosed space where our mail from overseas was confined before unknown eyes vetted it. Now, the building had been gutted to accommodate the new age of affluence, the corridors wider and the rooms, I was to discover, twice the size of the originals. This was all in line with the hotel's name change: 'Jinjiang Nanjing'. The private (of course) Jinjiang Group owns China's most famous pre-1949 skyscraper hotel in downtown Shanghai, until the 1980s by far the highest building in the whole of China. The 18-storey edifice dating from 1934 was one of the three Sassoon-owned hotels of the city. Back in 1972 when it was state-run, Ping-Pong Diplomacy had brought Richard Milhous Nixon and his entourage to the Jinjiang and the place had enjoyed the cachet ever since.

Modern-day traffic meant that Nanjing Hotel was now

a circuitous taxi ride from the glamour and buzz of the city's downtown. In an odd way, the place seemed to have assumed something of the exclusive role it quietly enjoyed in the Mao era. Certainly, in the mid-1970s it was the hideout of the illustrious commanders of the revolutionary committees of Nanjing and Jiangsu Province. Not exactly their private club, but a haven from the Cultural Revolution's dangerous turbulence. I had plenty of time to observe these potentates when the place was also our secluded compound. Indeed, it was our unwanted attention to the great leaders at play which caused our ejection from the hotel, and our isolation in a compound to the northwest of the city. Anyhow, forty years on, Nanjing Hotel was patronised by an elite of a very different genre. Lounging in the lobby bar were immaculately turned-out fashion icons and designer-clad matrons. Somehow, Nanjing Hotel had become the place to be seen. More than usual in today's China, I felt out of place, a peasant from another planet. My status as a guest through some cheap online booking agent had consigned me to a pleasant but smallish room in an annex. Puzzling about the unfamiliar familiar, I realised that this new building had replaced the European-style suburban detached villa, once the home to the benighted Zanzibari medical students who feature in the first volume of this China memoir.

I happened to have with me the PowerPoint slides which I'd used in the book's launch; a few were of Nanjing Hotel in the mid-1970s. Wandering into to the lobby of the main building to take advantage of its strong Wi-Fi, on impulse I loaded up my laptop and selected one of the images. The young woman at the reception desk who'd greeted me so pleasantly peered inquisitively at the screen. What she saw certainly wasn't the gleaming white frontage of today, but a rather dressed-down, concrete-grey Nanjing Hotel. Standing out in ancient Ektachrome was the Cultural Revolution slogan marching across the roof of the building in metre-high red characters, there to greet the odd member of the global bourgeoisie who happened to be wandering through the city. *Quan shijie renmin da tuanjie wansui!* yelled the huge characters: 'Long Live the Great Unity of the People of the World'. Not quite Marx' 'Workers of the world unite: you have nothing to lose but your chains,' but that was the general idea.

Ms Chen stared at the 1970s image and its long-decapitated slogan. 'Ah, that building looks familiar!' was far from her first thought. Rather, her eyes turned robotically to her outsized Huawei mobile, for surely the magic device would cast light on this antediluvian slogan. Perhaps the foreigner wanted a taxi to the building he was showing her? I almost smacked her hand and yelled 'LOOK! Use your eyes!' But finally she got it, beamed a smile and strode down the lobby to the manager's office to announce her unlikely discovery. Out came the be-suited youngsters in charge of the hotel. Not long ago you had to be in your sixties to run anything in China.

'A long time ago, this place was my home,' I told them. 'WAAH!' they chorused, as the image of the hotel as it once was sunk in. A great deal of Japanese-style bowing followed. I'd had no intention of casting off my lowly annex status. But the managers insisted my honourable self should be moved without delay to more fitting accommodation. In exchange, I was to present him with the historical images of Nanjing Hotel. I was happy to transfer a few of the images to one of their phones. On their offer, however, I demurred with a *mingtian*, which like the Spanish *mañana* is always a good standby. I had the contents of my suitcase strewn over every available surface and was quite comfortable where I was. But it was no good. The next morning a posse of managers and white-jacketed underlings cleared my room like locusts in a maize field. We marched in convoy over to the main hotel where, indeed, the presidential suite awaited me — on the upper floor of the rejuvenated building where long ago we'd always been forbidden to tread. And this is where I stayed, in the lap of luxury. But not entirely in peace, as the manager now demanded photographs, and he also presented me with a lavish gift of a satin-cushioned tea service. Every time I appeared in the lobby there were genuflections deserving of a prince.

———∽∽———

The Sichuan Airlines Airbus 320 was soon whisking me into another Chinese world where I no longer had to stride any stage, and was happy to find myself in a mere cubicle of a hotel room. Chengdu was the city of my grandparents, and my mother's birth too, but their quarters on Green Dragon Street which I'd once visited had long been cleared and redeveloped. A century on, my son's home was a rather different kind of exclusive compound, bearing the fancy name of *Ouzhou Cheng* ('European City'), just another of those enclaves for the new affluent class which dot every metropolises' suburbs, and built on land once supremely valuable for vegetables rather than real estate. What we used to call the 'greens zone'. Within Ouzhou Cheng's secluded walls you could wander through shaded pathways, and when the mood took you the swimming pool or tennis courts beckoned. Dinner with half-a-dozen of William's expatriate friends introduced me to the latest concoctions of Sichuan's fiery cuisine. The expat tribes, mainly young Westerners, were out in force in the bars and eateries.

'Chengdu now has over 30,000 foreign residents and half the U.S. Fortune 500 corporations have a presence here,' William told me. In 1979, when I'd first been in the city, there was not a single foreign resident amongst the-then 100 million people of

SHIFTING GEARS IN CHINA

Sichuan province.

My son's motorbike accident was several months behind him. The smashing of bones meant he was still on crutches, and I thought it best not to overburden him, exhausted as he was by eight relentless hours at the office and long taxi commutes on Chengdu's wild urban highways. In any case I had some unfinished business with the greatest of China's four famed Buddhist mountains. The only slight concern was that I'd recently registered some odd ECG's; they hadn't unduly alarmed the medics—nor me. Emeishan rises to over 3,000 metres, but there's actually a good head-start: the ascent really only begins at about 1,000 metres, so nothing much to worry about, an easy challenge which both my China-based children had recently tackled. Someone did suggest that a high mountain might not be a good idea in February, but Chengdu was sultry and weather problems hard to imagine.

Mount Emei had been in my sights for a while. In 1979 I'd been fortunate to be included in the first group of foreigners ('experts' mainly from Beijing) allowed on the newly opened 1,100 kilometre railway over the Yunnan-Guizhou Plateau. With a good part of its length either tunnels or bridges clinging to mountain cliffs, the Chengdu-Kunming ranks amongst the world's most spectacular feats of railway engineering. Back then, in China's late age of steam, we'd chugged past the smoke-wreathed Panzhihua Steel Works nestling in a valley deep beneath the line. The railway and the factories scattered in the secluded valleys were Third Front (*San xian*) projects, the secrets of which I'd introduced to a Western audience in a 1985 book on China's urbanisation policies. In the 1960s and 1970s, a huge proportion of national investment was buried in military strategic industries in the hostile interior. In the dying years of the Cultural Revolution when we'd been in Nanjing, the very existence of the Chengdu-Kunming railway was sometimes treated by our colleagues as no more than a rumour. It was once hinted to me that sabotage was behind the long delay in operating the railway. Former defence minister Lin Biao's people were behind the line's construction, and following his demise in 1972, which coincided with Deng Xiaoping's first rehabilitation, the strife in Sichuan intensified. At the height of the Cultural Revolution, the province had seen the heaviest fighting, its many armaments factories pilfered and pitched battles fought, often with heavy weapons and sometimes with fighter planes.

I recall that the railway's descent to the Sichuan Plain was sudden, unexpected. The train halted at the county town of Meishan, the station nearest the mountain. We badgered our guides to no effect: Emeishan, like all of Sichuan, was firmly closed to foreigners. As 'friends of China', there was special dispensation only for Chengdu, and the metropolis of Chongqing to its east. We were the first foreigners allowed to either city for years.

Now, any constraints on foreigners' movements in Sichuan had long since been thrown to the winds. My journey to the Buddhist mountain began with a long taxi ride to Chengdu's East Station. After a couple of hours and three halts in-between, we drew into the terminus, the imposing, vainglorious Emeishan station. The train had originated in a far corner of Sichuan and was packed, which is today the norm throughout China on the move. The crowds swarming out of the station surely weren't all would-be mountain climbing pilgrims? Certainly not the *nouveau riche* peasant woman with her high heels, bracelets and fancy handbag who was my neighbour on the train. Over the next couple of days I was to see a great many people like her, both female and male: rich in all but culture, it seemed. William later told me that urbanites unkindly stereotype this new rural class as *tuhao* ('earth bullies').

Outside the station with its vast, showy plaza was the usual taxi rank, though the cars and drivers were anything but usual: the vehicles were dilapidated hand-me-downs from the big city. I was surprised that their window stickers stated 5 *yuan* for the first 2 km; Chengdu was 8 *yuan* (and 10 *yuan* in sophisticated Nanjing—you could do a geographer's urban hierarchy chart from this kind of stuff). I was to find, however, that any tariff information was notional, as were the dashboard meters. The first two roughneck drivers refused to take me, no explanation. Did foreigners spell trouble? The third shooed me into the front seat, while in the rear were two students (apparently) at the Southwest Jiaotong University. It was odd to find the branch of such an august institution here in mountainous southern Sichuan—was this yet another legacy of the *San xian* strategy? Through the campus we mysteriously coursed for a good half hour, over numerous speed bumps and past multi-storey and apparently empty buildings. Having achieved nothing, and still with the 'students' on the back seat, we then left the campus area and headed for my hotel, or that's what I assumed was happening.

The roughneck driver rasped '*Daole!*'—'we've arrived'—and cheekily demanded double the fare I'd expected. I registered a wink from his back-seat passengers, their free ride courtesy of the witless foreigner. The place I'd chosen from dozens of hostelries with online profiles was just off the strip where peasants were hawking their wares—souvenir Emeishan cuddly-toy monkeys, Buddhistic trinkets, and exotic snacks of dried this and that in garish cellophane bags. In the side streets were a dozen guesthouses, each with its name emblazoned on an elaborate neon-lit sign. My chosen accommodation went by the appealing name 'Quiet Hotel'. The place, when I located it after asking around, hidden away as it was amongst a cluster of eateries and guesthouses, displayed on its signboard quite different characters. I stepped into a cool granite-built inner court with fountains and lush plants, and was shown up to a room with all facilities. At 95 *yuan* a night, a snip: my Ibis tower back in Chengdu was three times the price for a basic cell. I was planning to return in a couple of nights' time to the Quiet Hotel, a place so tranquil that I never saw or even heard another resident. This seemed quite acceptable to the laid-back youthful duo, who were either dozing with their heads on the paper-strewn check-in desk or canoodling in an adjoining closet. Even in super-charged capitalist China there seemed to be plenty of porosity in the system in which perfectly well-educated young people can earn some kind of living, whiling away the hours. A comforting thought in the hectic other-world of modern China.

It was the day for the mountain, and I breakfasted well at a place round the corner calling itself Teddy Bear Hotel. Owner Andy was the very study of a peasant entrepreneur, in his eccentric English trying every way to persuade me to sign up for a bed when, in a couple of days' time, I came down from the mountain. When I did return to his establishment but merely for his chef's excellent chicken supper, the famed *gongbao ji*, the man behaved as though I wasn't there.

I walked a few steps up the main street to the capacious Wannian bus station. The first bus was going to leave for the foot of the mountain at eight in the morning, and I had to be on it if I wanted to reach my bed for the night. On this journey, I was discovering a China in which surveillance was becoming ever more pervasive, which meant a constant need to prove one's identity. No bus ticket without producing my passport; after a ten-minute ride, the minibus dropped me in a large car park, the Wannian Temple terminus. In China's untrammelled enthusiasm for the market, things once taken for granted as public goods now had price tags, national parks included. I spotted a ticket office, and behind it a forbidding high metal fence. The only choice if you wanted to get onto the mountain was to first take a short ride in a cable car, which I could see rising on the other side. Pulling out my passport for the second time that morning, the woman behind the glass window surprised me by demanding a 160 yuan 'entering-the-park fee'. Emeishan didn't come cheap: that was almost two of my hotel nights in the town. Beyond her expectations of a foreign devil, I drew the woman's attention to a notice which, in a long list of rules and regulations in Chinese, also relieved any *foreigner over 65 years of age* from paying the exorbitant levy.

Hah-ha! Age had made me free. I shared my cable car gondola with four affable peasants with impenetrable dialects, up for a spot of religious tourism from the southern region of Guangxi Zhuang. I wondered at their spotless new clothing and sparkling white trainers. Later it dawned on me that these days, when people tell you that they've climbed a famous pilgrim mountain such as Emei, what they have actually done is ride on manmade contrivances to various scenic spots and temples gracing the slopes. And amusingly to me, they do so in everyday street clothes and footwear.

At the top of the short ride I headed off in the wrong direction and found myself at the crowded entrance to Wannian Monastery. Here, on the steep flight of granite steps up to the arched portal, a group of Buddhist pilgrims in full and matching grey gowns were making a fine show of measuring the length of their bodies on the ground in supplication. Retracing my steps, I soon found the track which skirted the broken-down perimeter wall of the monastery. I'd fully expected to be joining a throng of determined and happy pilgrim-climbers, but the path so far was eerily deserted. Soon the ascent on flights of steps began, their granite treads narrow and making for a tiring steepness which I knew I'd better get attuned to pretty quickly. At least I was lightly burdened with only a small backpack with water bottle, a waterproof (not needed as it turned out) and a down-filled zip-up jacket which turned out to be very much needed. Luckily, I'd borrowed one of William's sweaters which was never to leave me throughout the two days of my climb. My light-weight climbing boots and carbon-fibre walking pole were, unexpectedly, soon to repay the effort of packing them for China. As for supplies, a bag of sweet oranges and a few packets of dry biscuits were shoved into my pack; I was going to rely on whatever I could find on the mountain.

Chinese pilgrim mountains are invariably laced with paths, their steeper sections with flights of broad stone steps, often dating from antiquity. Taishan, which I'd climbed in the 1970s, I had cause to remember as one great staircase throughout its 1,500 metres. After a night at the summit, I'd made the mistake of descending in leaps and bounds. Halfway down, at the Nantian Gate, the tendons in my knees had become so overstretched that my legs disobeyed all commands. I crawled on hands and knees down the last 1,000 metres and had to be dragged to the university car. No chance of this on Emeishan, but I would be stuck with steps for a rather higher ascent than Taishan's. I was keen to start off with a rhythm, something to clothe the monotony of a mostly tree-clad and viewless mountainside. Sixty steps followed by a twenty second rest, which I found just about manageable until the altitude increased and my stamina dwindled, as did my pride, and I was reduced to thirty steps and longer to catch my breath. I was reassured by my only guide, a cartoon-like A4 sheet which Teddy Bear's Mr Andy had given me, Wannian Temple stands at 1,020 metres, so with no effort at all I was already one third of the way up the mountain.

The target for the first day was to get to the Xixiang Si, the Washing the Elephant Monastery, 1,050 metres above the bus terminus. As I laboured upwards, already hating the endless staircase, I calculated that with six of those steps for every rise of one metre, by Xixiang Monastery I would have covered 6,000 of the damned things. Son William had warned that the more usual western ascent was known for a really unforgiving staircase; I'd worked out from my flimsy chart that the eastern route seemed to promise a less painful climb. Perhaps there wasn't a lot to choose between the two paths, which I later saw merged anyway at around 1,500 metres where a local had strategically set up his rice stall.

The thing which kept crossing my mind on the first day was that I was hardly seeing anyone. Famous destinations in China are notoriously jammed with people, but where were they? Within ten minutes of starting the climb, a French couple passed me on their way down, and later a man on his own, also French. And an hour or so before I arrived at the day's destination I was passed by a rotund, jolly woman who wanted to engage me with her excellent English. Gloria – sports reporter from Beijing, her details scribbled on an old ticket which I then managed to lose. Neither she nor a rather camp young man who went past me at speed had anything much to offer about the path ahead, though Gloria warned me of a monkey troupe I was likely to meet. But the young man did do something which was later to prove providential. Wordlessly, as he passed me he thrust a pair of crampons into my hands – crude blacksmith's work, around twenty-five centimetres long, with four spikes and fraying red nylon cords. Yet the air was balmy, the sun was shining gently through the swaying bamboos along the path, the sky milky blue, and not a single snowflake in sight. 'Why should I need such exotic equipment?' I thought. A gift too bizarre to simply abandon, I thrust the crampons in my pack with the thought of keeping them as an Emei souvenir.

Earlier, the young French couple had recoiled when I'd mentioned monkeys. I'd anticipated cuddly little friends on the mountain, but not a bit of it. 'They jumped on my rucksack, very large, 'orrible,' the young woman said. 'You must 'it them with your stick.' It was only later that William told me that when he'd climbed Emei, a girl was being littered down with her breast ripped off by a vicious simian attack. I guessed that the more popular western route was likely to be more monkey infested and I'd cleverly avoided trouble on that score.

Well into the first day, and still no monkeys, though graphic cartoons of gaping jaws and bleeding hands were posted as a regular warning by the side of the path. The no-show by the monkeys was one thing, but wildlife in general seemed in very short supply and I barely saw a single flying insect. It was the absence of forest birdlife I found truly unsettling. At one point my path was crossed by a pair of brightly feathered creatures, jays perhaps, and later, much higher up the mountain, there was a family of what I took to be crows circling and calling. But that was about it. After four decades of agrochemicals on the once fertile plain far below, was China's 'birdless spring' to blame for this absence high above the paddy fields? In the 1970s, too, I hardly ever saw a bird in flight, either in the city where I lived or in the countryside where I was sent to work. Birdlife then had never had a chance to recover from the crazy mass extermination campaign which accompanied the Great Leap Forward way back in 1958. The over-use of fertilisers and pesticides as well as sheer population pressure hadn't allowed any revival. A bizarre comment on the state of nature was that in the township at the foot of Emei the only birdsong came, uncannily raucously, from loudspeakers strung from trees along the main roads.

The repetitive upward stepping induced a slightly dreamlike state; at one point I was surprised out of it by a tall young man carrying nothing with him, who passed me at great pace and without so much as a nod. Later in the day I encountered him again as he descended, equally silent. Another wordless climber passed by the shacks where I stopped for a cracked bowl of boiled aubergine and crusty rice, served by a taciturn toothless peasant who tried to fill my pack with his overpriced water bottles. As I rose up the mountain, I passed a few similar structures of crudely hewn planks which displayed ruinously coloured drinks and as well as water. By Day Two, for reasons which will soon be clear, the occasional shack was deserted, its rough panel door padlocked.

After lunch, my chosen route required a tough struggle up to a mountain crest which my 'map' told me was Huayuan Peak; annoyingly, I then had to lose perhaps 300 metres in height to regain the up-path. Finally, in late afternoon, poking through the trees I could see above me winged devil-roofs. A few steps on, the entrance to the Xixiang Monastery was heralded by a perimeter wall and archway gate, outside of which my first monkey family was assembled and waiting. Forewarned, I saw off an aggressive, penis-displaying male with my metal-tipped pole. But I wasn't quite through the monkey gauntlet. In the Monastery's lower forecourt was a concrete terrace with a few disconsolate apes flopping around the dried-up fountains. They quickly moved in for the assault. But by now I was safely into the concreted yard. A further short flight of steps led to the entrance where hand-painted signs spoke of accommodation and food.

I entered the portal, and through a window which served as reception a well-built young woman wanted to know what kind of accommodation I desired. The peeling tariff board announced that dormitory beds ranged from 30-50 *yuan* – hardly cheap. Outrageously, a single occupancy room would cost me 200 *yuan*. The interior of the monastery felt chilly, damp, and the prospect of a draughty dormitory shared with others (though where were they?) had little appeal. Yet 200 *yuan*? I paid up, comforting myself that I'd cleverly avoided the exorbitant mountain entry fee.

To get to my room I had to walk through the warm space of the office with its pot-bellied wood stove. An incurious knot of clearly secular locals seemed to run the place for the few monks in evidence. Here they whiled away the time, half-watching TV, one man repairing various electric appliances, others just sitting around and smoking. Some low-key exchanges were to be heard in the impenetrable Sichuan accent. My room was the first on a wooden corridor suspended over the mountainside. I was surprised to find hanging from its ceiling a huge and ancient reverse-thrust air conditioner. So electricity had somehow reached the Washing the Elephant Monastery! The evening was coming on and the mountain air damp. When I'd worked out how to activate the behemoth, I thought I'd just put up with its clutter and rattle and leave the heat on a low setting throughout the night.

Dinner was gonged in at 5:30 and served in a dim chamber with plenty of well-crafted and heavily red-lacquered furniture which would have looked more in place in a smart restaurant. Doubtless a gift from a faithful follower. Through a window from the kitchen, dishes were lowered onto a serving trestle: four vegetable concoctions and a watery soup. I handed over a 20 *yuan* note to one of the cooks who gestured that I should join the queue of half-a-dozen monks and the same number of lay people. Just one other person appeared to be a paying guest, a silent moustachioed Indonesian with whom I tried unsuccessfully to engage in conversation as we slurped our suppers at a lacquered table. Reminding me of food-deficient China of the 1970s, the people from the office and younger monks took their food while standing, their over-laden bowls empty in seconds. A few of the senior monks were allowed to retreat to the warmth of the kitchen above the dining room. Between the workers and the be-robed monks there was no chatter, and of course, no-one attempted to strike up a conversation with either of we two guests.

After dinner, from my cell's window I observed the staff, lay and monks alike, doing their hour-long after-dinner exercise, a rhythmic circling of the forecourt accompanied by a little banter and much chain-smoking. I guessed it was actually a subdued version of the regular Buddhist circumambulation. Electricity there might be but no bulb hung in the room; with fading light and only just enough to read I opened a travel adventure I'd filched from the lobby of my Chengdu hotel, but soon called it a day. The bed had one of those old-fashioned cotton-filled quilts and a pillow which was the usual solid lump, but all good enough for the weary. I crept under the bedclothes fully clad and soon drifted off to sleep. I'd expected bed-bugs, but the only disturbance of the night was my need to relieve myself. Reached by entering the bowels of the building down fifty metres of tunnel-like corridor, the monastery's latrines announced themselves well in advance. I was glad of my torch and when I'd found the right door, the medieval latrine was a long stone platform hanging out over the mountainside, receiving one's doings through a slimy slit.

I awoke at dawn in the semi-darkness with the monks chanting lazily in their temple chamber and its huge, gaudily-lit deity. Not only electricity, but Wi-Fi too: my phone had been chirping, the wake-up call coming in the form of a WeChat message from my Beijing- based ex-student and collaborator Wan Hong. I was surprised and pleased that he was promising to visit me when back in Chengdu. A flying visit, literally: he would arrive in the early hours of the morning after I got back, and then depart the same evening. Something to look forward to once the lonesome mountain experience was done with.

At the stroke of 6:30 the breakfast gong echoed around the corridors and I headed for the dismal dining room with its lacquered furnishings. Fortified by *mantou* and vegetables, all for 10 *yuan*, I was planning to waste no time in making tracks towards what turned out to be the false summit of Leidongping, 'Thunder Cave Peak'. The office people told me to expect a three-hour hike, but as it turned out my informants were either ignorant of the conditions above the monastery, or spinning the gullible foreigner a tale. I'd worked out from my flimsy map that it was there that I would find a bus to take me down the mountain. Peasant cultures are all about conquering raw nature; this goes very deep in China. Sacred mountains nowadays not only sprouted cable cars, but featured on Mr Teddy Bear's little chart was a highway winding up from the plain below almost to the summit.

It was 7am, and stepping out breezily, I passed through the tunnel-like monastery corridors and started up the first long flight of steps. Rounding a corner, I discovered why I was almost alone on the mountain. William had warned me about the weather, but I'd thought he was just scaremongering his old father. The vista ahead was of a smooth sheet of hard-crusted snow, and a very steep gradient with no steps to be seen. I tried to keep my pace and my walking pole with its sharp steel spike proved of some limited use. But after a few minutes of slip-sliding upwards, I remembered those crampons thrust at me by that strange young man who had rushed past me the day before. I sat on a rock and tried to work out how best to fix one of them to my left boot. I guessed that with one manageable foot and my sharp pole in my right hand I would be able to make progress. The crampon had somehow to be tied to the front of my boot, but I couldn't work out how best to do it and for a long stretch I had it coming loose every few dozen steps.

Not long into this stop-start routine, I found myself in the company of a nimble middle-aged monk in ochre robe, a rough character who told me he was on a pilgrimage from his monastery in Hubei Province. It's true that some youthful Chinese hikers nowadays look the part — after all, most of the world's finest hiking gear is China-made, but most people think nothing of tackling China's great outdoors in street clothes and flimsy footwear. Despite his impractical long gown, the sprightly Buddhist was wearing professional-looking leather walking boots to which were attached stainless steel crampons, sophisticated models fastened by strong nylon webbing. He observed dispassionately my painful struggle with my makeshift equipment. 'Perhaps he'll feel it his monkish duty to offer me just one of his lovely crampons,' I thought to myself. But some monk — there was nothing doing. After a few more trivial exchanges, mostly about the cost of this or that in England, I was bored with the man and wanted the peace of the mountain. By dawdling I let him get on ahead, musing a few anti-clerical thoughts as he sped on upwards. Whether East or West, the cloistered life bestows what the Chinese call the unbreakable 'iron rice bowl', to which moral vocation comes very much second for a lad from a poor farmer's family.

The next encounter was one which I didn't expect in the second decade of the 21st century. As mentioned, back in 1979 our broad-minded guardian at Shandong University had taken us to our first-ever Chinese mountain, Taishan. I recall being told back then (and on the quiet) how and why the large guesthouse at Taishan's summit was built. A year or two earlier, a visiting foreign dignitary — some president or other — had requested that he should witness the mountain's famed sunrise. He, of course, would be helicoptered to the summit, but his request demanded suitable accommodation. China's face had to be preserved: reminiscent of the pre-revolution French corvée, each adult inhabitant of Tai'an County was obliged to shoulder-pole a load of building materials up the 1,500 metres of this holy Buddhist mountain. In age-old Chinese fashion, the summit hotel was built, and in record time, and the president came and went, while the building remained for the use of lesser mortals including myself.

In 1979, the porterage method was still much in evidence. Vast and varied loads were being painfully inched upwards on the shoulders of ill-clad, wiry peasant wearing worn out plimsolls, each with a special resting pole somewhat like a crude hunting stick. These were portable body-rests on which they would balance their load every hundred steps or so. Now on Emei half-a-century later I was surprised to see the same thing, though why two bedraggled and silent men were bearing massive loads *down* the mountain bearing provisions to my monastery, no doubt, only dawned on me when I remembered that unexpected road to the summit. To their worn footwear they'd tied the same primitive iron crampons, with the same fraying red cord. Inching down the icy slope, they were so intent on not slipping that my own strange presence went unregistered.

After a while, the terrain levelled out and there were even

some gentle downward stretches. But then came an immensely steep flight of perhaps two hundred steps which were protected from rock fall by a kind of rising tunnel. Daytime melt-water from its roof meant that the steps now had a thick skin of transparent ice. Only by a handrail on the precipitous right side did I manage to claw my way up. At the top I rested, with the first real mountain vista before me, the roofs of the Xixiang Monastery shining in the middle distance. Once again my left boot had lost its crampon and it was here that I finally managed to fix it successfully, more or less, by winding the cord over and over through my boot laces. I decided to name the icy tunnel 'the Cresta Run'.

After a while I came to another stretch with some down-slopes. These proved to be unexpectedly treacherous and more than once I fell headlong. At a particularly long slope came a strange encounter with a young woman in a green woollen fashion coat and flat leather shoes. She was half carrying, half dragging a hugely heavy bag up the iced path, and moaning and crying out as she did so. I implored her in my best Chinese to go back, thinking of the dangers of the Cresta Run which lay a few hundred metres ahead.

'Do not care for me, do not care for me!' she shouted back in English. 'Leave me. I will go on!'

Nothing I, the ignorant foreigner, was going to say could change her mind, and my final view was of her sliding after her load which had cut loose. Continuing up and down various icy humps, I then met the last of my fellow strugglers on Emeishan, a couple and their teenage daughter, all in the usual light street clothes. Even worse, they were dragging between them a giant-sized suitcase. Again, conscious of what they were in for ahead, I warned them in a severe manner to return to Leidongping, but they smiled and slithered blithely on. Perhaps, I thought, they'd simply lost their bus fare for the journey back to base. The cartoon bus on Teddy Bear Andy's chart winding like a yellow snake down to the town below was probably going to be expensive.

The path once again levelled out, and I arrived at a section where on one side you could easily fall hundreds of metres; warning notices and fences at the worst parts were a useful reminder to keep one's footing. In fact, Emeishan's staircase from bottom to top had been peppered with signs—most warning against the monkeys, others against littering (ignored, despite the regularly-placed bins), and many, too, about the danger of fires and the need to protect nature. All to the good, though China's exhortation-weary masses probably looked on the lot of them with opaque eyes, for in town and village correct public deportment is belaboured at every turn. No cameras here yet, though of course in cities, towns and villages they were everywhere. Next time you went online to buy a train ticket you might be denied it, as a face-recognition street camera would have recorded your 'antisocial behaviour' (jaywalking, dropping a cigarette butt—even the traditional pastime of spitting, could penalise you).

After another half-hour, and having achieved around 1,000 metres that morning in five rather than the three hours promised at the Washing the Elephant Monastery, arrival at my destination was announced by sight of distant buildings. I rather wanted the climb to go on, feeling that any lapse in my pace would be anticlimactic. The final challenge came in the form of a troupe of sullen monkeys in the branches of a pine and in a cluster under some bushes. Again, the dominant male advanced on me until I made to lay about him with my pole: he backed off with bared fangs. Then from nowhere appeared a couple of fierce, shaggy-haired characters wearing scuffed formal Western jackets, oddly favoured by poorer rural males who long ago had discarded what we know as the 'Mao' jacket. The pair ignored me and marched towards the monkeys. With long poles (or were they the electric prods beloved of China's security patrols?) and with yells and fiery gestures the pair of monkey subduers set about bullying the beasts. Snarling their defeat, soon enough the whole troupe had retreated over the almost-sheer cliff.

It was nearly over. Passing by a large arched entrance to a monastery with a giant painted deity figure just visible in its first pavilion, continuing on I was soon striding across a vast grey-mudded vehicle park. At last, then, Leidongping, a complete village of hotels, restaurants, trinket shops, all jarring so absolutely with the quietitude of my climb. Incongruous, surreal! I was astonished to find a dozen coaches disgorging hundreds of that new breed of rich peasant, impolitely known as the *tuhao*. Young flag-wielding guides were marshalling the crowds. At least, I thought to myself trying to put a positive spin on the scene, the daily throng of tens of thousands of visitors offers the youth of Emei town far below a good and easy living. But after the lonely iciness of nature, the vista of lines of tourists shod in fashion shoes sloshing through the mud of a football pitch-sized coach park put the tranquillity of the Buddhist mountain quite out of mind.

A cold wind swept across the open expanse of the coach park, and yelling stall-holders were doing a brisk trade flogging the new arrivals plastic capes and rubber overshoes. Phalanxes of tourist-pilgrims could be seen heading off up a track for the final ascent from the bus compound to the peak, by way of yet another short gondola lift. A mountain mist was now wreathing itself around this spectacle. I was beginning to feel weary from my icy struggle, and quite disinclined to join the mass assault of the summit parties. I sat down for a few minutes and cast around the vast muddy plateau of a coach park and was suddenly in no mood to be on this sullied sacred mountain. I guessed the huge shed nearby housed the mountain's bus station and took myself towards it. By the time I realised I'd not picked up my expensive waterproof gloves and my fine pole and returned to retrieve them, they'd been snaffled by an old woman whom I could see rapidly shuffling off. I couldn't be bothered to chase her.

———∞———

Coaches were leaving every few minutes for the downhill ride. The bored female occupant at the ticket window demanded my passport and my park entry ticket. I surprised myself by finding the damp and crumpled slip still in my pocket, and presenting it along with 40 *yuan* was issued a bus pass. Did naughty people really course up that little mound of Emeishan without paying for entry? (Later, daughter Sophie told me that she and her friends were in the habit of doing just that kind of thing, climbing over mountain perimeter fences — in Taishan's case at night too). Perhaps the family with the suitcase had lost their park passes and their choice of descent was to avoid a large fine. Next came the inevitable X-ray conveyor for bags, its screen ignored (as ever) by the standard three uniforms who chatted smokily amongst themselves. In today's China every entry point to every transport mode, every public building of note — bus, rail, metro, museum, government office block — has just this scenario. I worked my way down a hundred-metre-long metal fenced lane, a bit like the cattle run in a slaughter house, towards the waiting coach. The road descent of Emeishan was ninety minutes of helter-skelter with frequent halts. The driver happily approached the defiles and hairpins on his brakes rather than his gears. In that respect nothing had changed over the past 40 years of my being driven in China. I found the Quiet Hotel again, but I'd overestimated the time needed for the mountain, and wasn't due back on the train until the next day. So I whiled away the time resting, exulting in a certain relief that body and spirit had held up on a wintry Emeishan.

An inveterate window gazer, the journey to Chengdu soon brought me back to China's realities. My Chinese interlocutors at that UN seminar in Nanjing had had much to say about their nation's super-urbanisation strategy, one which demands concentration of the whole population into townships, cities, and yet more megacities. As the train whizzed along at 250 km an hour, I noted that there was hardly a stretch of untrammelled agriculture to be seen. Uncontrolled development over the past let-it-all rip decades had produced a kind of unbroken semi-urbanism. It was a disorganised and messy jumble which stared back at me throughout the 150-kilometre journey over the Sichuan Plain. And I'd observed the same — worse even — on the high-speed train from Nanjing to Shanghai. Here, scarcely any of the traditional arable land remains — fields which for centuries have rotated winter wheat with two crops of paddy rice. The government's determination to concentrate China's population into urban centres implies reversing this unplanned occupation of much of the country's richest farmland. But its return to productive agriculture will demand huge remedial effort and massive costs, physically, economically, socially.

This was another of China's super-fast trains, and ever so suddenly we'd arrived. Descending from the great apron of Chengdu's South Station in search of a taxi, thoughts of that singular solitude of the icy mountain were rapidly dissipated in the restless roar of the megacity, China's chosen future.

About the Author

Richard Kirkby was born in Yorkshire, into a farming family with very strong China antecedents, and was educated at a Quaker school, at Bristol University and at the Architectural Association, London. Unlike many of his peers, he remembers the Sixties, when he was heavily involved in student politics. In the early 1970s, he spread his wings to Cultural Revolution China, with a quest centering on China's development model of massive industrialisation with little of the usually attendant urban squalor. He taught English at Nanjing University from 1974 to 1977, an experience enriched by spells of labour in rice paddies and a factory machine shop. After Mao Zedong's death but with China still in troubled times, he moved to Shandong University in Jinan city. Since 1980, the author has been a consultant on the Chinese economy, a director of a China firm, a writer of academic tracts (starting with his 1985 book *Urbanisation in China*, which is considered a foundation work in the field), and a broadcaster. In the 1990s, he exchanged his barefoot academic status for a fully shoed one at Liverpool University, directing a China research institute. In the city's Chinatown, he oversaw the creation of a ceremonial archway. He now focuses on Chinese art and the classical guitar, as well as fell walking in his home territory of the Lake District. He is married to museologist Louise Tythacott; his children are the fourth generation in his family to get the China bug, William living in Chengdu and Sophie studying at Nanjing University.

www.ingramcontent.com/pod-product-compliance
Lightning Source LLC
LaVergne TN
LVHW030317070526
838199LV00069B/6481